D1602307

4/21

THE OCEAN IS CLOSED

Journalistic Adventures and Investigations

Jon Bradshaw

PUBLISHED BY
Ze Books of Houston, TX
in partnership with Unnamed
Press of Los Angeles, CA

3262 Westheimer Road, #467
Houston, TX 77098
www.zebooks.com

CREDITS
Credits for visual content featured in *The Ocean is Closed* are included at the end of this volume. The editors would like to express their gratitude to rights holders who generously gave their permission. In particular, the editors would like to thank the Hugh M. Hefner Foundation and its Board of Directors for their courtesy and kind permission to publish the Hugh M. Hefner letters of December 23, 1975 and July 11, 1988.

BOOK SERIES DESIGN
With Projects, Inc.
www.withprojects.org

ISBN
978-1-733540-148

246897531
First Ze Books Printing:
March 2021

Library of Congress Control Number: 2020949790

Typeset in Janson and Univers.

Printed on 55LB. Rolland Enviro 100 Natural.

Printed in Canada.

ENVIRONMENTAL BENEFITS STATEMENT
New Society Publishing saved the following resources by printing the pages of this book on chlorine free paper made with 100% post-consumer waste.

TREES	WATER	ENERGY	SOLID WASTE	GREENHOUSE GASES
16 Fully Grown	7,427 Gallons	8 Million BTUs	497 Pounds	1,369 Pounds

Environmental impact estimates were made using the Environmental Paper Network Paper Calculator 3.2. For more information visit www.papercalculator.org

For Shannon

Table of Contents

Previous:
The final photograph of Bradshaw with his daughter Shannon. Photograph by Carolyn Pfeiffer

"He thought of the world as a marvelous jewel box and he just had to go and look for the jewels."

—Emma Soames.

PUBLISHER'S NOTE

I moved from England, where I was educated, to New York, where I was born, in the summer of 1975. It was two months after friends Jon Bradshaw and Anna Wintour had made the same move. Anna's brother Patrick was one of my best friends, and she was the ultracool older sister with equally cool and urbane boyfriends. Because they lived on the Upper East Side of Manhattan, at Sixty-Seventh Street, I took an apartment on Eighty-Second Street, even though I spent most of my evenings downtown at CBGB and other music clubs and at discotheques.

I had a few relatives in New York and a few friends to go and hear music with, but at least three nights a week, Bradshaw, Anna, and I went to Maxwell's Plum for dinner (free because Bradshaw had written a cover story about the singles bar for *New York* Magazine), to Nicola's on Eighty-Fourth Street (Bradshaw had a book cover on the wall), to a repertory cinema, or to the jazz clubs on Fifty-Second Street. I was reviewing third-string plays for the *Village Voice* and Bradshaw initially helped edit me. He was a different sort of father figure: erratic, insecure, loving but also melancholy, and in possession of a deep well of understanding and resignation at the folly of the world. Bradshaw was enjoying a certain success in the city with cover stories for *New York* Magazine and the simultaneous publication of two books: *Backgammon, the Cruelest Game: The Art of Winning* (with Barclay Cooke), a highly literary instruction manual, and *Fast Company: How Six Master Gamblers Defy the Odds—and Always Win*, a spellbinding tale of the oddballs whom Bradshaw loved to romanticize.

Bradshaw gave me a crash course in literature. I had studied French novels at university and had a standard knowledge of English and American classics. But he had me reading Damon Runyon, Ring Lardner, Budd Schulberg, Norman Mailer, and especially John O'Hara. He also introduced me to critics such as Cyril Connolly. He took me under his wing and provided an idiosyncratic but essential education that has shaped my tastes to this day.

In April 1976, at dinner after a Bob Marley concert at the Beacon Theatre, Bradshaw introduced me to Chris Blackwell, which changed my life. He was an old friend of Bradshaw's and the hero of my adolescence, since I lived for music and his Island

Records was my favorite label. Chris would eventually finance my own record label, Ze Records, and he remains one of my closest friends. Both Chris and I keep a picture of Bradshaw on our desks to this day—thirty-five years after his death.

After a long hiatus from the entertainment business, I started Ze Books to publish Glenn O'Brien, another close friend who passed away in 2017, because I wanted to honor his writing, and *Intelligence for Dummies* was released in 2019. This same impulse has led me to now publish *The Ocean Is Closed*. O'Brien wrote, "There is so much important writing in the magazines of the past that deserves to be exhumed," and it is my hope that Bradshaw will be remembered because of this book. Some of Bradshaw's writing is important as social history, but most of all it makes for a rollicking great read. Readers feel as if they are in the room with him and his interviewees.

Bradshaw was enormously empathetic, and he somehow managed to meld with his subjects no matter how different they were from each other. My favorite Bradshaw memory is of him sitting in my room in a small hotel in Berlin in 1978, on his way to connect with the Baader-Meinhof gang, the West German Far Left militant organization. He explained to me that he would be able to relate to Andreas Baader because they had come from similar backgrounds—raised by their mothers, given a peripatetic and unconventional education—and because they shared "the same simian good looks."

I want to thank Bradshaw's widow, Carolyn Pfeiffer; their daughter, Shannon; and Alex Belth for helping put this book together.

Michael Zilkha, Maine, September 2020

INTRODUCTION BY ALEX BELTH

Jon Bradshaw always said he would die young, but he probably didn't think he'd keel over on a public tennis court in Studio City a few weeks shy of turning forty-nine.

The smart money said he'd meet his fate on assignment in the Comoro Islands, where he'd interviewed a French mercenary for *Esquire*. Or at the Komische Oper opera house in then East Berlin, in clandestine meetings with members of the Baader-Meinhof gang. Or in a prison cell in the ancient Indian city of Gwalior, where he was the first American journalist to interview Phoolan Devi, the murderous bandit queen. But not while playing doubles with friends one autumn morning in the City of Angels.

Dying young fit the romantic image of the hard-drinking writer, and Bradshaw was a confirmed romantic who concocted his own literary persona: the magazine journalist as world-weary adventurer and dashing man-about-town.

In the 1960s, a handful of nonfiction writers emerged as literary rock stars. Magazines, then at the center of cultural conversation, delivered stories that were talked about for weeks, and for twenty years, Bradshaw cut a distinct figure in this world, delivering controversial cover stories and juicy character studies that were deftly written and intensively reported. Although he used the same novelistic devices of scene and dialogue that were the cornerstones of the so-called New Journalism, Bradshaw was not associated with any movement. He never wrote a bestseller or had a story turned into a famous movie. "He was in it for the fun of it," says writer-editor Lewis Lapham, "and for the learning. He delighted in the persona he presented but was not a self-promoter."

He was Bradshaw. Not Jon Bradshaw. Not Jonny or J.B. Just Bradshaw. Three packs of Rothmans a day, Johnnie Walker Black, two pieces of ice. Gambler, gossip, raconteur, playboy, and bon vivant, he fancied himself the last of the boulevardiers, "tripping the tightrope 'twixt insolence and insouciance," as he'd say with a smile in his winsome, mischievous way. A toothless bulldog—all snarl, no bite—he forever looked like a man up to something. "Your responsibility was to anticipate the self-interest and dubious privilege," says filmmaker Alan Rudolph. "It made his trustworthiness more profound. And you could trust Bradshaw as a friend when it counted."

If caught in a fabrication or a lie, as when he claimed to be the brother of NFL quarterback Terry Bradshaw, Bradshaw would wink: *You didn't really believe that, did you?*

Handsome in a rugged 1930s movie star way, and just this side of louche, Bradshaw was an American who adopted British manners and style without appearing effortful or ridiculous. An expansive storyteller, he didn't hog the spotlight, and he delighted in other people's stories. "Outrageous, that's just outrageous," he'd say, prodding them for more.

Above all he possessed that elusive quality known as charm, which may seem a superficial talent, though one well suited to a reporter. It was a quality laced with magic, especially when he trained its lights on you. "He was irresistible," says Barbara Leary, a friend. "It was very hard not to be attracted to him. He certainly got people to be comfortable."

"He was possibly the most social animal I ever knew," says A. Scott Berg, the decorated biographer. "He loved being surrounded by boldface names in large measure because they loved having him in their company. I think the happiest night of his life that I witnessed was at a party at which Mick Jagger came over and talked to him for about an hour."

Bradshaw loved the expense account life, the freebie, the harmless scam. He seemed to live on air, but that didn't stop him from spending other people's money. "Yes, of course we would tease him about being a flaneur," says writer and actress Fiona Lewis. "He had no shame about it, no, none whatsoever, which made it even funnier."

What kept him from being a schnorrer was that Bradshaw sang for his supper. He knew his worth and earned the drinks or the meal by flirting, cracking jokes, playing games—by being Bradshaw. Aristocrats, movie executives, and magazine editors wanted private audiences with him. Millionaires had him on their yachts for days just to play backgammon. "Part of his charm was that he was onto himself," says writer Anne Taylor Fleming. "He was amused, and maybe even needy about his persona, but part of the reason he was beguiling is because it wasn't a hard sell. There was a tenderness in Bradshaw. His charm wasn't acquisitive or operational or manipulative. With Bradshaw, it was in the bones."

"He had a somber side," remembers friend Lady Fiona Montagu, "and he would often gaze into the middle distance looking tragic before snapping out of it and cracking a little joke. There were lots of levels to Bradshaw. He was more interesting and deeper than any of his friends."

"Then he would sneak away to his typewriter, all affectation purged, and commence to write, cleanly and truthfully, enormously well," his friend Nik Cohn wrote in 1986. "In all matters literary, no man could have been more devout. Indeed, his passions for propriety in language, precision in expression, were almost fetishistic."

Weaned on Hemingway and Fitzgerald, influenced by the classics as well as such modern stylists as Nelson Algren, Evelyn Waugh, and Ian Fleming, Bradshaw considered himself a man of letters. He amassed an impressive collection of first editions. And while Bradshaw did not take himself too seriously, words and stories were another matter.

Writing was hard work for him, and it took forever for Bradshaw to deliver a piece, deadlines be damned. Getting things right mattered, and Bradshaw paid for the grind of a freelance life mixed with much hard living. There was no camouflaging his blues during a late-night conversation with Berg in the fall of 1986, when the subject turned to death and funerals. "Here's what I want at my memorial service," Bradshaw said. He had it all outlined, where he wanted it held—Morton's, a famous insider's spot in Hollywood—as well as who should speak and in what order. This didn't sound like some drunken riff. As soon as Berg got home, he wrote down everything he could remember.

A week later, Bradshaw was dead.

He had not joined the fitness revolution then sweeping the country. Booze, butts, heavy sauces, no salads. But he was competitive by nature, whether playing bridge, croquet, or Perquackey, and he wasn't going to embarrass himself by not hustling.

That's what got him in trouble that day when he took the court with his pals Dick Clement and Ian La Frenais, the British comedy writing team, and photographer Eddie Sanderson. It didn't take long before Bradshaw's heart gave out. According to the *San Francisco Chronicle*, Bradshaw invoked his wife: "Carolyn will kill me for this," he said, which is a pretty good line. Later, at UCLA Medical Center, his reported final words were: "Tennis will be the death of me yet."

If that sounds too good to be true, you're beginning to understand what made Bradshaw wink.

* * * * *

Jon Wayne Bradshaw spoke rarely of the past, and then only vaguely. "He wasn't even awkward about it," says Berg. "He just skipped right over it, as though he had sprung fully formed from the head of Zeus."

There was something of the fantasist in him, a little Walter Mitty, recalls his friend and occasional copy editor John Byrne. "When he said he'd passed through Columbia, was that an educational experience in New York, or had he stopped for a leak in South Carolina?"

We know that Bradshaw's father took off when Jon was young, and his mother, Annis Murphy—"Murph" to her friends—sent Bradshaw and his younger brother, Jimmy, to Church Farm, a small boarding school for boys from single-parent homes in Exton, Pennsylvania. Bradshaw was on the milk squad, up at 4:30, tending to the cows before first period, and one in a graduating class of five. His mother, meanwhile, settled in Manhattan, where she worked as a copy editor at *Vogue*.

After high school, Bradshaw took a few college courses but sought his education the old-fashioned way. He drove and hitchhiked across America—sleeping in a field in Illinois, making stops in New Orleans and Salt Lake City, living for months in Portland, Oregon, where he wrote poetry and helped a friend build houses. He worked as a soda jerk and short-order cook, then moved back to New York, where he landed a job as a cub reporter for The *Jersey Journal*, followed by a four-month stint at the *New York Herald Tribune*.

Already familiar with hangovers, romantic catastrophe, and sleeping on relatives' sofas in Manhattan, he took off for England in 1963, which would be his home base for the next twelve years.

Bradshaw arrived in the nascent days of the Swinging Sixties and started as a reporter for the *Daily Mail* before shifting to the *Sunday Times*. Through his mother he was introduced to Anne Trehearne, fashion editor at *Queen*, an old society magazine then in the midst of a revival, and Beatrix Miller, the much-beloved editor of *British Vogue*. By the end of the decade, Bradshaw was a freelancer writing about restaurants and hot spots and spaghetti westerns, profiling the likes of John Osborne, Norman Mailer, Julie Christie, and the Beatles. But his favorite pieces were the travel features that took him to Monte Carlo, Pamplona, Trinidad, Haiti, and Jamaica.

"There just weren't many people like Bradshaw," says Anna Wintour, who lived with him for five years. "He stood out. He would walk into a room and own that room. Living in London and being American—which added to his aura. The polar opposite of the upper-class English world that I knew when I was growing up. He was not so polite and not so careful, wore jeans, had that great smile, and was just much more open. And yeah, a little bit dangerous. He caused a stir."

When the *Daily Telegraph* sent him to Vietnam for a few months, Bradshaw turned up in Saigon in a brown velvet Carnaby Street suit. The other correspondents wore fatigues. "Well, here comes the correspondent from *Vogue* to cover the war," said the *New York Times* Saigon bureau chief A. J. Langguth, who would become a lifelong friend.

Bradshaw did not yearn to be another David Halberstam or Michael Herr reporting from the front lines. He had no more interest in politics than in going to the moon. He rarely left Saigon and instead went drinking and whoring with Nguyễn Cao Kỳ, the Vietnamese prime minister.

Back in the UK, Bradshaw slid smoothly into high society. At *Queen*, he was often paired with photographer Lord Patrick Lichfield, first cousin to the Queen. Bradshaw and Lichfield were on assignment once and, when they arrived at the airport, were appalled to find they hadn't been put in first class. This was Lord Lichfield, after all. They complained to no avail, then hit the bar before boarding. Lichfield promptly fell asleep, and when he awoke he found Bradshaw's seat next to him empty. Half an hour passed, no Bradshaw. Lichfield asked a flight attendant what happened to his friend. "Oh, that's Lord Lichfield," she said, "we've bumped him up to first."

Bradshaw was less lucky in love. First came a misbegotten marriage to Ann Wace, the skyscraping daughter of the governor-general of Trinidad and Tobago. It lasted eight months, capped by an extravagant divorce party she threw for him in London. Shortly thereafter, Bradshaw began dating Wintour, the daughter of Charles Wintour, the esteemed editor of the *Evening Standard*. "I was very young, and he was a larger-than-life figure," says Wintour, who was twelve years his junior. "I think a lot of times I didn't really understand what was going on. He was hopeless about money, he was addicted to gambling, but everyone always forgave him because he was so funny and charming."

Wace and Wintour were unable to corral Bradshaw into respectability, or even get him to take his talent more seriously, but they never doubted he had it. "He was a voracious reader," says Wintour. "He never lectured. I think he was always looking for himself in what he read."

And in those he wrote about as well—from the poet W. H. Auden to Al Seitz, the streetwise proprietor of the Hotel Oloffson in Haiti, to the wily grifters profiled in *Fast Company*, a succès d'estime that Nik Cohn called "a personal, and seductive, work."

Bradshaw returned to the States in 1975, as part of a "British invasion" of Clay Felker's *New York* Magazine that included Cohn, reporter Anthony Haden-Guest, and illustrator Julian Allen. First at *New York*, and then at *Esquire*, Bradshaw enjoyed his most sustained professional success. At the same time, his relationship with Wintour fizzled. This might seem the part of our story where everything falls apart, but here's a pleasant surprise: good fortune appeared in the form of Carolyn Pfeiffer, an old friend. They'd met years earlier as expats in the small London entertainment scene; now relocated to Los Angeles, Pfeiffer ran Alive Films and was an ideal partner. "He once said to me that he was a nonperson until he married Carolyn," says Leary. "He always credited Carolyn with getting him on the straight and narrow. I don't know what direction he would have gone in had he not married her."

"She's much too good for me," Bradshaw told another intimate.

Carolyn knew Bradshaw drank too much, but because he wasn't a mean drunk, it was easy to overlook. "In many ways he was shy and insecure, and I think the drinking helped him to shore himself up," she says. "I never remember thinking I lived with a depressed person, ever."

She was more concerned with the cigarettes, but he didn't have many sick days. "He was very self-motivating. For someone who'd take forever to write a piece, he was a busy bee around the house. It was great to live with him. He wasn't the kind of man who left the top off the toothpaste."

Bradshaw found himself in an unusual situation: domesticated. He'd begun to lose his youthful good looks but still had the carefree self-assuredness of somebody who had once been beautiful. "He was delicious company," says Anne Taylor Fleming, who was part of a group of women who would regularly have long, dishy lunches with him. "You felt safe with Bradshaw. The pounce factor wasn't there. You didn't see the flash of masculine power. You knew in Bradshaw's eyes he liked being around you and thought you were smart and funny and pretty. He didn't hold back on that, the appreciation part. But it didn't come with an expectation."

Although he put it down for not being literary enough, Bradshaw liked Los Angeles more than he cared to admit. Weirder still, he was now a father to a young daughter, Shannon, whom he adored.

Bradshaw spent most of this period laboring on a biography of Libby Holman, the torch singer and civil rights patron with a calamitous personal life, whom producer Ray Stark had suggested as a subject so that the book might be adapted into a movie. But drinks and conversation and laughter beckoned, all subversions of the discipline required to write a serious biography. Bradshaw was a sprinter, used to magazine deadlines. The Holman book is a good, dutiful one, but it didn't get rave reviews nor was it a bestseller.

He wrote the screenplay for *The Moderns* with Alan Rudolph—the movie came out in 1988—then tackled *Rafferty*, a would-be spy series for producer Thom Mount featuring a protagonist based on himself. Rafferty operated out of the in-terminal hotel at the Miami airport, where

Libby Holman book cover

Bradshaw and Carolyn made several research visits. One morning, Bradshaw noticed a sign at the foot of the beach that read THE OCEAN IS CLOSED. He loved that and planned to use it as the title for the first Rafferty book.

Carolyn doesn't remember Bradshaw morose, and neither do his friends. She was a little concerned about the pallor of his skin, but in the months leading up to his death, she was away on location. If you believe *the body knows*, perhaps mortality was on Bradshaw's mind when he mapped out his memorial for Berg. Heart disease ran in his family. One fall day, Bradshaw and Shannon drove to San Diego to fetch Carolyn; the next morning Carolyn remained in bed when he left early to play tennis. She never spoke to him again.

Neither Dick Clement nor Ian La Frenais have clear memories of what happened on the court. Only that Bradshaw said he wasn't feeling well, and they decided to stop. Clement offered to drive him to the emergency room, but Bradshaw said he just wanted to go home. Clement obliged. Once there, they called for an ambulance, but Bradshaw never regained consciousness. Three days later Carolyn made the wrenching decision to take him off life support.

Just as Bradshaw wanted, a memorial was held at Morton's. Three more followed, including a regal affair gossip columnist Nigel Dempster organized in London and a well-attended send-off at Elaine's, the famous literary saloon in New York. Finally, Carolyn and three-and-a-half-year-old Shannon returned to their home in Jamaica, where they buried Bradshaw under a huge bougainvillea bush in the garden with about forty Jamaican friends in attendance. The event was officiated by the local Seventh-day Adventist minister, who arrived in a pickup truck with a boys choir in back. The toasts and stories lasted well into the night, and in many ways, it was the purest of the Bradshaw farewells.

"I am a great man, you know," Berg recalls Bradshaw telling him. "Just look at who my friends are."

Talking to many of them some thirty-five years later—a wondrous cocktail party of smart, lively conversationalists—is to understand how much they adored him in return.

*****

"Bradshaw relished words," says John Byrne. "Given a new one he would swirl it in his mouth as if it were wine or bourbon." (It was Byrne who gave him "esurient"—a seventeenth-century word meaning "hungry, in a greedy way," which shows up in *Fast Company*.) But Bradshaw's love of words is not ostentatious, nor does it disrupt his otherwise unpretentious prose and keen observational eye. A feature about the Beverly Hills Hotel delivers a beaut: *Penthouse* publisher Bob Guccione by the pool one morning, sticking out among such suave record executives as Ahmet Ertegun and Clive Davis, "a piece of pork in a marmalade spread."

Bradshaw isn't a memoirist or a propagandist. He doesn't shove point of view in the reader's face. He's no showy stylist either. He writes, instead, in the understated magazine tradition of Lillian Ross, W. C. Heinz, and Gay Talese. We note his presence, but he tends to recede into the shadows so as not to get in the way of the story. Droll and deadpan, Bradshaw is a sturdy, amiable, booze-soaked guide.

Like most writers, Bradshaw had his beats. Thus we've divided this anthology into four parts: the literary world; the "scene" on both coasts in the '70s; his beloved gamblers and con men; and the adventure stories that gave him his bona fides as the Indiana Jones of journalism.

Bradshaw genuinely liked other writers, which is why his portraits of them are especially appealing. He doesn't kiss up to Auden or Tom Stoppard, he's not afraid to be critical, but you sense how much he admires them. "Isolation comes hard to him," he writes of Auden. "One feels he tastes the rancor of a prisoner, unjustly sentenced to thirty years at hard labor. He smiles, but the wizened face slumps with defeat and disappointment. His self-protective passion for rules, for form and punctuality, seems just that—self-protective—barriers built not to entice the ordinary literate person, but to keep the ordinary literate person out. There is something of the elderly sentinel about him, defending his own frontiers against enemies who will never materialize."

Although he worked from the '60s through the mid-'80s, most of Bradshaw's stories here take place in the '70s. The "Me Decade" was a lurid, cynical time, and beneath the cavalier veneer of free love, trouble bloomed. "In this age of so-called sexual liberation there are probably more lonely souls than there have ever been before," author and political speechwriter Richard Goodwin tells Bradshaw. With dispassionate calm, Bradshaw captures the "lonelies" in the feral lounge lizard scenes at Maxwell's Plum and the Polo Lounge at the Beverly Hills Hotel. "Nowadays, sex is a toy that everybody seems to have discovered *yesterday*," a sex worker tells Bradshaw at the Lounge. "It's out in the open now. You can smell it."

And there's a disquieting escapade in London one night with Hunter S. Thompson in full Dr. Gonzo mode, where it is tricky to discern outrageousness from possible criminality. "My dear friend, we live in *shoddy* times," Nigel Dempster tells Bradshaw. "At this moment in history, how else is one expected to behave but . . . *monstrously*."

That's exactly what Bradshaw's after in his ambitious, documentary-like portrait of the Baader-Meinhof gang and the history of German terrorism, and in "Savage Skulls," an immersive feature on gang violence and the urban chaos in American cities. It is also at the heart of his police procedural on the death of Don Bolles, an investigative reporter for the *Arizona Republic* murdered by the Mob for doing his job too well. Bolles and his wife had plans to see *All the President's Men* the day a bomb exploded in his car; and while nobody would mistake Bradshaw for Woodward or Bernstein, he sought a kind of truth too.

The reporter who tipped him off to Phoolan Devi said, "Her story is a classic Indian myth, an Eastern western, a fabulous yarn of love, betrayal, and revenge. . . . I don't necessarily believe the myth, but I'm hog-tied by it. And late at night with a couple of shots in my belt, I sometimes think it's true. Sometimes belief is better than investigation."

For Bradshaw, it was worth traveling halfway around the world to find out. Knowing was always better than believing. Devi turned out not to be what he expected, but he didn't leave disappointed. He went for the adventure and left with the stories.

The Literary Life

Young Bradshaw. Photograph by Gene Moore

Holding to a Schedule with W. H. Auden
Esquire, January 1970

"I don't believe that art is self-expression. If it is only interesting to yourself, keep it to yourself."

The table had been laid the night before. Now Chester has pushed his place aside; surrounded by scraps of paper and dictionaries, he toys with Sunday's crossword puzzles. He wears pajamas and a dressing gown. A gross, ungainly man, with dull and knobby eyes, he has the look of one become too old to play the naughty cherub anymore. Across the table, Auden's place is immaculate—the crockery and utensils fixed in neat formation, like chessmen in a game which is yet to be played. Volume X (Sole–Sz) of the *Oxford English Dictionary* lies, as it always does, on Auden's chair. Chester glances at his watch; the poet must be wakened soon. He belches and looks hurriedly round, as though the noise had come from behind him.

Auden enters at eight o'clock. Gruff pleasantries are exchanged—the A.M. utterances of old companions. They have been together for nearly thirteen years. His breath comes in little broken bursts, as though sleep itself had stretched him well beyond his limits. He stubs out a cigarette and lights another. Sitting on the *OED*, he pours some coffee, dolloping in the cream which Chester had whipped the day before. Leafing through the morning paper, he wipes his muculent eyes and peers at one of the photographs.

"Who is Ella Fitzgerald?" he rasps. "Is she well-known?"

Chester nods, assuring him the singer's fame is widespread.

"Never heard of her."

Chester asks for a nine-letter word meaning "prone to writing about tart-making." Auden says he thinks it is going to rain. He looks out the window. "I try not to read newspapers now," he mutters. "The only items which make sense anymore are the obituaries and the weather." Chester smiles.

Auden turns to the morning mail. There are bills and circulars and a few letters marked "Personal." One comes from a student, who is writing a thesis on the symbolic meaning of Auden's work. She implores the poet for clarifications. He pushes the letter aside. "They always want *me* to do their work for them," he says. "This symbol-hunting is an *awful* nuisance." There is also a note from the Pulitzer Prize Advisory Board inviting him to act as one of next year's judges.

Nervously, Chester bites his lower lip. "But, Wystan, *my* book of poems won't be out by then."

"Hurry up then, dearie," says Auden with a wrinkled smile.

"Oh, *Wystan*."

Auden lights another cigarette. The room is sick with the stale aroma of cigarettes. The tables, the floor, the chest and chairs are littered with paper, old British newspapers open to the crosswords, bills, and books. There is no telephone. One corner is shelved with record albums, mostly opera, arranged in alphabetical order from Bizet to Weill. There are cookbooks everywhere and dictionaries—Italian, English, Greek, and German. On the walls are pencil drawings of Strauss (by Munch), Stravinsky, and one of the young Yeats (by Augustus John), a present from Stephen Spender. There is a feeling of comfortable disorder. It is the room of a man in transit, a man who has left his few belongings where they fell. It is the room of a bachelor who knows the maid will appear in the morning.

Auden's workday begins promptly after breakfast. He sees himself as an artisan—clocking in at nine A.M., as any cooper, wheelwright, or topiarist would do. A man who makes words, the boss man of a dying cottage industry. "I am a professional, a man of letters," he says. But that, perhaps, is a modest assumption; one of his friends believes he sees himself as the giant private firm of Auden, Auden, Auden & Co.

At sixty-two, he feels he has reached the age when he can do and dress as he wishes. Wearing his tattered carpet slippers (he can't remember when he last wore shoes), limp, baggy trousers, an ancient jacket, frayed and stained, Auden shuffles into the garden in that slightly stooped, staccato walk of his—a grand old man in shabby clothes.

His workroom is reached only from the garden. Climbing twelve steep stairs at a corner of the cottage, he stoops through a tiny door, and there, among the eaves, is a wooden room—cluttered and cozy as any attic. A lifetime of litter has fallen here; the books are piled into makeshift bookcases, the bottom shelf sagging under the twelve volumes of the *OED*, papers and manuscripts are strewn across the floor, the table, the tiny bed. His desk is mounted on a platform beneath the room's main window and overlooks the hilly Austrian countryside. The room is chilly, but full of light—a far cry from his Oxford digs, described by Stephen Spender as "a darkened room with the curtains drawn, and a lamp on a table at his elbow."

He shows me his notebooks, filled with sinuous inscrutable jottings. He smiles hesitantly, as though he intended to apologize. "In the beginning, I don't like my writing to be too legible. It's somehow fixed then." He hates the typewriter. He works slowly, revising endlessly, and reckons to complete about seven poems a year.

"I rarely coin words. I believe in the *OED* and I like my readers to work. But one of my great ambitions is to get into the *OED* as the first person to have used in print a new word. I have two candidates at the moment, which I used in my review of J. R. Ackerley's autobiography. They are 'Plain-Sewing' and 'Princeton-First-Year.' They refer to two types of homosexual behavior."

He lights a cigarette. The ashtray is already full. "I was very lucky as a poet, you know, for some good reasons and some bad. But I never thought I wouldn't succeed. It's not a reasonable attitude, I know." He has also been financially successful, for him, perhaps, the weightier consideration. He exhibits not a little Midland common sense. He insists "one must pay his bills by return mail. It's the ethic of the professional middle classes in England." Poets, he feels, are luckier than novelists. "A novelist might make a fortune or he might not. Poets never will (though Ogden Nash might), so one arranges one's life not on the principle of a gamble. I make more than I used to," he adds.

He turns out anthologies "for fun and money," but poetry is another matter. "I write poetry because I like to, that's all. The world has changed, but my reasons for writing poetry are the same as they were forty years ago." In his fifties, one remembers, he was described as still the most promising poet writing in English. "Poems are verbal objects and they should be well-made. When I look at a poem, I immediately wonder how it's made, then what's said." Bound by domestic disciplines and rules, he treats his work with similar care. "One must have rules. Anyone who plays a game, plays with rules. The rules of baseball are different from those of bridge, of course. You can have what rules you like, but you must have them. Why shouldn't it be the same for poetry? In poetry, you have a form looking for a subject and a subject looking for a form. When they come together successfully, you have a poem."

Christopher Isherwood, at school with him, said Auden felt that form alone was significant. "Auden loathed (and still rather dislikes) the sea—for the sea, besides being deplorably wet and sloppy, is formless."

He is ruthless with his work and has revised or eliminated many poems, such as the famous "Spain 1937" and "September 1, 1939" from his *Collected Poetry*. "I eliminated those and others because they were either dishonest, bad-mannered, or boring. They were written in another hand, not mine. They were forgeries." Auden supports Valéry's dictum that a poem is never finished, it is merely abandoned. "One must be strict," he says. "I don't believe that art is self-expression. If it is only interesting to yourself, keep it to yourself. What one sees is a reality common to everyone, but from a unique point of view. That point of view can be interesting, even revealing, but I've never thought it would change the world. Anyway, a poem is meant to give pleasure. As for changing the world, my private utopian dream is that nothing will change until all foreign policy is taken out of the hands of men and given to married women. They're the only ones with a real stake in the future."

"I write poetry because I like to, that's all. The world has changed, but my reasons for writing poetry are the same as they were forty years ago."

He looks at his watch—one of the few machines in which he places any trust. He gasps. Unlike Carroll's white rabbit, whom he rather resembles, Auden is never late. It is time to go shopping in Kirchstetten, a rite obsessively observed each morning. Though Auden would call it a discipline.

In the kitchen, he picks up the green-black tartan bag he uses as a shopping basket. Chester is still in pajamas and dressing gown. He has put aside the crossword now and wrestles with a poem. As Chester does all the cooking, Auden asks for the shopping list. Chester looks up with a petulant air. "Food is more important than poetry," says Auden.

He shuffles down to the garden. Beyond—the orderly countryside. It would not be difficult to imagine this cottage in some such place as Kent or Dorset, inhabited by this same man, who has put aside his city clothes in order to cultivate the garden, to rest and read detective novels for the weekend. Auden consults his watch again: time enough to catch the 9:02 from Gillingham to Waterloo.

Kirchstetten is a village of five hundred people. There are six villages of that name in Austria and one or two of Auden's guests have ventured inadvertently to the wrong one—usually the Kirchstetten near the Hungarian border, a hundred miles away. Remote and tucked away, the real Kirchstetten is as difficult to find as Brigadoon.

Auden spends his springs and summers here, which fulfills his three prerequisites for living abroad—to live in a wine-producing country, near a flourishing opera house, and to be able to speak German, his favorite foreign language. A main rail line is nearby, and in the distance, corrupting the pastoral scene, runs the great autobahn from Salzburg in the west to Vienna, twenty miles away.

He uses a Volkswagen to travel the mile or so between his cottage and Kirchstetten. He wears dark glasses and one assumes he doesn't wish to be recognized, but no, they are prescribed. He has been myopic since sixteen—"probably as a retreat from reality," he explains, "a desire to shut the real world out. For protective reasons."

The village contains a post office, two grocery stores, three gasthäuser, a bakery, a butcher, an elementary school, and the beautiful onion-domed Gothic church. In each of these establishments, Auden is acknowledged as "Herr Professor." Speaking thus, the village men will doff their hats, the women will smile with downcast eyes. "In Austria," he says, "everyone must have a rank. Otherwise communications break down." He shops in the same small grocery, buying enough to last until the following day. The girls in the shop titter among themselves, drop his purchases into the tartan bag, tote up the bill, and with downcast eyes: "*Danke, danke, Herr Professor*."

Shopping completed, he stops at Franz Biber's gasthaus for sandwiches and beer. He has little company in Kirchstetten. Even if he wished to entertain, the local social customs limit the number of acceptable guests to the local doctor, the priest, and the schoolmaster. These are the Herr Professor's social equals. The mayor, whom Auden rather likes, is thought inferior, on a par with the farmers.

At Franz Biber's, Auden talks or nods to many people, irrespective of their station. He speaks slowly, his conversation dotted with irritating pauses, as though he were bored or simply stopping for a rest. He tends to hang an "um" or an "and" or a "but" at the end of his sentences, as though he were on the verge of additional revelation, but he always hesitates, lapsing at last into silence. His German is excellent, his English roughly inflected. It might be "transatlantic," if those two tongues had merged in him. As it is, his Yankee slang and short American *a*'s, coated with British intonation, give an impression of two people talking at the same time.

It was in 1939 that Auden and Isherwood left England permanently for America. Auden became an American citizen in 1946. "I don't think of myself as American," he says. "I'm a New Yorker, but my cadences, my handling of the language, is British." He left England for many reasons. "English life was a bit like family life for me and I didn't want to live with my family. . . . England is hopelessly vulgar. Look at the ads and the cheap press. . . . I'm absolutely horrified with British speech. No one has dialects anymore, just a kind of noise which to me is impossible. I'm not suggesting that everyone should speak Oxford English, but this in-between classless English is horrific. In America, they do at least attempt to teach the people a kind of standard American." It doesn't occur to him that standard American is an in-between classless English.

He keeps a flat in New York's East Village, where he spends his winters. Life is the same for him as it is in Austria, he claims. But not quite. Chester hates the city, preferring to spend his winters in Greece, so Auden lives alone and cooks for himself. He works, lectures occasionally, sees friends and editors he hasn't seen since the previous winter, and travels up and down the city in subways. "I love subways. I love being underground. I always have. Don't know what a psychiatrist would make of that."

He sits on one of the committees under the authority of the Standing Liturgical Commission. He was raised an Anglo-Catholic and both of his grandfathers were clergymen. Rejecting it, he came back to the Church at thirty-two. "There's a great deal of difference in believing something still and believing it again," he says. "That's Lichtenberg, of course. A marvelous remark."

Auden thinks himself a busy man, but his is private occupation and he's required to conduct his main concerns in the isolation of his home. At sixty-two, he is none too anxious that he should be alone for long. "I've often thought that I could have a coronary in my apartment in New York. It would be days before I was found. Your friends would ring up and just think you were out. Still," he says uncertainly, "my mailman might know."

Auden is very much a separate man—impartial and withdrawn—one of those early Church ascetics exiled into a demesne from which the vulgar world is barred. Fearing bad health and loneliness, he works at keeping busy. As a New Yorker, he puts himself into the hands of passing postmen. A poet whose popular works were written more than twenty years ago, he seems like some disenchanted Father McKenzie, writing the words of a sermon that no one will hear.

"I think a sense of isolation is peculiar to every writer. There is no audience now. Caring whether one is read or not is not a question you can fuss about. You can't be conscious of your readers; you don't know who they are. You might say I write for ordinary literate people. I think of myself as a person of general culture."

But isolation comes hard to him. One feels he tastes the rancor of a prisoner, unjustly sentenced to thirty years at hard labor. He smiles, but the wizened face slumps with defeat and disappointment. His self-protective passion for rules, for form and punctuality, seems just that—self-protective—barriers built not to entice the ordinary literate person, but to keep the ordinary literate person out. There is something of the elderly sentinel about him, defending his own frontiers against enemies who will never materialize.

Back at the house, unless it's "Campari weather," vermouth is served at twelve-thirty. "The vermouth's in," announces Auden.

"He means in the glass," says Chester. Chester has prepared lunch, which is served, as it always is, at one.

"Chester, do we have time for refreshers?" says Auden, looking at his empty glass. The two men look at one another.

"It's one o'clock," says Chester.

Chester always serves. There is meat and salad. "The lettuce is very undistinguished," says Auden. Chester grunts and mentions the time of the year.

The conversation is of literary figures, gossip, and reminiscence. Auden has an astonishing memory and can recite whole poems, aphorisms, lines of dialogue from novels and films appropriate to situations at hand. "When I was nine, I could learn thirty lines of Latin verse in twenty minutes. My memory's good," he says, "but not so good as it was, of course." He can remember the last line of the first poem he ever wrote. It went: "in the quiet oblivion of thy waters, let them stay." He can't remember who "they" were now.

"Sartre is an unattractive man," he says, between mouthfuls of what appears to be goulash. "Ugly beyond the call of duty. I know there's nothing wrong in being ugly, but it's almost as though it were Sartre's fault. . . . I don't judge my contemporaries. To the degree that anyone is good, they're unique. . . . Still, poor Cyril, it's rather sad to think he is merely England's best literary critic. . . . I'm on the shortlist for the Nobel Prize, I believe. I don't know how long that is, though. I don't think any Americans can win it now—at least until the war in Vietnam is ended. There have been some curious winners—Churchill, Bertrand Russell—but it is the highest honor. . . . What no critic seems to see in my work are its comic undertones. Only through comedy can one be serious . . . There's entirely too much sex in books today. So boring . . . There are only two kinds of people who read their own work badly. The person who is very shy like Marianne Moore and the person who is very conceited like Robert Graves. . . .

W. H. AUDEN

KIRCHSTETTEN (WESTBAHN)
HINTERHOLZ 6
N.-Ö., AUSTRIA

May 20th

Dear Mr Bradshaw:

Thank you for your letter of May 5th. You speak of 'driving': do you mean that you are having a car to meet you at the airport? If not, take a taxi to the Westbahnhof. (Ask the price first.)

If your plane is on time you should be able to catch the 14.10 which arrives at Kirchstetten at 15.13. If not, the next train is 15.35 arriving at 16.22. I will meet both. We can put you up. I think, though, we can get through any possible interrogation in two days.

Yours sincerely

Wystan Auden

W.H. Auden letter agreeing to an interview

Brecht was a horrid man. . . . Yeats and Robert Frost were horrid. . . . I like novels about Eden, which is what Firbank is all about. I like them to be short and preferably funny. I don't read many now. I rather like the ones I've read before. . . .

". . . You can never forgive those who had a bad influence on you. It's your own fault, of course, but never mind. Frost was a terrible influence. So was Rilke, who overused the definitive article. The worst influence was probably Yeats. He had an overinflated rhetoric, too noisy. Looking back now, I can see he was lying—and the fibs weren't even interesting. . . . In the end, art is small beer. The really serious things in life are earning one's living so as not to be a parasite and loving one's neighbor. My vocation is to write poetry, but one mustn't overestimate its importance."

* * * * *

After lunch, while Chester sunbathes in the garden, Auden shows one around the two-hundred-year-old cottage, described in *About the House*. Chester Kallman's is the only room not mentioned in the book. The rooms are small, but comfortable, containing few possessions. During a long life, Auden seems to have left things where he found them. He has always traveled light. In the years before the war, he traveled a great deal.

"The really serious things in life are earning one's living so as not to be a parasite and loving one's neighbor. My vocation is to write poetry, but one mustn't overestimate its importance."

"When I went down from Oxford in 1928," he has written, "my parents offered me a year abroad. For the generation of intellectuals immediately preceding mine, the only culture that counted was French culture. I was bored with hearing about it, and therefore determined that, wherever I might go, it would not be Paris. Where then? Rome? No;

Mussolini and fascism made that impossible. Berlin? That was an idea. Why not? I knew no German and hardly any German literature, but then, nobody else I knew did either. . . . Perhaps, also, I had an unconscious bias in favor of Germany because, when I was a little boy in prep school during the First World War, if I took an extra slice of bread and margarine, some master was sure to say: 'I see, Auden, you want the Huns to win'—thus establishing in my mind an association between Germany and forbidden pleasures."

He spent two years in Berlin and was joined by Isherwood in 1929. In 1936 he traveled to Iceland with Louis MacNeice, in 1937 to Spain for the revolution, and in 1938 to China with Isherwood to write a book about the Sino-Japanese War.

In 1936 he had married Erika Mann, the daughter of Thomas Mann; she was running a cabaret in Amsterdam, when she lost her German nationality. Passportless, she couldn't leave the country. Isherwood, who happened to be in Amsterdam, wired Auden in England suggesting he should marry her, in order to give her British citizenship. Auden, who had never met her, wired back: "Delighted. Wystan." "In fact," says Auden, "Goebbels removed her nationality the day we were married." Why marriage? "It was a peculiar period. It had to be done." They remain married, though they rarely see one another. "She is in Switzerland now. Just the other day I heard she was dying." (Erika Mann died last August.)

Over China tea at four P.M., Auden talks of his "declining days," a subject Chester considers morbid, "really morbid, Wystan." He plans to live until he's eighty-four. "I'll have said everything I want to say by then. On the whole, I've had a very happy life. I can't say I haven't. I've been very lucky. And luck is a fact; I can't deny it." He wants to retire to Christ Church, Oxford. "After all, Cambridge did as much for Forster. Next time I'm there, I think I'll broach it to them."

He came down from Oxford forty-one years ago. "I went up as a scientist and found I simply wanted to read. Needless to say, I got a rather bad degree. But I always felt that one was wasting one's parents' money. I had a good time. Eighteen to twenty-one was a very happy period, though I suppose it is for everyone. Oxford was a place for England's elite. Which was all right. People can't be equal, it's absurd. We had certain advantages, no doubt unjust, but I had them and I'm not sorry I had them. As late as 1928, we lived as in prewar England. The older generation knew something had changed, but at Oxford the surface of life was the same."

Stephen Spender, meeting him at Oxford in 1928, found him interested in "poetry, psychoanalysis, and medicine. . . . At this early age, Auden had already an extensive knowledge of the theories of modern psychology, which he used as a means of understanding himself and dominating his friends."

They never listened to popular music or read the newspapers. "We were interested in the arts and personal relationships," says Auden.

C. Day-Lewis said, "It was his vitality, rather than his intellectual power, which most impressed itself on me at the start—a vitality so abundant that, overflowing into certain poses and follies and wildly unrealistic notions, it gave these an air of authority, an illusion of rightness, which enticed some of Auden's contemporaries into taking them over-seriously. His exuberance redeemed too, for me, the dogmatism, the intellectual bossiness, and the tendency to try and run his friends' lives for them, all of which were by-products of this excess of life."

Louis MacNeice, also at Oxford with Auden, saw him as "by nature partly a buffoon, and largely a gossip. Auden, then, as always, was busy getting on with the job . . . dressed like an untidy bank clerk and reading in a self-imposed blackout all sorts of technical unaesthetic matter or flapping his hands while he denounced the wearing of bright colors or the cultivation of flowers."

Day-Lewis describes him in 1927 taking his favorite walk past the gasworks and the municipal rubbish dump—"moving with his phenomenally long, ungainly stride, and talking incessantly, his words tumbling over one another in the hurry to get out, a lock of tow-colored hair falling over the brow of his rather puffy but wonderfully animated white face. As likely as not, he was carrying a starting pistol and wearing an extraordinary black lay-reader's type of frock coat which came halfway down to his knees and had been rescued by him from one of his mother's jumble sales."

Auden's first poems, twenty-six of them, were hand-printed by Spender on his press at Oxford in 1928. There were fewer than forty-five copies and the volume was dedicated to Isherwood. By now, he was taken with Eliot. "I sent Eliot my poems in 1929 and he asked me to come and see him. Later, he became my editor at Faber." Auden's reputation seemed to mushroom overnight. Quite suddenly, he, Spender, Day-Lewis, and others became a movement. "But there was no gang feeling among us. Writers of any particular period are going to have certain things in common, but that's the least interesting thing about them. It's their differences which are interesting." He doesn't know why he and the others were called the "Pylon Poets"—though Spender did write a poem called "The Pylons." "My own poetry is often pre-Pylon—the age of steam."

Until his sixteenth year, Auden's interests were almost exclusively in the age of steam. His father was a doctor, a professor of public health at Birmingham University and the school medical officer for the City of Birmingham. His mother had been a nurse. As a boy . . . his great loves were machinery and mines; he wanted to be a mining engineer.

Isherwood described him at school as a "sturdy, podgy little boy, precociously clever, untidy, lazy, and, with the masters, inclined to be insolent. His . . . playbox was full of thick scientific books on geology and metals and machines borrowed from his father's library. . . . With his hinted forbidden knowledge and

> stock of mispronounced scientific words, portentously uttered, he enjoyed among us, his semi-savage school-fellows, the status of a kind of witch doctor. . . .
>
> "Auden could never understand how anybody could long for the sun, the blue skies, the palm trees of the south. His favorite weather was autumnal; high wind and driving rain. He loved industrial ruins, a disused factory or an abandoned mill; a ruined abbey would leave him quite cold. He has always had a special feeling for caves and mines. At school, one of his favorite books was Jules Verne's *Journey to the Center of the Earth*."
>
> Auden has described himself at the time as "the son of book-loving, Anglo-Catholic parents of the professional class, the youngest of three brothers, I was . . . mentally precocious, physically backward, shortsighted, a rabbit at all games, very untidy and grubby, a nail biter, a physical coward, dishonest, sentimental, with no community sense whatever, in fact, a typical little highbrow and difficult child."

* * * * *

Tea is cleared away, the dinner table set. Although it is not yet dark, the curtains are drawn for the "cocktail hour." Auden makes the martinis himself; they are strong, often four-to-one. He has iced the glasses and always puts in two onions. One martini at six-thirty, another at seven—dinner promptly at seven-thirty. Ritual runs rampant. Exotic smells drift in from Chester's kitchen; he bustles in and out of the room. "Are you nearly finished, dearie? It's cocktail time," says Auden. Chester seems stricken; he looks at Auden piteously, as though he alone were heir to the mysteries of cooking Indonesian stew. "I can't do *every*thing," he says.

Chester returns to the kitchen; Auden sits primly on the edge of a chair, his thick, octopal hands wrapped around his tiny glass. He has been talking about his family and can drag up incidents which occurred before he was four.

"One of the games I love to play is the people my ma and pa should have married. Ma should have married a robust Italian who was very sexy and cheated on her. She would have hated it, but it would have kept her on her toes. Pa should have married someone weaker than he and utterly devoted to him. But, of course, if they had, I shouldn't be here. It's quite absurd.

"I remember at the age of seven seeing Ma and Pa in drag and bursting into tears. She had on his clothes and a false mustache and he was wearing hers. They were going to a masquerade, I think, and I suppose they thought it would amuse me. I was terrified. It was one of the last times I saw him as a child. My father was away during the 1914–18 war and I'm sure that's why I am the way I am. A child needs a mother up until the time he's seven. After that, he needs a father and mine was gone.

"I was brought up in a family which was more scientific than literary. As a boy, I constructed a private landscape based on the Pennine moors and lead mining; I was the sole autocratic inhabitant of a dream country of lead mines, narrow-gage tramways, and overshot waterwheels." The titles of his original nursery library bear this out. They included such things as *Icelandic Legends; Machinery for Metalliferous Mines; Eric, or Little by Little; Lead and Zinc Ores of Northumberland and Alston Moor; The Edinburgh School of Surgery; Hymns, Ancient and Modern;* and *Dangers to Health*—a Victorian treatise on plumbing.

He got on famously with his family—no rebelliousness there. "I never questioned my family's values, either as a child or an adult. It seems to me that the happiest relation, between parents and adult children certainly, is one of mutual affection and trust on the one hand, and of mutual reticence on the other. I was a precocious child. I didn't know what the word meant, of course, but I did know at the age of six that most of the adults I knew were stupid. I realized they knew more than I did, but only because they had lived longer. I was a little monster. I talked extravagantly. Adults never seem to realize that when a child uses four-syllable words when one syllable will do, it's a sign of a love for the language. That sort of thing is a vice in an adult, but a virtue in a child."

Following dinner, there is music, usually opera, and gossip. Bottles of Valpolicella are opened. Auden sits and smokes, lazily nodding his head. As the music crashes across the room, he seems to drift away, his partially closed eyes becoming just two more wrinkles in his lunar features. It's a face which invites outrageous metaphor—a savage geography, the sort of terrain which cavalry strategists or astronauts would avoid. A lonely face, as bleak and beckoning as the Pennine moors from whence he came.

Occasionally, he conducts a bar or two or hums snatches of the melody. Both he and Chester are notorious opera addicts. They've collaborated on the libretti of numerous operas, including Stravinsky's *Rake's Progress* and Brecht's *Seven Deadly Sins*. Chester was responsible for interesting Auden in opera. But opera, one feels, is just another of his shields, another of his ways of keeping busy in order to keep the world at bay. It follows the sort of formal principles he admires and conjures up a settled, sensible past, which he remembers with more than a little longing.

"My family seemed sanity itself compared to stories I hear about children's families today. Then, a lot of people might have been stuffy, dull, and repressed, but they had values and financial probity. I suppose that began to die in the '30s, though.

"The world of today is a little strange, but you cope with it. The young's lack of interest implies a lack of interest in the future. They want everything now. It looks as if traditional morality is to be succeeded by fashionable morality: heroin and de Sade will be in one year, cocoa and virginity the next. Moral decisions, of course, must always be taken in a basic context; but the context has disappeared.

"The so-called rebels of today are rebelling against permissiveness, which is so vague. You can't be a rebel anymore, because there's nothing fixed to rebel against. Look at that off-Broadway play, *Che!* They shouldn't have arrested the cast, they should've arrested the audience. I admire the young when they're anti-money, but what they mustn't do is take money from Papa and then criticize his way of life. The young have no humility. I think humility is the supreme virtue, just as pride is the major vice. It's the one virtue one ought to have and hasn't. But it's difficult to recognize. Often, you can't tell whether a humble person is humble for reasons of pride."

At Auden's request, Chester plays an Elaine May–Mike Nichols album. Auden particularly admires the possessive dialogue between a mother and her grown son. "The dialogue in this is better than most modern plays," he says between spasms of gruff laughter. Other records are played. The room is smoky, warm. Auden pours the last of the wine. He autographs a copy of *About the House*, tracking through its pages to alter words, often crossing out whole lines, inserting others in the margins. Presumably, the lines were "forgeries," "bad-mannered." Auden looks up. "You must learn to choose the truth before aesthetic preferences."

"I think humility is the supreme virtue, just as pride is the major vice. But it's difficult to recognize. Often, you can't tell whether a humble person is humble for reasons of pride."

Chester begins to talk of films and Auden looks into the distance, disinterestedly. He detests films, finding the medium "too naturalistic," the subject matter "too violent." Suddenly:

"I'm implacably conservative," he says. "It's not the world I knew." Chester yawns. "But I'm not going to give in." He looks away. "One fights little rearguard actions—for language, for civility."

There is a short silence: Chester picks up where he left off. Auden looks at his watch. Getting up, he empties the ashtrays, collects the empty glasses, and shuffles to the door. Chester agrees to wake him at eight A.M., to turn off the lights and the gramophone. At the door, Auden waves his hand tentatively, as though he were about to board a train on the other side. He and Chester exchange grim smiles. There's a little look of resignation in Auden's face. It's difficult and a bit bad-mannered to take the world too seriously at ten P.M.

Auden died three years after this article was published, at the age of sixty-six. Not everyone was enamored with Bradshaw's "lion-in-winter" tribute. "I'd read your profile of Auden in Esquire,*" Graham Greene wrote Bradshaw several years later. "He may have liked that sort of thing, but I certainly don't. I happen to think that one has a right to one's own private life." Greene didn't consent to an interview, but later, he and Bradshaw exchanged friendly correspondence.*

Tom Stoppard, Nonstop: Word Games with a Hit Playwright

New York, January 10, 1977

"Hello, I'm from journalism. I've come to inspect you. Take off your clothes and lie down."

The Quality Inn is an inferior hostelry in the upper reaches of Regent Street. Two men entered the inn and took a booth toward the back. The taller man, a playwright, carried a large leather bag. For reasons which later escaped him, the shorter man, a journalist, assumed it was filled with plays; he had been drinking seriously since noon and his perceptions were not what they had been before lunch. The playwright wore a blue imitation-leather suit, purple shoes emblazoned with red stars, and a black-and-white striped scarf into which was knitted in red the word "travesties." The journalist was certain of that. He drank his tea. The tea was rank and bagged. Lifting his hand, he summoned a waiter.

"May I have a drink?" he said.

"Only if you have something to eat."

"I don't want anything to eat."

"Suppose *I* have something to eat," said the playwright. "Can *he* have something to drink?"

"No, it's against the rules."

"Suppose I have something to drink," said the journalist. "Can *he* have something to eat?"

"I don't understand," said the waiter.

The journalist pushed the tea bag through the murky tea.

"Well, where shall we begin?"

"Why don't I give you a prepared statement?" the playwright said. "Actually, I'm quite prepared for interviews. I'm always interviewing myself. Or at least I used to. I don't have to interview myself anymore because people come and do it for me." He grinned. "Mind you, they don't do it as well as I do.

"I must tell you," he continued. "There's something you should know right away. I'll say *anything* to an interviewer, but somewhere in the middle of the piece, there ought to be a warning, like on cigarette packets. A warning which states: This profile is in the middle truth range. Don't inhale. And that's the point, since a profile shows just *one* side of somebody . . . a very good term for this particular *kind* of journalism."

"And which side did you intend to show?"

"The outside. That's what I like about interviews. Now, I suppose you'll want some sort of background. The facts. The wheres and whens?"

"Yes, I suppose. But don't exaggerate."

"Oh, I'm very good at giving boring interviews," he said. "I can say, yes, my name is Tom Stoppard and, yes, I'm thirty-nine and, yes, I left school at seventeen and joined the *Western Daily Press* as a junior reporter in 1954 and joined the *Bristol Evening World* in 1958 and, yes, I began to write *Rosencrantz* and *Guildenstern* in 1964. I'm very good at that. No problem. Wait while I get some cigarettes and I'll tell you some more."

He walked off to the back of the restaurant. The facts, to dispense with them immediately, were more than a little surprising. He was born in Czechoslovakia in 1937. Both his parents were Czech. He had an older brother. Shortly before the outbreak of World War II, the four of them were sent to Singapore, quite the wrong place to go since shortly after, the Japanese invaded it. The Stoppards were evacuated to India. Stoppard's father remained behind and died in Japanese captivity.

They spent the rest of the war in India—in Calcutta and in Darjeeling, where Stoppard attended an American multiracial school. In late 1945 his mother married an Englishman serving in the British army who early in 1946 brought them to England. "My stepfather's name was Stoppard," the playwright said, returning to the booth. "My father's name was Straussler, like the composer with *ler* at the end." He smiled. "As you can see, Tomas Straussler sits before you."

"Is that all?"

"Yes, I'm afraid that's it. I have never starved, never lived in a garret, and I've never had TB."

The playwright ordered another cup of tea. "When I left school," he said, "I wanted to be a great journalist. My first ambition was to be lying on the floor of an African airport while machine-gun bullets zoomed over my typewriter. But I wasn't much use as a reporter. I felt I didn't have the right to ask people questions. I always thought they'd throw the teapot at me or call the police. For me, it was like knocking at the door, wearing your reporter's peaked cap, and saying, 'Hello, I'm from journalism. I've come to inspect you. Take off your clothes and lie down.'

"But I wasn't much good at it and I never got to Fleet Street. Early on in my career, I had an interview with Mr. Charles Wintour, the editor of the *Evening*

Standard. At one point, Mr. Wintour asked me if I were interested in politics. Thinking all journalists should be interested in politics, I told him I was. He then asked me who the current home secretary was. Of course, I had no idea who the current home secretary was. And, in any event, it was an unfair question. I'd only admitted to an interest in politics. I hadn't claimed I was *obsessed* with the subject.

"But I'm through with all that now. I gave up journalism and became a playwright."

"But you have no objections to seeing journalists who have come to inspect *you*?"

"No, but I'm wary of them. Do you see what I'm saying?" The playwright paused to light a cigarette. "I feel I should preface this with an epigram, which is: Nothing is more studied than a repeated spontaneity. And on that note I'll repeat what I said to you the other day. You see, the unstated supposition to any interviewing situation is that I know the answers to the questions you're asking. And there are certain kinds of questions to which I do indeed know the answers. If you ask me how tall I am, I'll say six foot one, and tomorrow if you ask me again, I'll say the same thing . . . unless, of course, I've grown. But if you ask me what I think of Virginia Woolf, then the answer would have a different *status*."

"I now have a repertoire of plausible answers which evade the whole truth. The truth slips away and becomes something you probably won't mean tomorrow."

"What *do* you think of Virginia Woolf?"

"Well, in my opinion, Virginia Woolf was the tallest woman writer of the '20s."

"Are you quite sure?"

THURSDAY 21 APRIL

1977 111th day – 254 days follow

Paris

1:30 Fly to New York.

Drinks – Madam – Guest

Esquire – Byron Dobell

"Yes, yes. My information is that Katherine Mansfield was only four-foot-eleven and Edith Sitwell was only five-foot-three. But Virginia Woolf was six-foot-eight, a fact not commonly known." The playwright laughed. "Actually, life would be very simple if writers were judged by measurable criteria. Now as a matter of fact, I don't know if I'm six-foot-one, because I haven't measured myself lately. But then I would be being merely inaccurate, which is a different kind of a mistake. Do you see? I often give a frivolous answer to a serious question, which is a kind of a lie. I don't lie about my age or the number of bathrooms in my house, but if you ask me whether I write comedy because I am too insecure to make a serious statement, well, that's a complex question and rather than getting into it, it's much easier to say yes. One doesn't tell lies. I now have a repertoire of plausible answers which evade the whole truth. It just goes wrong. The truth slips away and becomes something you probably won't mean tomorrow."

"You could, of course, have a prepared statement, and when a newshound knocked at the door you could slide it out to him," said the journalist.

"Yes, or it would be very funny to have the answers written on cards and do tricks. You could say to the interviewer, 'Now listen, take a card, any card. Okay? Don't tell me what it is. Okay? Now ask me a question. Right. Now, look at the card. Got it?'"

The two men paid the bill and left the restaurant.

"You know, if every card said 'maybe,' you could get away with that," the playwright said.

* * * * *

The large stone Victorian house is situated near a busy traffic circle in Buckinghamshire. Tom Stoppard has lived here for four years with his wife and four children. During the week there are a nanny and a secretary in attendance. As the two men entered, little shrieks of welcome emanated from down the hall and the four children came rushing in. The journalist was introduced and the two men retired to another room.

"This is really a parlor sort of room, which I very rarely use," said the playwright. He seemed concerned. "I can put you into a more interesting room if you like."

Observing a bar in the corner, the journalist assured him the room was more than adequate—grand, even, in its way. Barnaby, the seven-year-old, came in.

"Daddy," he said, "when is Mr. Bradshaw leaving?"

"I suppose just as soon as we can get rid of him," his father said.

"Get *rid* of him?" said Barnaby.

Since the two men were going to a performance of *Dirty Linen*, an early dinner was served in the spacious kitchen. Miriam, the playwright's wife, served spaghetti. (Miriam, a doctor, author, and business executive, has become something of a British-television personality answering questions on popular medicine.) Everyone ate together at a large round table. Having set out the food and wine, Miriam sat down and said, "Tom, Mr. Bradshaw's not asked a question for some time."

"He's going to ask the questions later," said the playwright. "First he's collecting the incriminating domestic evidence."

Looking up from his plate, Barnaby watched his father eat spaghetti. "Daddy, why do you twist your fork like that?" he said.

"Because if you kept the fork still and twisted yourself," said the playwright, "you'd get dizzy and fall into the spaghetti."

After dinner the two men drove up to London. During the trip the playwright recalled the success of his first play. "In 1965 I began work on a novel called *Lord*

Malquist and Mr. Moon," he said. "I just couldn't write it. Time passed and I finally started it two days before it was due. I worked out that if I wrote thirty thousand words a day, I could still get it done in time." It was about this time that he also began work on *Rosencrantz* and *Guildenstern Are Dead*. "I believed my reputation would be made by the novel. I believed the play would be of little consequence. They both appeared in the same week in August of 1966. I remember taking the train back to London from Edinburgh, where *Rosencrantz* had opened at the Edinburgh Festival. I looked through the pages of the *Observer*. There was no mention of the book. But there was a photograph of me with a caption which said, 'The most brilliant dramatic debut since Arden.' And I thought to myself, 'I didn't know Arden had written novels.' But, of course, they were referring to the play. When I went to bed that night I remember thinking that some monstrous hoax had been perpetrated on me. The novel, on the other hand, did very badly. It sold about 688 copies and I'm told it did very well in Venezuela. I'm very big in Caracas, you know."

"In Caracas?"

"Well, not exactly *in* Caracas. Near Caracas."

It began to rain, and slowing down, the playwright turned on the windshield wipers. "I became a playwright," he said, "almost as the result of a historical accident. I began writing during a period when young writers in England wanted to be playwrights. In the late '50s, the playwright was the hottest thing in town. It's true. I promise you. Pinter, Osborne, Arden, and Wesker were the four hoarse men of the new apocalypse. Now, that's a truthful answer, in a limited way, as to why I write plays."

"And the rest of it?"

"Well, when I seriously consider why it is that I write plays, it has nothing to do with the social history of England or with what other people were writing around 1958. I'd rather write for the stage than television, for instance, because in a theater one has the full attention of one's audience, whereas while watching television one tends to glance at the newspaper, to talk, or to answer the telephone. I'm not terribly keen on having my plays performed in that sort of situation. And I'm not terribly attracted to writing novels because their impact is dispersed over the time it takes someone to read them. And could I trust my readers to lock the doors and take the telephone off the hook? I could not. There is also the fact that I like theaters as places. So one begins to see that my plausible answer turns out to be very much like a lie.

"*Rosencrantz* came about in a curious way. I was riding back from one of the commercial television stations with my agent, where I had failed to convince them that I was *the* person to write an *Armchair Theatre*. We were talking about a production of *Hamlet* at the Old Vic. He said there was a play to be written about Rosencrantz and Guildenstern after they got to England. What happened to them once they got there? I was attracted to it immediately.

"The play had no substance beyond its own terms, beyond its apparent situation. It was about two courtiers in a Danish castle. Two nonentities surrounded by intrigue, given very little information and much of that false. It had nothing to do with the condition of modern man or the decline of metaphysics. One wasn't thinking, 'Life is an anteroom in which one has to kill time.' Or I wasn't, at any rate. God help us, what a play that would have been." He paused to light a cigarette. "I think I've actually seen one or two of those plays," he said. "But *Rosencrantz* and *Guildenstern* wasn't about that at all. It was about two blokes, right?

"But there you go. There's a deep suspicion among serious people of comic situations. The point is that good fun is merely frivolous. There was something I said the other day which bears repeating. The trouble is that I think I said it to you. Never mind. I think I used to have a redeeming streak of seriousness in my work and now I have a redeeming streak of frivolity. That's a neat way of putting it and I wouldn't say it represents the *precise* truth of the matter. But that *is* the tendency.

"I'm stuck with the kind of plays I write. I'm stuck with the level I write on because I enjoy humor, I'm good at humor, and I enjoy it being performed and laughed at."

"I tend to see everything through a comic prism. *After Magritte*, for example, sprang from a friend's story about the morning he was shaving when he saw from the bathroom window his pet peacock leap over the garden hedge and make off down the road. Peacocks being rare birds, he dropped his razor and, barefoot and lathered, he pursued it, caught it, and returned with the peacock under his arm. Now, I tend to write plays about people who drive by in a car at that particular moment. They see a man in pajamas, bare feet, and shaving foam, carrying a peacock, for about a third of a second. They never see him again. They never quite understand what it is they've seen. They probably wouldn't even agree on what it was.

"You see, I know what I'm after. And it's like this. I'm stuck with the kind of plays I write. I'm stuck with the level I write on because I enjoy humor, I'm good at humor, and I enjoy it being performed and laughed at—ironic juxtapositions, all that sort of thing. And that's what I've got to do. Because if I decided to write a modern Greek tragedy in blank verse, I'd just write rubbish. You see, I want to demonstrate that I can make serious points by flinging a custard pie around the stage for a couple of hours. In other words, I want to write plays that are just funny enough to do their jobs but not too funny to obscure them. My line at the moment would be to try to reduce weighty preoccupations about the way the world is going to an extended exchange of epigrams with a good first-act curtain."

"Your plays aren't peopled by what one would call *real* people. Why don't people interest you as much as words?"

"I don't know. I don't know. I mean you're wrong actually to put it in quite those terms. I'm not a lexicographer. I'm not interested in words as such, I'm interested in ideas. But there's no other way to express an idea except in words. It's a distinction worth making. I'm not being pedantic. I'm not James Thurber, who, if he couldn't get to sleep, thought up ninety-three words beginning with *pqu* or something. That's not it at all. Couldn't care less. Never do crosswords. Don't care."

The car crossed the Hammersmith cloverleaf and moved into central London. "It doesn't interest me in any way to create *characters*. In *Dirty Linen*, the Chairman is off the shelf and Miss Gotobed is off another shelf. She's not a *real* character. What interests me is getting a cliché and then betraying it. Miss Gotobed is a busty lady who triumphs in the play and she's sharper and brighter about a lot of things and that's fine, but it doesn't mean she's a real character at all. In fact, it probably means that she's *less* real than anybody else.

"Incidentally, it's worth pointing out that you make it sound as though I belong to some rather exclusive little club who write plays which aren't about real people. Without making too much of it, it *appears* that my plays which aren't about real people go down well with enormous numbers of real people. Now you tell me why that is."

"Well, perhaps characters in a play are never *real*. Have you met anybody who's reminded you of Oedipus Rex lately?"

"Only my father. God, I should say immediately into this tape recorder that it's not true, I have a weakness for wisecracks which I don't sometimes have the tact to withhold. I always think that mere untruth is a very poor reason for restraint. Let me rephrase that. Accuracy is a high price to pay for truth. End of epigram." The playwright laughed and then in a solemn voice said, "This epigram has been brought to you by Hitachi.

"You know, the kind of joke I enjoy the most is a tautology. When I was at school we used to listen to

He was very generous, spirit-wise. That doesn't come naturally to a lot of writers but it came naturally to Bradshaw. It wasn't always about himself. He was genuinely interested in other people and not what he could get out of them.

Lewis Lapham

The Goon Show, and I remember they were doing a sketch on colonial India and there was this joke. One of the Goons, Spike Milligan, I suppose, said, 'And then the monsoons came, and they couldn't have come at a worse time, bang in the middle of the rainy season.' Now, that to me is a perfect joke. My kind of joke is a snake in a funny hat eating its own tail. Tautologies, right? And for reasons which may be very uninteresting indeed, I'm very fond of them."

"You do speedwriting, I suppose?"

"Yes, if I'm given enough time."

"How long have you been a pedestrian?"

"Ever since I could walk."

"And how do you see yourself in the scheme of things?"

"*Je suis, ergo sum.*"

"I *thought* so. It's a theme that runs throughout your work."

* * * * *

The two men walked hurriedly up Great Newport Street. It was still raining and they were late for *Dirty Linen*. "It's raining," the playwright said. "Let's duck into the nearest theater."

Entering the crowded theater, the playwright was recognized by several of the lingering astute and a flurry of whispers rose in his wake. The two men retreated to the upstairs bar.

"How many times have you seen *Dirty Linen*?" said the journalist.

"Twelve," said the playwright, "and it gets better every other time."

Moments later, the bell rang and the two men took their seats. The playwright took pen and paper from his leather bag in order to make notes on the performance. It was a habit of his to stop in from time to time to assure himself (and the actors) that matters were running smoothly. The houselights went down. The play began and one was soon immersed in jokes—tautologies and puns, wisecracks and japes, non sequiturs, absurd conceits, and epigrams—followed about an hour later by the curtain and much applause. A man sitting two seats away turned to his wife and said, "Is that the *end*?" The two men returned to the bar.

"*Dirty Linen* sort of grew like Topsy, really," the playwright said. "Ed Berman, the director, would have been perfectly happy if I'd turned in a twenty-five-minute sketch, which is all I'd intended to do because I didn't have any ideas and because I couldn't think of a sketch relating to his own particular needs, which were for a season of plays about America or something to do with America. I ended up using an idea I'd saved for some other occasion and that idea was to have a play about a committee of very high-powered people. I was thinking of the archbishop of Canterbury and the prime minister, the equivalent of Einstein, some guy doing nuclear physics, a theologian, a philosopher, and they were going to have this committee meeting on some topic worthy of their brain power, and there was going to be this staggering bird, who was there to sharpen the pencils and pass the water carafe around, and I was going to have her correcting them on points of theology and nuclear physics in a very bland sort of way.

"I hadn't developed the idea beyond that single notion of dislocating the category of dumb blondes, you see. Finally, out of despair—you know, the usual deadline trouble—I began writing that play in the form of a committee meeting to debate Ed Herman's application for British citizenship. Got sick of that, decided to hell with Berman's American problem, and just wrote *Dirty Linen*. And then, you see, because there is a God and he *does* look after writers, I realized that all I had to do was to have an adjournment, put in fifteen minutes about America, and I'd solved Berman's problem as well. And the whole thing is a nonsense, of course, little more than an extended joke."

"What are you doing next?"

"What next? Well, I've written a sort of play which involves six actors and a symphony orchestra. The setting is contemporary, political in its implications, to do with human rights, and the treatment is tragi-comic. The idea, which was suggested by André Previn, appealed as much as anything to my incipient megalomania, I think. I just love the idea of having a hundred musicians in a play. And I'm very in awe of conductors. Apart from Evel Knievel, I think the conductor of a great orchestra is the most awesome figure on earth.

"You see, ultimately, before being carried out feetfirst, I would like to have done a bit of absolutely everything. Really, without any evidence of any talent in those other directions, I find it very hard to turn down offers to write an underwater ballet for dolphins or a play for a motorcyclist on the wall of death. That's why I did this thing with André Previn. No one ever asked me to write a play with a symphony orchestra before. Probably no one ever will again."

The theater was empty now but for a few of the actors who had come up to the bar to chat with the playwright and to have a drink before going home. "Are you bothered much with urgent requests from people seeking *meaning* in your work?" the journalist said.

"Not often, but often enough to be irritating," he said. "You see, plays are written to entertain, they're *theatrical*. I don't want to be disobliging or churlish to people who are invariably nice and are paying me a real compliment in asking academic questions about my plays. But I do insist on making the point that they aren't written to be studied and discussed. No plays are written to be studied and discussed any more than pictures are painted to be discussed. The lit-crit industry is now approaching the dimensions of ITT. It reminds me of a very good footnote to an edition of Goethe's letters. Goethe was saying something like 'And now, I fell in love for the first time.' And in the footnote, the editor said, 'Here, Goethe was mistaken. In 18 . . .'" He laughed. "You know?"

"What about the style of your work? You've been accused of being all style and no substance," said the journalist.

"Not quite. In my own work, I think if you took away the style, the gift for putting things in certain ways, if you took that away and rewrote everything so that it was pedestrian, but said the same thing, then you would have a residue of a certain number of things worth saying, but not worth listening to. I don't think I would say that of, say, Oscar Wilde. I think Wilde was *motivated* by style, which is a different thing. With Wilde, style was not merely the means, it was the end. In my own work the distinction between style and substance is never quite as clear as an academic might wish it to be. I'm not a writer who doesn't care what things mean and doesn't care if there isn't any meaning, but despite myself I *am* a kind of writer who doesn't give a fair crack of the whip to that meaning. The plays tend to give an impression of effervescence and style and wit for their own sake and thereby obscure what to me is the core of the toffee apple."

"There's no point in being quoted if one isn't going to be quotable."

"The toffee apple?"

"A toffee apple, American readers, is a sort of hot dog, taken from Sanskrit. . . . *Tof* meaning 'hot' and *ap*, a sort of dog."

"Are you prepared to stand by that?"

"Well, I write fiction because it's a way of making statements I can disown. And I write plays because dialogue is the most respectable way of contradicting myself."

"Not bad," said the journalist. "May I quote you on that?"

"There's no point in being quoted if one isn't going to be quotable," the playwright said.

Bradshaw playing softball with expats in London

Dirty Linen was not a huge hit, but fear not, Stoppard had plenty more success in his future, including *The Real Thing*, which had a memorable, award-winning production in the early '80s featuring Jeremy Irons and Glenn Close, directed by Mike Nichols. Two decades later, he won a Tony again for Best Play with *The Coast of Utopia*. In addition to his theater work, he's written many radio plays and screenplays, including cowriting *Shakespeare in Love*. He's even had his hand in the *Indiana Jones* and *Star Wars* franchises.

Hunter Thompson, on a Bat: Fear and Loathing in Mayfair

The Village Voice, May 19, 1975

"He's never been this bad. I've never seen him go this far before. Christ, in Zaire he was an absolute menance."

We were somewhere deep in Berkeley Square in a dive decorated to look like an early '30s cocktail lounge when the malaria began to take hold. Dr. Gonzo leaned wearily against the bar and wiped his forehead with the back of his hand. "Great creeping Jesus," he screamed, "it's the *cold* sweats this time. They're the fucking worst. This town is diseased. You'd think they'd protect tourists from vicious bugs. The fucking things are everywhere, Ralph. Ralph, where the hell are you? I need a fucking doctor. Immediately!"

Ralph Steadman, artist and amiable patriarch, sat next to Gonzo at the bar scanning the gigantic drinks list. "Have a drink," he said. "This list says you can have anything from tequila sunrises to scorpions. Have them both. They'll do you some good."

"I'll have three Bloody Marys," said Gonzo to the startled barman. "And I want a lot of lime in them. The little fuckers hate lime. Takes the poison out of them. And, Ralph, if that doesn't help, I'll need a doctor. I think I need a doctor anyway. I need a massive jolt of tetracycline. I *know*. I've had malaria before. It's not the sort of thing you fuck around with."

Dr. Gonzo and Mr. Steadman had flown into London two days before from Zaire, where they had gone to report the George Foreman–Muhammad Ali fight. Now, sitting in this darkened bar, the talk, whenever Gonzo could take his mind off his galloping malaria, was of the fight and their deadline for *Rolling Stone* the next day. "Shit, I've got ten thousand words to write for tomorrow," said Gonzo, "and I haven't even started yet. There's not a lot of time, and what do I come down with in this poxy town? Fucking malaria."

According to the heated accounts of the intrepid duo, Zaire had been an ominous assignment. They had had to fight their way out of the country—"hand-to-hand combat" is how it was described—just managing to catch the last plane out to Lagos and New York. At Kennedy airport, customs officers confiscated a pair of Gonzo's recently acquired elephant tusks, though he managed to retrieve them by sneaking into the customs shed when the officer had his back turned. In New York, they learned John Daly, one of the fight's promoters and a key figure in their story, was in London and would talk to them there. Arriving in London, they learned that Daly had flown to New York. Now, hunkered down in Brown's Hotel, they seethed and awaited his return.

"We're lucky to be alive," said Steadman. "Zaire was a narrow escape. Quite naturally, when we get off the plane and walk into Brown's at nine in the morning, Hunter orders three Bloody Marys, a dozen beers, a bottle of Scotch, a bottle of Wild Turkey, and the number of the nearest brothel. They thought he was crazy and it was all downhill after that. Last night he was accused of trying to rape one of the maids and of shooting pigeons on the window ledge with a Magnum .44. This morning I find him in bed with a girl. At some point during the night, he had drawn a swastika on her ass in indelible ink. She dropped her drawers to show it to me. She said she would wear it forever. I don't know how much longer London will put up with us. I don't like it. We're getting a lot of weird looks in the hotel lobby."

Dr. Gonzo orders another two Bloody Marys and says he's going to the toilet. "Keep your eye on the bartender," he says to Steadman on the way out. "I think he's trying to cheat me on the lime. If he doesn't put in enough, shoot him."

"How long can he go on like this?" someone asks.

"Well," says Steadman, "it's not good. I'd say another fifty years. He'll beat himself to hell, die peacefully in his sleep at ninety, and everyone will say he got exactly what he deserved. But he's never been *this* bad. I've never seen him go this far before. Christ, in Zaire he was an absolute menace."

Dr. Gonzo returns to the bar, takes a sip of his drink, and glares at the barman.

"There's not enough lime in here," he says. "Do you want the little bastards to escape?" He is wearing Levi's, a checked shirt, a kind of smart Canadian lumberman's jacket with an obscure foreign press badge on the pocket, tennis shoes, and tinted glasses. Balding, he has the look of an elderly athlete with perhaps another season in him.

"Shit, I feel terrible," he says. "I haven't slept for three days. And now this malaria. I deserve better things. Ralph, goddamn it, get a doctor, will you? I want him here now. Tell him to bring some tetracycline with him. I know how to deal with this thing. And I'll need some coke. I may as well take every precaution I can. It's a fucking twisted world we live in. I need protection."

Steadman goes to find a telephone.

"I need an Irish coffee," he says to the barman. "But I don't want any scum on top. Just whiskey, sugar, and hot coffee. I've got the cold sweats. Jesus, I'm beginning to have visions."

"How was the fight?" someone asks.

"What fight?" mumbles Gonzo, swilling down the Irish coffee. "I never saw the fucking fight. Who won? I don't like fights anyway. Thirty minutes before it started, I gave our tickets to some crazy wino I found in the hotel lobby. My mind was on other things, important things. I'd bought $1,000 of grass the day before and was ripped off. It was bad stuff. Ugly. So I cast it over the waters of the hotel swimming pool and went swimming until the fight was over. Under the circumstances, it was the only thing to do. It's not the sort of country in which you have a lot of choices. A savage place filled with a lot of malignant mutants. I was lucky to escape with my life, believe me. Thirty years of hard labor at best. You're looking at a man who has looked into the face of death—and then kicked him in the balls. I'm lucky to be here. Listen, one night, kicking down the door in my hotel room, because I'd lost my key, I heard this awful growl in the hallway. It was pitch dark because the fuses had blown. I flashed a light and there was Foreman walking down the hall with a huge German shepherd beside him. I thought I was having hallucinations. I wasn't. He walked up and down that dark hall every night—brooding. It was all like that. It was a savage place."

* * * * *

Steadman returned to say the doctor insisted on looking at Gonzo personally at six that afternoon. Steadman himself would have to leave. The art deadline was imminent. There were a lot of lunatics in San Francisco screaming like banshees for the cover and Steadman didn't want to be too late. He begged Gonzo to take care of himself, to go back to the hotel, lock himself in, rip out the telephone, and do some work. Gonzo nodded and ordered another Irish whiskey.

"Are there any girls in town?" he asked when Steadman had gone. "I want to rape someone. I need about 113 orgasms before I can do any serious work tonight." He looked out the window. "What's the penalty for rape in Berkeley Square?" he asked.

Two Irish whiskeys later, he seemed to have forgotten girls and began to talk of tailors. He needed a suit, he said, possibly two. "Let's get a few bottles of beer and find a tailor. We'll need something to drink while I'm being fitted. You know what tailors are like. Mean bastards. Never keep drink on the premises." He turned to the barman. "Bartender," he shouted, "I'll need eight bottles of beer, Tuborg will do, and a brown paper bag to transport them." He reached into his wallet, extracting his last bill—a Zaire ten-franc note. "Look at this," he said. "You're not allowed to take the fucking currency out of the country. I forgot. Good thing they didn't find it on me. The penalty's life imprisonment." He handed the note to the barman. "Bartender, here, I think this will just about cover the beer. If there's any change left, keep it, you deserve it. You have a dirty job. You must get a lot of maniacs in a place like this." The barman elected to consult the owner. "If they cause any trouble," whispered Gonzo, "we'll take both the bastards outside and execute them. Castrate the fuckers. On second thought, it might be easier to shoot them. We don't have a lot of time."

But the owner was persuaded, and, taking the Tuborg in a blue polythene bag, we set off for the tailor's. In the backroom of the tailor shop, the proprietor listened patiently. "Listen," said Gonzo, sipping beer, "it's ridiculously simple. I need two suits, one maybe in white and one in black. You can put in some stripes if you like, or some polka dots, but nothing fashionable. They have to be boss gambler's suits. That's the main thing. I use them on my lecture tours. They have to create an immediate effect, you understand. Give me a pencil and I'll draw them for you."

After a loud and complicated conversation and a series of surrealistic drawings, the wild-eyed tailor began to scream.

"Listen," he said, "I don't know who you are or where you came from, but I'll tell you where to go. Go to Hollywood and look up one of the studio costumiers. They'll have exactly what you want, whatever that is. They'll probably even have it in stock. Try MGM. They did a lot of Mississippi gambler pictures."

"Christ," said Gonzo out in the street. "There's a lot of hate in this town. A lot of dingbats and freaks. We'll have to be careful. It's a weird place. That tailor should be locked up. He needs electric shock treatment right away. That's my advice. Zap him—a thousand volts twice a day. He'll never make it otherwise. Did you see his eyes? Ugly. Really ugly."

Memories of the rest of the day are extremely hazy. At an Italian restaurant, Gonzo offered the proprietress the opportunity of an afternoon in bed with him in exchange for a free meal. The doctor provided him with a battery of pills, an ounce of coke, and vials of vitamin B12. We finished off the bottles of malt whiskey and Wild Turkey in his room at the hotel and arranged with an escort agency for five girls to meet us at midnight. Toward eleven in the evening, we attended a crowded dinner party in Belsize Park. We had only been there for fifteen minutes when Gonzo began to growl, his eyes shifting to the top of his head.

"Christ," said Gonzo out in the street. "There's a lot of hate in this town. A lot of dingbats and freaks. We'll have to be careful. It's a weird place."

"What sort of weird place have you brought me to?" he shouted. "They don't have any ice in this joint, not a cube. And worse, there's no whiskey. Christ, you can't take any chances in this town. You've got to carry your own booze with you at all times. Let's go out and get some drink. Where the hell are we anyway?"

At this point, a chubby but pretty girl, who at some particularly decadent stage in her life had read a few of the doctor's mad scribblings, offered to take us back to her flat promising as much whiskey as we could drink. En route in the car, Gonzo extracted the vials of vitamin B12 from his pocket. "Shoot some of this," he said, "it's a great high. Keeps you going for days. It's absolutely essential. Keeps your mind on the key issues."

The girl—she was called Sara or Emma or Annabelle, we were never certain—had a penthouse flat in Belgravia. She provided whiskey and a lot of ice. Gonzo produced his coke and passed it round on the end of a switchblade. For about five minutes it was peaceful. But Gonzo, now into his third Scotch, suddenly asked the girl if she would like to be raped.

"You'll like it," he said. "You have that look about you. I always recognize it immediately. You can see it in the eyes. It's a fearful look."

The girl giggled but declined. "Why use violence?" she purred. "Can't we just fuck normally?"

"Normally?" he shouted. "What the hell does that mean? Are you some sort of weird freak? I want to rip off your clothes, rape you, tear you limb from limb, and throw you into the street. You'll like it. Believe me, goddamn it, I'm an expert. I *know* what I'm doing."

This time, the girl did not giggle. Rather nervously, she suggested it was time for us to go and edged toward the telephone. "No, I think *you'd* better leave," she said.

"I'm beginning to like it here. You can have my room at Brown's. It's a nice hotel, a little crazy, a lot of freaks in the lobby and roaming the halls, but perfectly safe. I'll stay here. Just show me the bedroom before you go."

The girl, however, seemed adamant and began to scream. Filling her crystal glasses with enough whiskey to last the journey, we left. Gonzo left her a five-franc note for the glasses.

"Shit," he said, on the way back to Brown's, "have you ever run across a weirdo like that before? A raving lunatic. Must be the lack of sun. This is the coldest town I've ever been in. My soul is cold. And all these crazies running round. How do you manage it? I couldn't live here unless I was heavily armed at all times. Wouldn't be safe. There are a lot of weird hostilities here. I can feel them everywhere."

Dr. Gonzo's hotel room looked as if it had been burgled only moments before. There was litter everywhere—empty whiskey bottles, numerous files on the fight in Zaire strewn on the unmade bed and the floor, clothes, newspapers, magazines, and a purple bra which had been ripped in half. "The maids don't set a foot in here anymore," he said. "They're terrified. I've only been here for two days and they sent me a bill this morning. Is that normal?" On the desk was a large IBM typewriter which had been sent over by *Rolling Stone*. "On that machine," he pointed out, "I can type as fast as I can think. And I'm going to have to think fast. I've only got nine hours till my deadline." Above the desk on the wall, Gonzo had pasted a large poster of the fight, and perching precariously on one of the pictures was a long sign which said ANGER—HIGH VOLTAGE. The room looked like that of a man who had been there for several months.

In the bathroom there was about a half an inch of water on the carpeted floor. "Look at that," he shouted, "there's no overflow outlet. Every time I turn on the bath it overflows onto the floor. The guy below must be going crazy. Two days of that and I figure the water must be over his head by now. And the miserable geek hasn't even bothered to inform the management. Stiff upper lip. The English are crazy."

Toward 3:00 A.M., the savage drama was coming to its end. All the whiskey had been consumed and four hysterical phone calls to the night porter had failed to provide any more. Gonzo now decided that he would have to return home immediately.

"I want you to get me on the first plane out to Woody Creek, Colorado. Offer bribes. Just get me on anything going west. And be quick about it, goddamn it. I've got a deadline to meet."

"Shit," he screamed, throwing his mess into a battered case, "I can't get anything done in this town. There's nothing left to drink in the whole country, the hotel is repressed, the streets are filled with bands of armed masturbators. It's a twisted place, teetering on the brink of insanity. It's ugly, *very* ugly. There's only one thing to do. Go home. I'll never work otherwise. Great creeping Jesus, it must have cost *Rolling Stone* $10,000 already on this story. I'll have to give them something. I should've hired somebody to write the fucking thing and saved myself a lot of trouble."

He banged the telephone receiver up and down. "This is Dr. Gonzo," he said, "I want you to get me on the first plane out to Woody Creek, Colorado. Lean on those fuckers at the airport. Get heavy. Offer bribes. Just get me on anything going west. Get me on anything going west. And be quick about it, goddamn it. I've got a deadline to meet."

Thompson didn't meet the deadline, and his failure to deliver a piece on the Ali-Foreman fight, which attracted literary big shots such as Norman Mailer and George Plimpton, stands as one of the big misses in an otherwise prosperous career. Arguably the most famous American magazine writer of his time, Thompson died of a self-inflicted gunshot wound to the head at the age of sixty-seven in 2005.

MARCH **11** FRIDAY

New York

1977 70th day – 295 days follow

Esquire Magazine

Shopping with Anna

Drinks, Nick Cohn, The Russian Tea Room

(Anna)

London Taxi to Airport –

TWA – Air France to Paris

Richard Goodwin: The Good, the Bad, and the Ugly

New York, August 18, 1975

"You must have a kind of defiance in the end. That and the ability to struggle with your own insanities. That's what keeps me going."

They had all been taken by surprise. It was an accident, of course, an absurdity, although later the older man recalled that these were the sorts of accidents that seemed to disturb his most innocent adventures. Not more than twenty minutes before, he had cut the engine; jumping into the shallow sea, he had guided the boat to the beach. The younger man, the two women, and the boy lurched over the side and waded ashore. Taking the anchor, the older man sank it into the sand. He had hired the boat for the day in order to take his son fishing. He had even bought two fishing rods and some hideous though colorful plastic lures. But they were to have lunch first, and they trudged up the beach toward the high bluffs behind. Not more than twenty minutes could have passed. It was the boy, Richard, who saw it first; jumping up and down, he screamed that the tide was going out. The four adults turned around. The boat, the goddamn fishing boat, was high on a mud flat several yards away from the receding sea.

They ran down the beach, the older man, Goodwin, running ahead. Heaving the boat in semicircular motions, they managed to move it several yards; but they could not keep pace with the sea. Lighting up an old cigar, Goodwin suggested they have lunch in the boat, a long, leisurely lunch, and wait on the turn of the tide. They took their places in the boat—Richard Goodwin, Doris Kearns, a young friend, Anna Wintour, who was a fashion editor at *Harper's Bazaar*, and the other, younger man—your correspondent. Only Richard, Goodwin's nine-year-old son, who was afraid of the sea, refused to sit in the boat. He sat instead on a nearby sandbank reading *The Making of Kubrick's "2001."*

They were mired on the eastern edge of Great Island, which jutted into the bay near the village of Wellfleet in Cape Cod. Across the wide harbor was Lieutenant's Island, where Goodwin and Kearns had taken a house for the summer. They had come to Cape Cod to escape Washington, where they lived for most of the year, or, as Goodwin liked to put it, "to escape this tidal wave of bullshit that threatens to engulf us." He referred to the press and the strident publicity surrounding their work-in-progress, their "psycho-history" of Lyndon Johnson. But their retreat had not been successful. Even here, on the barren reaches of Cape Cod, the telephone daily announced the latest Byzantine turn in the plot, and journalists and photographers came and went with the regularity of commuters. Even now, at this very moment, another viper was in residence, sprawled in the goddamn boat, quaffing vodka and filling his face with food. Goodwin and Kearns had come to work, and little or no work was being done. Goodwin looked at me suspiciously. "I'm not talking to anyone else," he growled. "I'm drawing the line with you." Goodwin growled with great charm, like a retired general. But he was not to be taken literally. Others, I knew, choked with cameras and questions, would almost certainly follow me; and Goodwin, despite his best intentions, or perhaps because of them, would not resist their blandishments. He was not a man who spurned seducers.

Concerning the book, much of the publicity had been uncomplimentary. As Robert Kennedy's former press secretary, Frank Mankiewicz, had pointed out: "For people who know as much about public relations as those two, they're not winning any of the battles." And they could not resign themselves to that. They had, they said, made final statements and had nothing more to say; and they kept on making them. Doris Kearns wanted only to complete her book, achieve tenure at Harvard, marry Goodwin, and drop, however momentarily, from view. Richard Goodwin, having publicly announced that he would no longer coauthor the book, wanted merely to sail, to play electronic tennis in the local groggeries, to get on with his own writing, and to bar his door to the world. The matter had been given over to lawyers. Only that morning, their lawyer, Edward Bennett Williams, had telephoned and said, "Dick, leave everything to me. I've set up a suing office down here in Washington and, goddamn it, we're going to sue." And there, for the moment, the matter rested.

In New York, Cambridge, and Washington, however, the matter, or "the scandal," as it was often called, had not been so casually forgotten. In those literary, academic, and political circles where gossip is the only real form of conversation, one invariably encountered splendid displays of indignation when Kearns-Goodwin were mentioned. One remembered the journalists, the professors, and the politicians greedily disemboweling Goodwin—ridiculing his warped charm, his maniacal lust for power, his arrogance, his Machiavellian manner. One remembered the sorrowful references to "poor, poor Doris," how she had been seduced, manipulated. In those provincial feuds which occasionally erupt in New York, there was little doubt that Richard Goodwin had become the villain of the piece—"Rasputin out of Frankenstein," as one of his admirers liked to put it. For the moment, however, sitting in his bathing suit in the back of the boat, he looked more like a choleric troll. "The gossip round Cambridge," he said, "is that Doris has been enslaved by the potent sexual powers of Dick Goodwin." He stood up and looked out to sea. "How did they find out?" Doris Kearns laughed.

Despite his humor, Goodwin was secretly enraged. This literary imbroglio, he felt, had cost him considerable time and money. It is not every day, after all, that a writer returns a check to his publisher for $75,000. "This book of ours, which is rapidly becoming an underground classic," he said in a flat Boston accent, "this 'leap of greed,' as the newspapers would call it, has put me deep in debt. True, I was in debt before it happened, but it was the kind of debt you could pay off over a period of time and still live well. Now, considering the time I spent on the book, sending the money back, and the lawyer's fees, I'm irremediably, irretrievably, irrevocably in debt. So

(oops!)

THE AMERICAN CONDITION

To John Bradshaw

Among The chosen few who understands even as he embodies The American Condition.

From his friend,

Richard N. Goodwin

Richard Goodwin inscription

much for my alleged financial prowess. Listen," he said to me, "let's go out and buy a boat tomorrow, a big boat, a boat that won't bog down. The fact that I'm overwhelmingly in debt should be no deterrent."

Goodwin had a genius for controversy. As speechwriter for John Kennedy and Lyndon Johnson, as political strategist for Eugene McCarthy and Robert Kennedy, he had provoked wonderful dissensions. Quarrels, estrangements, debt, and death had dogged him throughout his long career. He had an aptitude for trouble as other men have aptitudes for music or architecture. It created uncomfortable conundrums. On the one hand, he seemed to me a man with no more than his share of the usual vices and virtues—a man who disliked himself no more than he approved of others; a shy man who mumbled fluently; calculative but sincere; self-conscious yet self-absorbed; intelligent with a sure sense of the absurdity of things; no more arrogant than any journalist, no less persuasive than any parish priest; a man who used his complicated charm to conceal himself while influencing his enemies—on the whole an agreeable man. And yet, the legions of people to whom I had talked took particular pleasure in denigrating him. Goodwin had been variously described as a marvelous reptile, a gunslinger, a shark, a warped genius, a mythomaniac, an intellectual quack, a wily Svengali, and even, I remembered, with considerable envy, an antichrist. Everyone, it seemed, who had come into contact with Goodwin had carried away some secret consternation, some ugly doubt, some rich disgruntlement, which over the years had left multitudes of anti-Goodwinites across the land. Everyone loved to hate him.

Sitting now in the back of the boat, the antichrist took the sun and puffed at his cigar. He dismissed his reputation with a kind of wry insouciance, although it puzzled him somewhat. "God knows," he said, "but Goodwin doesn't care. It's very odd, you know. Wherever I go, that small black cloud appears. Trouble arises from my most innocent encounters. I've never quite understood it. But the trouble's always there, practically at my heel, like a faithful hound."

* * * * *

In 1961, when John Kennedy became president, Goodwin was named assistant special counsel. And still he remained uncertain that that was what he should be doing. "I had ambivalent feelings about getting stuck in politics," he said. "I was twenty-nine and I thought I would like to do other things. But I was a classic liberal Democrat and I actually thought that if good guys like us could get our hands on the controls we could do good things. But it soon became clear that it was very difficult to get your hands on the controls. You know, people really come to Washington believing it's the center of power. I know I did. It was only much later I learned that Washington is a steering wheel that's not connected to the engine."

"Wherever I go, that small black cloud appears. I've never quite understood it. But the trouble's always there, practically at my heel, like a faithful hound."

To be twenty-nine, the youngest man in the White House, to be well paid, but not overly, to have men raise their hats as you walked by, to have the tedious bric-a-brac of your life attended to by lifting up the telephone, to have aides and limousines at your disposal, who would not have flourished? And he probably went too far. He certainly came in for violent criticism. "Some, especially in those early years, found his personality, in a favorite Washington word, abrasive," said Arthur Schlesinger Jr. "He was certainly driving and often impatient; those whom he overrode called him arrogant. But he was a man of uncommon intelligence, perception, and charm. Above all, he had immense facility, both literary and intellectual. Kennedy liked his speed, wit, imagination, and passion. . . . It seemed to me that in many ways Dick Goodwin, though younger than the average, was the archetypal New Frontiersman. . . . He was the supreme generalist who could turn from Latin America to saving the Nile monuments at Abu Simbel, from civil rights to planning the White House dinner for the Nobel Prize winners, from composing a parody of Norman Mailer to drafting a piece of legislation, from lunching with a Supreme Court justice to dining with Jean Seberg and Romain Gary—and at the same time retain an unquenchable spirit of sardonic liberalism and an unceasing drive to get things done. . . .

"I think Goodwin probably lacked tact and finesse," said Schlesinger. "He had friends in high places and could therefore cut through the sort of red tape that bogged down others, and they, of course, resented him for that."

And Goodwin paid. "I did a range of things in the White House," he said, "but Latin America became more and more consuming. I was also very involved with civil rights and domestic programs and wrote a lot of speeches.

"It was a very exciting period. At the time, Bobby Kennedy had much the same reputation as I did, but he, of course, was untouchable. I was not. I was oblivious of my age. I never thought about it. And I suppose I had the kind of arrogance one might expect from a man of twenty-nine."

Goodwin later worked for Lyndon Johnson. His chief function was that of speechwriter, and he occupied an office on the second floor of the White House's West Wing. Johnson believed Goodwin to be "the fastest speechwriter in the country. He can write a better speech than Ted Sorensen and in one-fifth of the time," he said. Ultimately, Goodwin would be responsible for most of Johnson's major speeches on Vietnam, poverty, and civil rights.

Goodwin liked Johnson. "He was brilliant," he said, "a great raconteur, cunning, forceful, funny, a strong man. He would have been a great president if it had not been for the war. Now I know that's like saying if he had had three right arms he would have worked wonders, but he would have been.

"I liked the style of writing for Johnson, although it wasn't his real style, his country-western style. Very direct, very simple statements. We discussed most of the ideas for a particular speech beforehand and sometimes in the White House pool. I remember one occasion particularly. It was just after his election and he was swimming naked, as he liked to do, around the pool, and he talked about how he had fulfilled Kennedy's program and how he now wanted to begin one of his own. It was the inception of the whole Great Society program and how it would be constructed. It was always difficult to get his full attention. He talked incessantly on the telephone. He kept a phone on an inflatable raft in the pool. With politicians, a phone is a kind of extension of their ear—and with Johnson more than most. To deny Johnson his telephone would be like denying Jefferson his quill."

Goodwin was to work for Johnson for nearly two years, and again, as in the Kennedy administration, his manner and his methods attracted criticism. Historian Eric Goldman, who worked in the White House at the time, later described Goodwin as roaming "the corridors of power like a court manipulator out of the Middle Ages—dark, disheveled, brilliant, and sardonic. . . . A good deal of the distrust of Goodwin resulted from something quite different—his chameleonlike air, the feeling that he was a good bit of an adventurer, with a highly developed ability to confuse advancing policies with advancing Dick Goodwin, and no great fastidiousness in the methods he used in either case. . . . A connoisseur of the latest in literature and art, who, at the age of thirty-two, last week's soup stain on his suit, puffing his cigar and twirling his gold chain enigmatically, talked of power and policy with a faintly weary smile."

Goodwin was particularly amused at that description. "Under Johnson," he said, "I didn't do too well advancing myself or my policies, which calls my competence into question, doesn't it? I had a hell of a run at it, though, but it was the run of a bluefish on the hook."

"I found him fascinating," said Jack Valenti, who had been a special assistant to Johnson. "When he was disengaged from his hesitancies, he was a near genius. But he was difficult to work with. He had a larger dose of the ego disease than anyone I knew. He was a man of immense and persistent skill, and, ironically, he was given far greater leeway with Johnson than with Kennedy. But Johnson always had some instinctual distrust of Dick. I don't know why. I think he felt that Dick would have preferred a Kennedy in the White House."

"Dick was a loner," said Larry O'Brien. "He was widely regarded in Washington circles as an opportunist, self-centered and self-promoting, and in Washington, once that's suspected, people come to believe it very quickly. But Dick took it with a smirk and a knowing look."

* * * * *

There was cold lobster for lunch and dollops of Miracle Whip and a bottle of iced vodka. Someone had forgotten to bring plates and cutlery, and Goodwin heaped the lobster on the lid of a plastic container and everyone used his fingers. Occasionally, between bites, Goodwin would stand in the back of the boat and assay the state of the sea. It was not propitious. The tide neither ebbed nor flowed.

Dressed only in his bathing suit, Goodwin still managed to look untidy. His male detractors thought him an unattractive man, ugly even. Given the remnants of youthful acne on his face, the long, unmanageable black hair, the uncommonly pale brown eyes, he did look like an irascible churl. Some years before, a group of reporters had seen him board a plane with Robert Kennedy. Not knowing who he was, they consulted one another, finally deciding that he was an Italian journalist with a hangover. And there was something old and Latinate about him; he looked like the second lead in an opera buffa—one of those shy and watchful conjurers with the pronounced aura of Weltschmerz in the eyes.

Sitting in the boat, Doris Kearns read *The Scarlet Letter*. A pert and pretty thirty-two-year-old, she had been known in her younger Washington days as "Little Orphan Annie with eyes." The elegant fashion editor pretended to fish with one of the rods, a blue-green plastic fish dangling from the line. Looking around him, Goodwin suddenly laughed. "Have you noticed?" he said. "This is the quintessential film set. A gem. But you've got to see it from the camera's point of view. A long shot. Desolation everywhere. Long stretches of empty beach, the sinister mudflats, the ominous low tide, the treacherous dull sea. No place for man or beast. The camera focuses on an open boat, mired in the mud with four hapless people in it, one of whom is fishing. It's a scene out of Antonioni, a classic scene reflecting the tedium and futility of our lives. It's intended as a symbol of the modern world. Nothing happens. Nothing will ever happen. That's very important. Monotony is the key to success in films." Goodwin puffed at his cigar. "I tell you we've got a box-office smash on our hands," he said.

"No one is responsible anymore," he added. "There is no social commitment, so there can be no social power. In this age of so-called sexual liberation there are probably more lonely souls than there have ever been before. More and more the search for private pleasure becomes a compensation for civic, communal behavior which has broken down or disappeared. When James talked of the moral equivalent of war, he talked about some kind of shared enterprise above and beyond our own lives. What you get today is the frantic pursuit of private pleasure, which is only a substitution after all."

Goodwin continued to talk. He talked volubly of politics, of society. It was only when the past was raised that a yawn or sarcasm crept into his voice. He had a habit of talking about that other, younger Goodwin as though he were talking about a stranger—an obscure figure he had met in his youth and had never seen again. Occasionally, Doris Kearns looked up from her book and listened with mild misgivings. That morning she had told me that she was unaware of what she called "that side of Dick's life." She did not understand the old rumors of animosity, the tales of arrogance. But she was both fascinated with and curiously disturbed by what she was learning. She returned to *The Scarlet Letter*. The fashion editor continued to fish. The two men talked. The tide had still not turned.

* * * * *

In the summer of 1972, Goodwin met Doris Kearns at Harvard's Institute of Politics. Kearns, born in Rockville Centre, Long Island, had attended Colby College and Harvard Graduate School. Early in 1967 she had been nominated for the White House Fellows program, which each year selected a few young people to work as special assistants to the president or to members of the cabinet. She first met Lyndon Johnson at a White House dance on May 7, 1967, and the result of nearly three years of conversation with him was her book, "the psycho-history." Her meeting with Goodwin would result in their brief and misbegotten collaboration.

It also marked the beginning of their love affair. Goodwin's wife, Sandra, had been ill for a year or two, her illness having been diagnosed as paranoid schizophrenia. For two years she had been in and out of various Boston hospitals. In December of 1972, Goodwin and his son, Richard, had taken a brief holiday in Martinique, where they were later joined by Doris Kearns. On December 17, Sandra Goodwin talked her doctors into granting her a short leave. Despite the fact that Goodwin had left his number with the doctors, they never called him. Arriving at her home in Beacon Hill, Mrs. Goodwin found no one there. She locked herself into the house, took an overdose of sleeping pills, and died. After the funeral Goodwin returned to Maine and Kearns dared not leave him alone. Nor was she able to continue her book on Johnson. In late December, Johnson telephoned and asked her to come to Texas before he died. She told him she was not able to. On January 22, 1973, Lyndon Johnson died. Kearns did not attend the funeral. And her "psycho-history" remained incomplete.

The book had become almost obsessive to Doris Kearns. Not only would it ensure her tenure at Harvard as a full professor, but it was her first book and five years is a long time on the job. In addition, she had been given insights into Johnson's private life and thoughts that no one, with the possible exception of his wife, had had. She looked on her book as a valuable document. She remembered the day in April of 1968 when the president called her into the White House Oval Office and told her that he had nine remaining months in office without an election and he wanted her to help him. He wanted, he said, to do everything he could to make the young people of America, "especially you Harvards," as he called the enemy, understand just what the political system was all about. And Doris Kearns was given an office just two doors away from the president.

At nine or ten, two or three evenings a week, Doris would sit for an hour or two in the little sitting room next to the Oval Office while Johnson recounted his day's activities. He would tell her whom he had seen and what he had said to them, reading from stacks of memos and letters on his desk. She never fully understood why Johnson had selected her specifically. She had been publicly critical of his policies, but she had attended Harvard and Johnson must have felt that by talking with her he had acquired a direct line into the enemy camp. She was also young and pretty, she was a good listener, and she made no demands. And Doris Kearns liked the dying president, appreciated what she called "his colorful, coarse, yet gentle manner."

While attending Colby College, Doris had worked for two summers as a private secretary and knew shorthand. While Johnson talked she invariably took notes. Sometimes he would say to her, "Now, I don't want you to tell this to anyone in the world, not even your great-grandchildren." And moments later, he would contradict himself and say, "Hey, why aren't

A politician is the sort of man to whom you can speak gibberish and you can always count on him to say, 'It was good to talk with you.'
I suppose they assume *their* gibberish passes unnoticed too.

Richard Goodwin

you writing all this down? Someday, someone may want to hear it." He understood she might want to write a book one day. "He was not one of 'those Harvards' who wrote books," she said, "but I could do it for him."

It was not until after his heart attack in the spring of 1970 that the nature of their conversations began to change. No longer did he talk of his presidency, of the mistakes he may or may not have made, the misdeeds of his opponents. Rather, he began to talk of his past—an unhappy boyhood, a failed father, a demanding, unyielding mother. He was beginning to die and he knew it. They usually talked in the early morning, and after the heart attack a curious ritual developed. Doris would awaken at five and get dressed. "At five-thirty Johnson would knock at my door," she said, "dressed in his robe and pajamas. I sat in a chair by the window, he climbed into bed, pulling the sheets up to his neck, looking like a cold and frightened child. He spoke of the beginnings and ends of things, of dreams and fantasies—particularly of a dream he had had night after night as a child in which he would see himself absolutely still in a big straight chair. The chair stood in the middle of the great open plains. A stampede of cattle was coming toward him. He tried to move, but he could not. He cried out again and again for his mother, but no one came. He was all alone. He also talked of his early days in Washington, the time in the Senate and his vice presidency." Kearns knew she had a good book and now, some four years after she had begun, she wanted to get it done.

In the summer of 1974, Goodwin and Kearns moved to Washington. Goodwin was writing a series of essays for the *New Yorker* and Kearns commuted between Washington and Cambridge in order to fulfill her teaching obligations. Last April, the feud with Basic Books erupted, and in June, Goodwin renounced coauthorship, writing an open letter to Simon and Schuster announcing his abdication. Among journalists, it became known as "that Prince of Wales communication," and David Halberstam and Sandy Vanocur composed a telegram to Goodwin which said, "Congratulations on your appointment as governor-general of the Bahamas," though at the last moment they grew wonderfully politic and didn't send it. But the gossip grew, the rumors multiplied, and the New York literary world wallowed in its first decent scandal in years. In late June, Goodwin and Kearns retreated to Cape Cod.

* * * * *

Now, in spite of the tide, in spite of the journalists, in spite of the fact that there would be no fishing that day, Goodwin felt better than he had felt in months. His days were rich and regular. He liked to rise early and would eat a breakfast he had taken over from Richard Nixon—cottage cheese sprinkled liberally with ketchup. "It's two-thirds of a very patriotic breakfast," he liked to say. Over breakfast he normally read the *Boston Globe* and the *New York Times*, pausing with particular mirth over the reported "philosophy" of Gerald Ford. "A politician," said Goodwin, "is the sort of man to whom you can speak gibberish and you can always count on him to say, 'It was good to talk with you.' I suppose they assume *their* gibberish passes unnoticed too. Have you ever noticed how often Ford uses verbs such as 'polish' or 'varnish' or 'shellac'? That's because he's from Grand Rapids, America's furniture-making capital. Ford goes to extraordinary lengths in order to say nothing. Instead of reporting his every word, the *Times* ought to have a box on the front page each morning that says, 'Today, the president said nothing of note.' It would save everyone a lot of time."

Goodwin stood up in the back of the boat and thrust his cigar at the sea. "As I predicted," he said, "the sea returns." It was four o'clock and the sea had now returned to where it had been nearly five hours before. Doris Kearns had finished *The Scarlet Letter*. The fashion editor had caught no fish but had managed to coax Goodwin's son into the boat, and the boy watched the retrenching of the tide with a solemn face. I told Goodwin I would probably leave in the morning.

"How long have we been together now?" he said. "A week? Listen, this story has been told already. It was called *The Man Who Came to Dinner*. As a result of all this, I know more about myself than I did before, you know."

Despite his lingering fascination with politics, he no longer believed they mattered one way or the other. He believed the country had hit a crisis point and politics could do nothing to overcome it. "There's a lot of impotence and fear in the country today," he said. "People's general impotence is being translated into fear. The sense of paranoia has been validated by Watergate. Now people believe anything is possible, the worst iniquities, whereas before Watergate they would have sneered at such things as bugged telephones.

"You should learn how to read statistics. It's not very difficult. If you can play backgammon, you can read a computer printout. Seventy to 80 percent of most people's energy is spent on economic considerations. Getting and spending. Getting and spending they lay waste their powers. And you've got to find out how they waste them. There are radicals and dangerous radicals. The dangerous radical is the one who talks about money. I must say that over the years if I had had a lot of money, no one would have dared, or would have wanted, to open his mouth against me. It would have been very easy to have made a lot of money. The problem is that you would have had to have worked at it full time."

"There's a lot of impotence and fear in the country today. Now people believe anything is possible, the worst iniquities, whereas before Watergate they would have sneered at such things as bugged telephones."

Full time? No, that would not have done. Over the previous week I had often wondered what would become of him, whether he would return to public life or whether he would continue to write in private.

He was an unpredictable man—unsettled and hence unsettling. One never knew, with any certainty, where he would wash up next—toward what strange windmill he would set his course. "Dick is like one of those old sailors who used to sit around the port in Genoa in the fifteenth century," said one of his detractors. "They had maps then which ended at the edge of the world—beyond which it said in Latin, 'Here Be Demons.' Well, what always worried me about Dick was that he would actually sail off the edge looking for those demons. He believes they exist."

"Dick's smart, that's his talent," said Frank Mankiewicz. "I'll tell you one thing. If I were doing anything, overthrowing a government, starting a revolution, or running a campaign, I'd sure as hell want to know where Dick Goodwin was."

The sea now swirled around the edges of the boat. Goodwin watched it, a puzzled look on his face. He often had that look—the puzzled look of a man who knows that something has gone wrong, or is just about to. "Listen," he said, "all of my ideas are either pretentious nonsense or they're very accurate. You must have a kind of defiance in the end. That and the ability to struggle with your own insanities. That's what keeps me going."

The boat was now afloat. Goodwin retrieved the anchor and put to sea. Not more than five minutes had passed when, in an otherwise perfectly blue sky, a large black cloud began to form and slid down the horizon to conceal the sun. Looking over his shoulder, Goodwin puffed at his cigar and said he didn't think it was going to rain. It rained within the hour.

The joke went: Bradshaw went to Cape Cod to do an interview and he stayed for the summer. That's how well he got along with Goodwin and how much Goodwin liked him in return. Long after the profile appeared, Bradshaw remained friends with Goodwin, who died in 2018 at the age of eighty-six, and Doris Kearns Goodwin. Her book Lyndon Johnson and the American Dream *launched her storied literary career.*

Sucking in the Seventies

A Bold Gossip, a Heroic Journalist, or a Detestable Snoop

New York, June 7, 1976

"No one can appeal to my better nature . . . because I don't have a better nature."

Regine's has been open for about a week, and the club is crowded with the usual motley of stupefied white and Third World night crawlers. It is practically dark, and against the *lac d'ambre* plastique walls it is difficult to tell one from the other. Wandering from the bar through the dining room to the discotheque and back again are clusters of starved and foppish girls, hairdressers, actors, designers, entrepreneurs, the idle rich, their courtiers—the sort of people the trendy tabloids have taken to calling the hep elite.

In a corner of the main room stands a youngish man who manages to keep a furtive eye on the crowd without appearing to move his head. There is nothing particularly remarkable about his appearance; he looks as any Englishman of his type might be expected to look—the Savile Row suit, the Gucci shoes, the Turnbull and Asser tie, the Sun-Dym tinted glasses, the dark hair worn short, though more as a result of age than fashion. He might be a stockholder or a junior underwriter at Lloyds; he might, in fact, be anything in the head-office variety, since he has the tired and guarded look of an employee. He is talking to a girl, and in a loud, tendentious voice he explains that because he works some fourteen or fifteen hours a day, he doesn't have a lot of time for his radio and television commitments or for the surefire bestseller he is at present writing. The girl looks sympathetic.

His name is Nigel Dempster. He seems to know everyone, and, moving about the room, he makes a point of talking to them. He has a trick of talking that enables him to listen to several conversations at the same time. He is by trade a gossip columnist—a species that, depending on the company you keep, is defined as either a scandalmonger or an investigative reporter. His "Diary," as it is called, appears five days a week in the London *Daily Mail*. As London's leading gossip columnist, Dempster has at one time or another attacked most of Britain's sacrosanct figures and traditions.

In December of last year, for example, he announced that Prime Minister Harold Wilson would retire three months later on the eve of his sixtieth birthday. Dempster was promptly served a writ alleging libel and demanding substantial damages and an immediate retraction. Dempster ignored it. Three months later, Wilson resigned. Earlier in the year, Dempster revealed that Lady Antonia Fraser, wife of an aristocratic MP and mother of *six*, was conducting an affair with playwright Harold Pinter; for reasons of limited space, he wrote, he could name only six of her previous lovers. And went on to do so. In February of this year, he let his readers know that a well-known Labour MP had left her husband for a female contributor to *Sappho*, Britain's only lesbian magazine. As a result of such attacks, Dempster's adversaries have called him everything from a despicable snob to an intellectual pervert. He has his champions, however, foremost among whom is Auberon Waugh, the well-known columnist and novelist and son of the late Evelyn Waugh. In a recent column in the *New Statesman*, Waugh described Dempster as "the only one among my contemporaries who has yet achieved heroic stature; he's a better journalist than any of his detractors." It is a clipping Dempster rarely strays far from home without.

*****

Dempster has arrived in New York only late this afternoon on assignment to write two of his typical columns for this magazine. He intends, he says, "to savage what passes for society in New York, to bring it to its knees." He has come to Regine's not merely to socialize, but to work, to gather information, to elicit some particularly droll rumor, which he will run down and insert in his column.

"I am the prophet of my time. I am the harbinger of doom. I've warned everyone. I've given them notice. But will they listen?"

There is about him a certain rude charm and limitless effrontery. He is bright and what is known as likable. He is, by his own admission, industrious—ambitious, even. One day, he explains, he will be the editor of one or another of London's great newspapers. It is, in the nature of things, a matter of time. For the moment, however, with thirteen years as a gossip columnist behind him, he is content with his fearsome reputation.

"I am the prophet of my time," he says. "I am the harbinger of doom. I've warned everyone. I've given them notice. But will they listen?" He looks around the room. "No one in this joint's listening, that's for sure. Look at them. Hardly an acceptable name in the place. Who wants to write about these Americans anyway? They're upstarts, socially uneducated, and their names are totally unpronounceable. I met a man tonight who told me his name was Slumberjay. I later learned it was Schlumberger. *Totally* unpronounceable. Let's go. There's no decent dirt in here. Let's go to Elaine's. It won't be social. One will be reduced to starlets and posturing litterateurs, but there might be some laughs and a little conversation."

At the door, having avoided Regine, Dempster stops and says, "Listen, in England I write the sort of column which, if syndicated here, would earn me $100,000 a year. In America, I'd be *big* news. As it is, I only have five and a half million daily readers." He sighs. "It's not easy for a young man to make his way in the world."

* * * * *

It was G. K. Chesterton who pointed out that "journalism largely consists in saying 'Lord Jones Dead' to people who never knew that Lord Jones was alive." The gossip column is a decadent variation of the same principle. Nigel Dempster's "Diary" in the *Daily Mail* is a kind of social comic strip. In it he amuses himself with the foibles and faux pas of the well-known and well-to-do, publishing an endless parade of what he calls "my harmless indiscretions." Thus he takes a perverse delight in announcing (always "exclusively" and "for the first time") marriages and marital disputes, financial falls from grace, divorces, love affairs, the *real* names of actors and actresses, the number of former wives, husbands, lovers, and illegitimate children. Essentially his column is the grim account of failure, shot through with a manic glee that such defeats should actually have taken place. It is more of a jeer than journalism.

Daily, Dempster trumps up a world he has come to believe exists. And so, presumably, do his readers. It is a limbo through which floats a succession of doomed and misbegotten figures—bankrupts, lechers, gamblers, transvestites, alcoholics, and tax evaders. Moreover, on the premise that he is portraying "real life," Dempster has assembled a permanent cast of characters whom he moves on and off his stage with the dexterity of an amateur playwright—the Gettys, the Onassises, the Rainiers, the Fords, the Rockefellers, the Kennedys, a galaxy of film stars, and, inexplicably, at least once a week, Big Daddy Amin. If his columns are any guide to his tastes, it would seem he spends the majority of his time at Ascot, fashionable London restaurants and discotheques, embassy parties, and film premieres. In a typical column earlier this year, he mentioned the Duke of Grafton, the Duke of Sutherland, Lord Cottesloe, Lord Montagu, Viscount Newport, King Constantine, Richard Chamberlain, Taryn Power, Mickey Mouse, Donald Duck, and Martha Mitchell. It is this world that he has come to see as the real one.

For one who believes himself to be a perceptive chronicler of the monied classes, Dempster has had a curiously underprivileged background. He was born of Australian parents in Calcutta in 1941—the sort of background one is more likely to encounter in Somerset Maugham than in Evelyn Waugh. His idiosyncratic use of the English language is better understood when one learns that his first language was Hindustani. Dempster came to England when he was four, and it was not until he was eight that he learned to read and write English with any facility. He attended St. Peter's School in Devon and in 1955 acquired an obscure scholarship to Sherborne School. Three years later, he was expelled for "gross indiscipline" and with a heavy heart set off for London to make his way in the world. At the age of sixteen he became a porter at the Westminster Hospital, "carting the stiffs around." He remained there for a year, and in 1959, deciding that the future lay not in undertaking but in underwriting, he joined Lloyds of London and promptly went out and purchased fifteen old school ties. They were to become an essential part of his disguise.

"In 1959," said Dempster, "the old school tie was a passport which enabled me to travel safely throughout the aristocratic highlands. I also took the precaution of memorizing the public school yearbooks."

Such dodges produced much business for the ambitious broker. The disguise was so convincing that to this day Old Etonian, Old Harrovian, and Old Wykehamist underwriters with whom Dempster once worked will walk up to him and say, "Correct me if I'm wrong, but weren't we at school together?"

But by 1960 Dempster had tired of the game, and he left Lloyds for a brief fling in the stock exchange. Within months, however, he was asked to leave, the senior partner of his firm saying, "Young man, you would be better off as a car salesman."

Later that year he became the personal assistant to the Earl of Kimberley, doing public relations for such clients as Smirnoff vodka and Sam Bronston, the film producer. He worked with Kimberley for three years. During this period he met many of the earl's social friends and became an informant for the William Hickey column in the *Daily Express*. "I suddenly found that all those people I was meeting, I could write about. It was in the days when earls actually counted for something. I can't imagine why, but I decided to milk it for all it was worth."

In 1965 Dempster became the London correspondent of Igor Cassini's now-defunct *Status* magazine. He also moonlighted for the *Evening Standard*, calling himself the "deb-season correspondent."

During those years, in fact, his chief obsession was the London social season. "I social-climbed for seven years to get where I am," he admits. "From 1959 to 1966 I went to about eight hundred deb dances and about fifteen hundred deb parties. That's why I know everyone today. Everyone worth knowing in England today is either a close friend or a close personal enemy. I prefer the enemies. You can always judge a man by his enemies. I insinuated myself into the upper classes, and I didn't like what I saw—or overheard.

"But from April to August I was there. I stole my first tie and tails. The days were always the same. Up late and take the bus to Harrods. The day began by getting your shoes polished on the lower ground floor, thence to the health-juice bar, then up to the record department to listen to Buddy Holly and the Crickets, Ricky Nelson, Cliff Richard, and Tommy Steele. Then down to the main lobby in the bank where by one o'clock you were guaranteed to meet at least twenty debs. I went through that routine for seven years, getting the lie of the land, meeting the daughters of the aristocracy, eating their food, drinking their drink, improving my knowledge and my position. I was invited everywhere, and when I wasn't, I gate-crashed. I gate-crashed parties because I knew that had my hosts had the good fortune to have met me in the first place, they would certainly have invited me. Eventually, they stopped sending me invitations altogether, since they knew I would turn up anyway, and besides, it saved them a threepenny stamp."

According to his friend the Earl of Lichfield, however, "His hosts were delighted to meet Dempster because he was the last mint condition of an almost extinct social phenomenon—the cad, alias the bounder. Dempster may well be the last of the prewar cads."

In April of 1966, Dempster joined the William Hickey column, where he was to remain for the next six years. "I wasn't just some ordinary gossip columnist," he likes to remember. "I wasn't some guttersnipe arriving at the door with scuffed shoes. No one has the memory bank I have. Where have the rest

42

Articles in 1965 —

Number	Magazine	Article	Date Due	Words	Price	Mile[illegible]
1	King Magazine	'Bouncers and Barmaids'	Jan. 10th	3099	£100	—
2	King Magazine	'English Spoken Here'	Feb. 20th	4152	£100	—
3	Queen Magazine	'Downs and Outs'	April 5th	4498	£75	12,10
4	The Sunday Times	'The World's Fair'	April 13th	731	£25	
5	The Sunday Mirror	'Bunny Escapades'	April 14th	621	£30 ⊗	
6	Lee Lustig	'Dick Haymes Biography'	May 20th	19,181	—	
7	King Magazine	'Northern Clubs'	May 25th	2935	£100	
8	King Magazine	'The Pretenders'	June 12th	1935	£63	
9	Queen Magazine	'Status Restaurants'	May 7th	5224D	£60	
10	King Magazine	'Wared in Morocco'	May 24th	3761	£50	
11	London Life	'John Osborne Interview'	June 28th	1673	£10	
12	Queen Magazine	'Society: The Index'	June 30th	3454D.	£300	
13	King Magazine	'Gambling in Britain'	July 5th	2257	£25	
14	King Magazine	'Pamplona Festival'	August 15th	9650	£75	—
15	Queen Magazine	'The Death Business'	September 20th	6232	£200	
16	Twentieth Century Fox	'Modesty Blaise Profiles'	September 20th	5349	£300	
17	Queen Magazine	'Married With Profile'	September 21st	1310	£75	
18	Queen Magazine	'Iwang'	December 31st	12,174	£500	—
				91,106	£2,869	

Articles in 1966 —

Number	Magazine	Article	Date Due	Words	Price	Mile[illegible]
1	King Magazine	'Monte Carlo Rally'	February 2nd	2756	£25	
2	Queen Magazine	'Candy Mossler Trial'	March 15th	12,161	£500	—
3	Queen Magazine	'Casino Royale'	—	—	£700	
4.	Rediffusion Television	'Synopses of T.V. Shows'	April 15th	678	£100	22,80
5.	Vogue Magazine	'Cordobés'	May 5th	378	£10	
6.	King Magazine	'Mini Skirts'	June 14th	3,491	£60	
7.	Weekend Telegraph	'Italian Westerns'	August 1st	2,158	£125	
8.	Weekend Telegraph	'British Bullfighter'	August 6th	2,068	£125	
9.	American Vogue	'Marquess of Bath'	September 1st	2,758	£200	
10.	British Vogue	'Articles and Editing'	September 26–	—	—	
11.	[illegible]	[illegible]	–December 31st	3,334	£700	
11.	Queen Magazine	'Alvaro's'	December 21st	3,998	£150	
12.	Queen Magazine	'Last Exit to Brooklyn'	December 28th	14,622	£300	—
				48,402	[illegible] £3,005	

Articles sold in 1965 and 1966

of them been? What have they done? I can ring up Paul Getty today and say, 'I was at your party in Sutton Place in 1959.' They can't do that. My memory is long. I had been in strict training for seven years. I knew what I was writing about. I didn't have to guess. I was one of the first journalists to write about people I was friends with. Unfortunately, what I wrote soon changed that.

"And gossip columns were changing. In 1965 an Old Etonian took over Hickey. Imagine! And there I was, an upstart gentleman who had been to every top public school in the country at least once. In those days, gossip columns were straightforward who's-left-who stuff—marriage, divorce, and close companions. Everybody married in those days. It wasn't until 1965 or 1966 that people openly admitted to living together. The gossip columnists were louts wading into the upper classes; they wrote marriage-breakup columns. It was a straight war between the heavily armed upper classes and the lower-class winkler.

"I don't write many British social stories anymore. As far as I'm concerned, the aristocracy is dead (in America it never existed) and to concern oneself with it is tantamount to necrophilia. The aristos have been cashing their class like a check for centuries and today the checks are bouncing everywhere. You can hear the thud in the streets. In these times they have a minus all across the board—Old Etonian, private incomes, stately homes, it just doesn't work anymore. The last wicket is about to fall. I am about to bowl them out. And when I do the game is up, the upper classes are out.

"There are those, of course, who find me offensive. Imagine! Who do I offend? Only the upper classes. As they are only 1 percent of the population, that hardly counts, does it? Ninety-nine percent of the population adore me. I write about 1 percent for the other 99. You don't believe me? Listen, you can walk into the Victoria Coach Station and shout the name of Nigel Dempster and a horde of ruffians will rise to their feet, cheer, and wave their *Daily Mails*."

"Through me all my readers lead a vicarious life. They believe they are connected directly to the heartbeat of every nuptial bed in the land. And in a way they are. I'm living their life for them, living out their fantasies."

There are more than a few of Dempster's colleagues, however, who would question his motives, journalist Anthony Haden-Guest among them. "Really," he says, "Dempster mustn't be allowed to get away with all that reformist rubbish about flagellating the upper classes. The irony is that the only way he can get as close to the upper classes as he likes is by feeding off them and the only way he can keep his self-respect is by attacking his host. Gossip columnists, as our parents used to say of the Germans, are either at your throat or at your feet."

"My column is successful for very simple reasons," says Dempster. "The hallmarks of my column, you could say, are money, sex, and innuendo. It is written in a style people can read without pausing. It's fact, well constructed and simple, and all the questions are answered—how much money? did she sleep with him? how old is she? how many children?—in the minimum of words and the maximum of flow.

"Through me all my readers lead a vicarious life. They believe they are connected directly to the heartbeat of every nuptial bed in the land. And in a way they are. I'm living their life for them, living out their fantasies. I am employed to spy on behalf of my five and a half million readers in order to amuse and inform them about a world they can never hope to enter. It's a real world because they believe it to be. They know that given better fortune, a better background or breeding, it's a world they might have inhabited themselves instead of being sentenced to a drab existence in Blackpool. I can show them that world because I know it intimately. I write the truth and I realize that it is often embarrassing. I would never not print a story for that reason, though.

One of Dempster's rivals sees his column in a somewhat different light. "You could call his column," he says, "an antiquated world digest. For all his ranting about exclusivity, his stories have beards on. They're spin-offs. Most of them come from upper-class snoops who, because they lack upper-class means, inform on their friends for the cash. His column is the epitome of keyhole journalism."

But Dempster feigns indifference to the gibes of his

rivals. Or he will attack them in print. There has been a long tradition in Fleet Street that dog shall not eat dog, but Dempster admits he never entered that bargain. "Most of the gossip columns in England and America are parochial, illiterate, and very boring," he says. "Upstarts writing about upstarts. Occasionally in my column I will reprimand them, poor things. It is not enough that I succeed," he maintains. "Others must fail."

In 1973, using his *Daily Mail* column as a base, Dempster branched into other areas. He did a few radio broadcasts and was invited to join a television talk show, which, because it failed to make the grade, was scrapped. He also began to write the "Grovel" gossip column in the infamous British satirical magazine *Private Eye*. There, he was permitted to attack his targets with greater impunity and to indulge in the sadomasochistic pleasures of reviling himself. Thus, in the pages of *Private Eye*, he likes to describe himself as "a fortune hunter," as "Fleet Street's most notorious drunk, gambler, and lecher," or more flatteringly as "the *Daily Mail*'s rakish diarist."

As a direct result of his rude assaults, Dempster has been banned from two of London's most fashionable clubs—Burke's and Annabel's; he has made powerful enemies within his own profession and more than a few of his victims have seriously considered the possibility of sending round the heavies to the offices of the *Daily Mail*. The rakish diarist remains indifferent and looks to the future with odd equanimity. "Who else is going to be remembered in my generation of popular journalism? No one. The *Mail* is sending me to America, and by the time I've dealt with that country and exposed its ass off, I'll be famous."

Opposite:
Nigel Dempster,
by David Levine

* * * * *

It was nearly midnight when Dempster walked into Elaine's. The groggery was full, and packs of the disgruntled milled at the bar. Jim Brady of the *National Star* and a loud claque of professional gossips sat at a table near the bar and waved Dempster over. He sat down between Brady and Jack Martin, Rona Barrett's right-hand man. Tonight was a choice occasion, Brady explained; the joint was jammed with stars. Sidney and Gail Lumet were giving a party for, among others, Vanessa Redgrave and Sue Mengers. The Arthur Schlesingers and the Steve Smiths were dining together. At the very next table were Kevin McCarthy, Betty Comden, Adolph Green, and George Plimpton. "I must be in America. I've never heard of any of them," said Dempster. "But order champagne and I'll stay."

As Dempster drank champagne, he noted that the real time, London time, was 5:00 A.M., and, since he was in training, he would have to leave in an hour. Someone laughed loudly at the next table and Dempster turned round. "Who is that man," he said, "and where did he get his teeth?" It was explained that the man was Adolph Green. "I don't know who he is," shouted Dempster, "but that man is walking around in someone else's teeth." Brady blanched and hid his head in his hands. It was true that Green's teeth were lustrous and oversized, but he appeared not to have heard, since he continued to flash them round the room. Dempster was not to be deterred. "They're someone else's teeth," he shouted. "Elaine, arrest that man for petty theft."

At the back of the restaurant, the Lumet party had broken up. Sue Mengers came slowly down the aisle nodding to friends and clients en route. She was introduced to Dempster. She smiled brightly and had half extended her hand when his name seemed to trigger some wild, belated response. Withdrawing her hand, but continuing to smile, she said, "Uh, I was just on my way out, Mr. Dempster."

"You've not heard the last of me," Dempster shouted. "When I've exposed New York, I'm heading west. No one escapes, no one gets off, not even you." Miss Mengers did not look back.

Around the table, all the gossips were laughing. Earlier this evening, at a party, Dempster had been introduced to George Plimpton and had offered him personal amnesty in exchange for any available literary dirt. Plimpton had laughed and muttered cautious courtesies. Now, Dempster repeated his offer and Plimpton jokingly said that he didn't bargain with newshounds. It was the opening, apparently, that Dempster had been waiting for. Suddenly, he fell to the floor on his hands and knees, began to bark, and, lunging at Plimpton, bit him savagely in the right calf. Plimpton managed to pull away. "He's a paper lion," shouted Dempster, "he's a paper lion." Plimpton smiled, but there was fear in his eyes.

Dempster barked again for good measure and returned to his table. The gossips were cackling among themselves. One of them asked Dempster if he always behaved so badly. "My dear friend," said Dempster, "we live in shoddy times. At this moment in history, how else is one expected to behave but . . . *monstrously?*"

Dempster and Bradshaw were great friends. When Bradshaw died, it was Dempster who organized a memorial for him in London. Dempster, a legend in his field—editor and writer Tina Brown called him "the boss of gloss"—reported on many famous breakups, including that of Prince Charles and Lady Diana. "There is a holiday in my heart when I discover another marriage break-up," he once said. Dempster passed away at the age of sixty-five in 2007.

The Action at Maxwell's Plum

New York, June 16, 1975

"Man, you get a lot of freaks in here."

It is just before midnight on a Friday night and the bar at Maxwell's Plum is gorged with what Jesse, the head barman, calls the BBQs—the shrill and gaudy youth from Brooklyn, the Bronx, and Queens. There are more than 150 predators jammed up against the bar, and for the second time that night the traffic controller has been compelled to bolt the restaurant's front door. The crowd is wild and inconsolable. It is the sort of crowd one used to find at public executions. Jesse is unperturbed. He has seen it all before. Black and bearded, with tinted glasses and a golden hoop in his ear, he looks wonderfully cool.

"Hey, this is nothing, man. This is *slow*. These cats is foreigners. Most nights this place is tripping with models and stewardesses. Hip chicks. Most nights you get a lot of overseas talent. And a lot of girls from Seattle. Yeah, Seattle. Hey, I've seen the second-richest woman in the world in here. I know. I've been around. I mean, I've *traveled*, man. Come back during the week. We're having a run on girls from Paris. That's because of all the *bo*-tique shows in town."

In the back room of the restaurant one of the dinner-jacketed captains looks with a kind of fond distaste at the bar jam. By inclination an actor, he works at Maxwell's most weekends and refers to himself as Captain Napkin. On weekends he's a star. The Andrews Sisters won't *set foot* in the place unless Captain Napkin is on the floor. "Let me tell you," he says, nodding at the bar, "these kids are *kids*. They're amateurs. No self-respecting hooker would be caught dead in here. This singles thing is a con. I don't think anybody actually gets laid at the bar. Not *laid*, honey. What they get is a lot of bump and grind . . . and a few bruises." Captain

Napkin laughs. "Maybe that's all they want.

"Look at them," he says. "This is the home of the heavy macho look. All these guys come into the bar in the same clothes—the shirt split to the navel, the chest hair parted in the middle, and round their necks they always wear a gold chain with an ivory tooth. You can count on it. It's very macho, man. Oh, yeah, and the place *reeks*. Can you smell it?" Captain Napkin lifts his fine nose in the air. "It's a distillation of eau de Flatbush."

At midnight the restaurant still swarms with late-night revelers. Even the back room, the classy part of Maxwell's Plum, is infested with balloons and the remnants of a birthday party who have just ordered two more bottles of Dom Pérignon. Maxwell's seats 240 people, and today, Friday, has served 1,500 meals. It has been a perfectly average day. In the nine years since the restaurant opened, it has become one of the city's four largest-volume producers—the others, in no particular order, being Mamma Leone's, Lüchow's, and "21." Nearly a half a million people a year walk in and out of Maxwell's Plum. Last year it did a $4.1 million turnover, and it's doing considerably better in 1975. What began as a joint for junk food and the singles trade has now become an East Side institution—a circus of bearded barmen and balloons, ceramic animals, clowning captains, a sideshow at the bar—and beloved by . . . well . . . by people who believe that food need not necessarily be the main event.

* * * * *

Maxwell's Plum was opened by Warner LeRoy on the night of April 6, 1966. Until then, Warner, the son of Mervyn LeRoy and the great-nephew of Jack Warner, had been a film editor, a stage manager, and a producer and director in the theater. In 1959 he took over the York Theatre on First Avenue, producing and directing plays, and in 1964 converted it into the York Cinema, where he ran a series of highly successful film festivals. Next door to the cinema, on the corner of First Avenue and Sixty-Fourth Street, there was a tiny luncheonette. "It was a really bad luncheonette," LeRoy recalled, "the E + B Luncheonette or something. It was crummy, really crummy. It sat about twenty people. I'd always wanted to open up a café. I didn't know anything about the restaurant business, but I began to think about New York as a scene, I mean physically almost, I mean trucks and taxis and people going up and down First Avenue, the whole scene, and naturally enough I thought, 'I'll do a sidewalk café and I'll make it pretty and interesting.' First Avenue was really interesting to look at then. It was a kind of theater to me . . . a spectacle. It dealt in all the senses. It was a slice of New York life, and I loved it. Christ. That was it. The E + B Luncheonette.

"In 1965 First Avenue was a bad, bad area. Nobody came to First Avenue. But I bought a long lease on that luncheonette. At the time I didn't know all these airline stewardesses lived around here. I didn't know about all those nurses and secretaries. And it was just about the time the Pill was coming into fashion and the women's lib movement was getting off the ground. I didn't know what to call the place. I was looking for names with double meanings. I remember I toyed with the 'Shanghai Hippopotamus.' I toyed with the 'Silver Cherry.' In the end I decided on 'Maxwell's Plum.' It doesn't mean anything. It isn't supposed to mean anything. It's just a feeling I get. Y'know?

"Anyway, we opened. We didn't advertise or anything. We still don't. Oh, we had a sign outside for about a week before, saying 'Get Ready for Maxwell's Plum.' But that was all. I didn't invite a soul. I wasn't even going to go, but finally, around eleven, I went down expecting to find about eight people, maybe nine people, who couldn't get in anywhere else. But it was jammed and there was this crowd outside in the street. I never even went in. Forget it, a mob, I couldn't believe it. The place was meant to seat eighty people. The kitchen was ten-by-seven. Three cooks and two dishwashers. I thought we'd serve twenty meals a night, thirty tops. Wrong. I was really wrong. For the first two or three years we did about ten lunches a day, but it was always a success at night. Listen, we've never had a night that we didn't sell out at least two sittings. Not once. And that includes recessions, inflations, depressions; that includes blizzards on Christmas Eve. Nothing affects us, not even the weather."

> To enter Great Adventure or Maxwell's Plum is somehow to blunder through the Looking Glass; and LeRoy himself bears more than a passing resemblance to Tweedledum.

By 1969 the restaurant was doing so well that LeRoy decided to convert the York Cinema next door into a bigger and better Maxwell's Plum. Warner LeRoy is an oversized and amiable man of some 250 pounds, a fact he likes to blame on Maxwell's Plum. But he doesn't frequent the restaurant as often as he used to. Occasionally he'll come in with his second wife, Kay, a former TWA stewardess whom he met in the original, smaller Maxwell's, and when he does, it is impossible to miss him sitting in the back room wearing one or another of his favorite outfits—the Moroccan outfit with copper water cups and flashlights and the outsized hat festooned with silver bells, or the western outfit with sequined lions' heads on the back, or, more often than not, the black velvet dinner jacket emblazoned with huge, almost luminous, pink, lilac, white, and orange flowers. In his younger days, LeRoy (who is now forty) drove to Maxwell's in a white pimpmobile splashed with bright red stars—but no more. He has, he feels, settled down.

LeRoy is a man who likes to embellish reality with bizarre effects. To enter Great Adventure or Maxwell's Plum is somehow to blunder through the Looking Glass; and LeRoy himself bears more than a passing resemblance to Tweedledum. "I tried to create a mood, a spectacle in here," he says. "I wanted it to be a happening. I'd say we're successful not only because of the decor but because of the quality of the food and the mix of people. We think of ourselves as a neighborhood restaurant. We draw a lot of people from across the street, but we try and wear as many different hats as possible in order to get the mix. We get the celebrities, the models and stewardesses, the neighbors, the tourists, as well as the singles crowd. Maxwell's Plum is the melting pot of New York and of those who come to New York.

"From the very beginning the young people came and

they were single or posing as single. We've never done anything to promote them. Not that we've been against them, but we've done nothing to promote them either. We have a better-quality singles crowd than we used to have, but it's a very small part of our business. Hell, we have to have *something*. The average gross sales per year are about $17,000 per seat in here. That's a lot of sales. One of the main reasons for our success is that we're very efficient. This restaurant is *well run*. You wouldn't believe the mechanics of this place. I mean its day-to-day management. It doesn't just happen, y'know. It isn't an accident. We can't afford to have accidents. Running Maxwell's Plum is like running a goddamn hospital."

* * * * *

The dinner rush at Maxwell's Plum begins promptly at six o' clock, and as at lunch, the restaurant is practically full some thirty minutes later. Already at 6:30, the heavy jostling for position has begun to occur at the front door. Although many customers book, particularly in the back room, the allocation of tables is a difficult problem at Maxwell's Plum and has, in the past, required patience and more than a little managerial cunning.

Warner LeRoy assures one that there is no preferential treatment at Maxwell's Plum. "We try and be democratic," he

Bradshaw. Photograph by Patrick Lichfield

says. "No one gets special treatment, and reservations are honored. Because there are no minimums here, you can come in and order a cup of coffee and stay as long as you like. The people at the front desk are fired if we discover them selling tables." Maxwell's normally allows ten minutes for customers who have made bookings and are late; after that, unless they telephone or the weather is particularly bad, the table is given away. John Sutcliffe and Werner Mair, Maxwell's two comanagers, know the regular customers and make an effort to seat them quickly. It is customary for those who haven't booked to wait for long periods of time.

The back room is the premier part of the restaurant. With twenty-six tables seating some ninety people, it is run by the six-foot-six-inch Van Ribblett, a forty-four-year-old former hairdresser and part-time painter. He prefers to be called the "director" of the back room. He looks on it as a kind of stage and likes to choreograph it accordingly. "Seating the room is an elaborate chess game," he says. "We do our best to honor all reservations, but on the other hand, you can't tell the sister of the Shah of Iran to stand at the bar till you make room for her. You make room for her right away. My customers are a total cross section of humanity and they treat this room as they would their own home. They're always showing it off to newcomers. They even give them tours. Friday and Saturday nights are a madhouse. The better class in New York don't go out on those nights." And neither, presumably, does Van, since those are his nights off.

Warner LeRoy's assurances to the contrary, there are "good" tables at Maxwell's Plum—particularly the four tables overlooking the west side of the bar. There is even a list of special customers with three ranks or gradations—PPX, PX, and Forget It. PPX stands for preferred personal extras, and PX for personal extras. The latter is self-evident. The list contains some 450 names, of which fifty PPX names are starred. "It's your standard everyday name-dropping list of stars," says Captain Napkin. "That means, when one of the celebs orders his meal, the chef comes in and makes sure all the shrimp are facing north." Despite the list, Van insists that all his customers are treated with "gentility and good grace."

By ten o'clock the restaurant is so crowded the traffic controller has locked the front door. It is a common occurrence on Friday nights. "The only time I remember a quiet night in this place," says Captain Napkin, "was the night they showed *Godfather I* on television for the first time. All New York was quiet that night. Listen, Maxwell's is one of the longest-running hit restaurants in town. There are a lot of hit people in the neighborhood and they come in for the mystique of the place, to have a good time or to spot the stars. Some people come in, sit down, and before ordering a drink even, they say, 'Who's here tonight?' You get a rich crowd in here. They can drive you nuts. We're very polite. You notice I smile a lot? But there's none of that sycophantic '*Pardon, monsieur*' stuff. You don't get a lot of Côte Basque bullshit in here. You get a performance. Being a captain in Maxwell's Plum means coming in, changing into costume, and going out and performing. It's a six-hour stand-up comic routine. Let me tell you, honey, even Bob Hope couldn't hack that."

"Being a captain in Maxwell's Plum means coming in, changing into costume, and going out and performing. It's a six-hour stand-up comic routine. Let me tell you, honey, even Bob Hope couldn't hack that."

The type of clientele changes from meal to meal. The waiters seem to prefer Sunday nights, not only because the kitchen closes at midnight, but because the crowd is nicer, more of a family crowd, and not so loud and vulgar. On weeknights the dress is gaudy, clusters of Gucci, Ricci, and Pucci labels in evidence—a style Captain Napkin calls "East Side plastic."

"You don't get what you call a chic crowd in here," he says. "Very few of your genuine chicees here. The neighborhood is riddled with nurses and stewardesses and hip actor-model types, a lot of nouveaus in the high-rises. We get them. This place is outrageous. You get a lot of heavy-duty partying. People sometimes come in here and ask me for a quiet table and I say, 'Hey, honey, you're in the wrong restaurant.'"

sort of thing. The chicks in here don't wear bobby sox and chew bubble gum, y'know. They're *sophisticated*. A lot of guys come in here whacked out of their heads, man. I mean buzzed. A lot of guys come in here who have their wives stashed somewhere else. Yeah, we get a lot of lonelies."

The pandemonium at the bar continues. The kitchen closes at 1:40, but the bar won't close till 3:00. The four closing waiters have arrived and will stay till the last customer leaves. The night maître d' will check the locks and the toilet for drunks and sleepers and will leave just as the two stove-cleaners come on duty. The night cashier will have completed a cover check and a menu breakdown, and the night steward, who is in charge of night security, will remain till five. But at the moment all the action is at the bar.

"It's always the same," says Jesse. "Monday, you get the out-of-towners; Tuesday, the women who come in after the theater or the cinema; Wednesday, the regulars, the New Yorkers; Thursday, the businessmen, the divorcées, and the wives looking for a little extracurricular activity, though they have to catch the ten o'clock train home to Long Island; and Fridays and Saturdays, the BBQs.

"We refer to people by what they drink," he says. "Miss Dewars-and-Water always sits on the south side of the bar and looks off into the distance

* * * * *

By eleven o'clock the bar is jammed to capacity, and just before midnight the front doors are locked again. The men outnumber the women by three to one. One of them, a sullen youth, stands at the east end of the bar wearing a World War I aviator's helmet, black goggles pulled down over his eyes, and a long white silk scarf around his neck. He is drinking brandy. Occasionally, he looks hastily over his shoulder into the street as though he has just heard the scramble alarm. "He's nothing," says barman Jesse. "You should've been here the night the guy who skated from California on roller skates came in here. Skated right up to the bar. First drink he'd had since Sacramento."

"Outta sight," says the flier.

"I remember the night a guy gave a chick a hundred dollars to streak. She disrobed and bolted around the bar like a bunny in heat. This is an 'in' place. You got to expect that and don't say nothing. She always brushes off the first three guys who come up to her but starts talking after that. Red Wine over there is a divorcée, real nice, a talker, a mover. Rusty Nail down at the end is a hell-raiser. Just as soon kick you in the balls as not."

"Outta sight," says the flier.

Toward two o'clock the bar is thinning out. Perhaps twenty men hungrily eye the two remaining women. At the north end of the bar, where most of them are gathered, an argument erupts between two of the men. "I'm terribly sorry," says one of them.

"You're sorry?" screams the other. "You piss on my date and you say you're *sorry*?"

"Man, you get a lot of freaks in here," says Jesse.

"Outta sight," says the flier.

Maxwell's Plum had a massively successful twenty-two-year run before shutting its doors in 1988. Warner LeRoy went on to have success at other New York restaurant institutions like the Russian Tea Room and Tavern on the Green. He died at the age of sixty-five in 2001.

Bradshaw and Carolyn's wedding

Inside the Special World of the Pink Palace on the Hill

New West, May 10, 1976

"Nowadays, sex is a toy that everybody seems to have discovered yesterday. They can't leave it alone. That's what the Polo Lounge is all about. It's out in the open now. You can smell it."

"What? Whatwazzat? Whatwazzat?" Instinctively, one of the diners, a Canadian, ducks behind his bowl of soup. And again, this high and hideous wail pierces the Polo Lounge like a cry for help, like the swan song of a parakeet that has spotted a cat in the parlor: "Mistafeelds . . . tellafuncahl fah Mistafeelds, pleese." It cuts through the room like a plastic whistle. "Jezus," says the Canadian, "whatwazzat?" The insistent squeaks seem to emanate from a tiny costumed man, mousing tentatively among the tables like an actor who has wandered into the wrong play. He is just over four feet tall. He wears a red jacket embroidered with black welted seams, brass buttons, and black trousers with a red stripe down the sides. He is the hotel's official page. He must be sixty-five. He wears spectacles, and, as he gads through the Polo Lounge, he clasps his hands behind him in the manner of the Prince of Wales. "Mistafeelds," comes the plaintive pipe again. "Tellafuncahl fah Mistafeelds."

Mr. Freddie Fields is sitting in the premier booth of the Polo Lounge, and, affecting a little look of irritation, he takes the call on a pink telephone at his elbow. He is having lunch with me and with Charlie Joffe, who produces Woody Allen's films. We have waited thirty minutes for Fields to arrive, and after his first drink he announces that he will have to leave within the hour—for Paramount. Formerly an agent, Fields has recently produced his first film. As he prattles into the telephone, I look distractedly around the room.

There is pandemonium in the Polo Lounge. Already, at 1:30, all the booths and the tables in the lounge, the loggia, and the patio have been taken. It is not quite spring and the temperature is 82 degrees. There is a confusion of the seasons in Beverly Hills that creates confusions in the local dress. Here, at lunch, the men dress much alike; occasionally, one sees a man in a suit and tie, but more often than not they appear to have purchased their clothes from the same shop—the trousers in various violent colors, open-neck shirts, and woolen pullovers thrown carelessly round the shoulders and loosely tied in front. The men with tans, transplanted easterners, wear Gucci shoes without socks. The women favor long white dresses, T-shirts and French jeans, or slacks and Missoni tops. The women who have *traveled* wear rather warmer clothes, usually with long sleeves. Most of the younger women wear their hair long and straight with dark glasses thrown to the tops of their heads. It is the look of studied nonchalance.

Perhaps it is the assorted suntans and long blond hair, but everyone in the room seems *familiar*. It seems that if you are not someone in Beverly Hills, it is more than passingly important to look like someone. But the Polo Lounge has always been famous for its faces—Charlie Chaplin, W. C. Fields, Errol Flynn. In booth number two, one recalls, Ehrlichman, Haldeman, and Mitchell were taking lunch when the call came through that Watergate had broken. Even in these bland times, in the less conspicuous booths or at corner tables, it is just possible to make out Raymond Massey, Petula Clark, Peter Ustinov, Donald Pleasence, and Doris Day. Sitting in booth number three with two young blondes is Eli Robbins, known as "the patriarch of the Polo Lounge." Now ninety-four, he has been dining here regularly for nearly forty years. He is dressed—as he always is—in a dark suit and bow tie, a white boutonniere in his lapel, and an emerald-and-diamond ring given to him by Marion Davies. It is not entirely clear what Eli Robbins does, or has ever done, but he tells me he lived with one of Bela Lugosi's ex-wives for thirty-two years.

After some minutes, Freddie Fields replaces the telephone and sips moodily at his drink. As he has so little time, I am rather anxious to get to the point of our lunch, but my opening sally is promptly turned aside. Easing out of the booth, Fields smiles and says, "Excuse me, uh, while I do some cheek-kissing." He shrugs, as if to say there are some duties a man cannot evade. "Do you see that blonde over there?" he says. "She is my absolute fantasy lady." She looks perfectly ordinary to me, but Joffe appears to understand and Fields walks across the room smiling easily at people en route. In the corner booth there are three girls, presumably starlets, each of them blond and pretty; they look almost precisely alike. As Fields approaches, they begin to effuse, to percolate; their preening and simpering is exquisite—and excessive. They have probably not seen Freddie since yesterday. Freddie, as he has promised to do, kisses each of them perfunctorily on the cheek. It is like a Beverly Hills benediction.

The mighty studios may have been chopped into parking lots and shopping malls, the film stars may have been replaced with music moguls and television chiefs, but the Beverly Hills Hotel keeps up appearances.

It is like a scene in an old movie. But scenes of this kind are as common in the new Hollywood as they were in the old—particularly in Beverly Hills. The mighty studios may have been chopped into parking lots and shopping malls, the film stars may have been replaced with music moguls and television chiefs, whole worlds may have shifted out there in the *rest* of the city, but the Beverly Hills Hotel keeps up appearances. It remains intact and insular, fashionable, yet old-fashioned, a kind of duchy, a preposterous little raj cocooned in the hills of Beverly. Nearly a third of its clients are regulars; they fly out from New York, from Chicago and Washington, check in, conduct their labyrinthine business at the pool or the Polo Lounge, and rarely leave the premises. They take up residence like émigrés in their favorite foreign country.

The Beverly Hills Hotel was built in 1912, at a cost of $500,000, on fifteen acres of land then known as the Rancho Rodeo de las Aguas. The surrounding area was farmland, producing lima beans. Sunset Boulevard was an obscure bridle path. There were only 550 people living in Beverly Hills when it was incorporated as a city in 1914, but as the film business became an industry, actors and actresses began to move in. In 1919 Douglas Fairbanks and Mary Pickford built "Pickfair" in the hills behind the hotel and it became known as the "White House of Hollywood." Between 1925 and 1930 Buster Keaton, Marion Davies, Harold Lloyd, John Barrymore, Charlie Chaplin, Will Rogers, Gloria Swanson, Hoot Gibson, Buck Jones, and Tom Mix constructed extravagant mansions within blocks of the hotel.

Over the years, the hotel changed hands frequently. But for a new wing added in 1949, the hotel has remained relatively unchanged; its day-to-day life, though accelerated and more sumptuous, resembles the humdrum life of a country town. During the last sixty-four years, people have been born here, have been schooled and nursed and doctored, have been engaged, married, honeymooned, cuckolded, and have waited out divorces. Its guests have conducted business and love affairs, written books and screenplays, composed scores, and painted pictures. They have gone into hiding, been burglarized (there are two or three *reported* thefts a month), played tennis and swum and partied. They have grown old and died. The hotel itself has often been filmed, most recently in *Funny Lady* and *Once Is Not Enough*. The action of Neil Simon's current play, *California Suite*, is set in the hotel. It has had, in fact, an unusual (if predictable) history, and though Dorothy Parker liked to say that the Beverly Hills is the place where the elephants go to die, the owners continue to feel it is one of the world's great addresses.

* * * * *

The hotel is secluded and self-sufficient. One need not actually leave it for any reason or spend cash while one is there; everything can be charged. In the promenade, there is a travel agency, a beauty salon, a barbershop, men's and women's clothing shops, a drugstore, a coffee shop, and a private screening room. The screening room contains fifteen leather armchairs and may be hired, with projectionist, for $150 an evening. MGM people often hire it to see their dailies, and Elizabeth Taylor, when she does not wish to be seen in public, has screenings here. There is also a jade store and a flower shop on the main floor. For the rest, any real or eccentric whim can be ordered from the outside world.

The Beverly Hills is not considered to be one of the world's great hotels. It is not in the class of the Connaught or the Plaza Athénée or the Gritti Palace, but it is a luxurious little inn and, given the occupancy rate, often as difficult to enter as a private club. And, as in any private club, there are few irrevocable rules. Conventions are not permitted, nor men with name cards on their lapels. Until two years ago, pets were registered at $5 a night. But it made for difficulties. The fourteen-year-old son of Ali Ipar of Turkey smuggled a bear cub into his room. The Duke and Duchess of Windsor always traveled with their pugs. Each evening, an order was placed with room service for three sirloin, carrot, and pea burgers, cooked *saignant*. It was not for some time that the kitchen discovered they were for the pugs. Pets are not permitted now.

Idiosyncrasies of this nature are noted scrupulously by the hotel management. Anyone who has ever stayed at the hotel has a "guest history card" on file. The hotel claims to have one hundred thousand of them. The cards note all guest preferences. One lady, for example, will permit only oranges in her room; all other fruits disturb her. Elizabeth Taylor demands little bowls of pistachio nuts waiting in her bungalow. One entrepreneur requires facilities for laundering his Rolls, a task he prefers to perform himself each morning. Howard Hughes demanded that upside-down cakes be held in readiness. Van Johnson will use only red napkins, and a certain Mrs. Ziv refuses to have a rose on her room-service tray as it upsets her when it dies.

A Texas oilman once ordered bear steaks. There were none. Now, when he arrives, bear steaks are flown in from Alaska. Violet and gold tulips were planted in Queen Juliana's bungalow garden the day before she arrived. Gauloise cigarettes were flown in from Paris for Lord Snowdon, and because General Sarnoff preferred suite 486 in a wing of the hotel that was not air-conditioned at the time, special 220-volt lines were run up to the room and an air conditioner installed. Further eccentricities are noted, such as guests who arrive with their own security guards, or, in the case of Sukarno, his own personal food-tasters. Some celebrities insist on anonymity and "no information" is noted, while other celebrities prefer the world be made aware of their arrivals and "notify press" is written down. For all that, there are those perfectly ordinary people who prefer the shield of anonymity, who are repelled by what seems to be an implied familiarity. On arrival, they become discomfited, suspecting their references have been checked; they develop the sorts of ugly insecurities that spring from straying into someone else's party. For the rest, however, the Beverly Hills is approximate bliss, a place in which their merest whim is, as it should be, gratified.

By three o'clock, lunch in the Polo Lounge is nearly over. Freddie Fields has left for Paramount, but not before he insisted on signing the three blondes' luncheon bill. A terrific altercation flared up between Fields and the waiter. The waiter claimed, as a matter of politesse, he would have to consult the ladies first; Fields demanded the bill—immediately. There was much dispute. Happily, the blondes were soon won over and traipsed across to his booth in order to admire his style, his savoir-faire, in order to kiss *him* on the cheek. "I'll tell you what," said Freddie. "Meet me at the airport this afternoon. TWA, four-thirty. We'll fly away for the weekend." The girls giggled in unison. "Just bring your passports," he said, "we'll pick up whatever you need when we get there." Again, the girls giggled, mentioning husbands and pets and other niggling obligations. Freddie shrugged and the blondes slithered back to their table. Looking hastily at his watch, Freddie said he was late and would have to leave. Joffe and I were left to ourselves. It just wasn't the same without Freddie.

Bradshaw with A. Scott Berg at Bradshaw's annual birthday dinner

*****

Around ten in the morning, the eastern moguls begin to gather at the sunny side of the pool. Their tycoonery is conducted in bathing suits, dark glasses, and Cartier timers. Nat Cohen, the British film producer, is on the telephone to London, and next to him Mark Goodson talks sharply to New York. Between them, Goodson's secretary waits, presumably for directions. Two chaise longues away, three pallid men speak solemnly of stocks and shares. Mark Goodson spends nearly six months a year at the Beverly Hills Hotel and the remainder of his time in New York. California is for the body, he likes to say; New York is for the mind. He has been coming to the hotel for more than twenty years; he has probably spent enough money here to have bought three houses in Malibu and a couple of sailing ships. But there are no regrets; it is an old-fashioned hotel, an old-fashioned habit. "In twenty years, the only things that have changed," he says, "are the prices and the Polo Lounge."

Ten years ago these businessmen would have been in films; today they are mainly in music. One sees just as many copies of *Billboard* as *Variety* at the pool. At ten in the morning on this particular day the upper cabanas are occupied with the likes of Ahmet Ertegun (Atlantic) and Clive Davis (Arista). And curiously in their midst, like a piece of pork in a marmalade spread, is Bob Guccione, the publisher of *Penthouse* magazine. For reasons best known to himself, he has registered in the hotel under a pseudonym. Standing now at the railing of his cabana overlooking the pool, he wears swimming trunks; his dark matted chest is aswarm with golden chains.

"Wearing all those chains," says pool manager Svend Petersen, "he'll be a hunchback in a year or two." And so it continues throughout the afternoon. Depending on the weather, Svend will close the pool around six. But by then the action has moved elsewhere—back, in fact, to the Polo Lounge and the tumultuous cocktail hour. During the '20s and '30s, Le Jardin, the bar at the Beverly Hills Hotel, was frequented by a little group of nobs and polo players. Having galloped through their Sunday chukkers, they would drive over from what is now Will Rogers Park in Pacific Palisades to drink and reminisce. Toward six o'clock, Le Jardin was crowded with such players as Darryl Zanuck, Will Rogers, Tommy Hitchcock, Walter Wanger, Robert Stack, and, though he was not one of the better horsemen, Spencer Tracy. It was not until 1941 that Hernando Courtright decided to change the name of the bar to the Polo Lounge; and by then, polo was rarely played in Los Angeles and a new group of drinkers had taken to roistering there.

Willie "Pancho" Holguin, a Polo Lounge waiter for thirty-eight years, remembers the period well. In the Palm Terrace, before it was renamed the Persian Room, there was live music, and when the band had finished its gig and the customers had gone, Howard Hughes slipped in and paid the band for another session. Hughes liked to sit in the empty room and listen as Pancho poured him champagne. In the Polo Lounge, Charlie Chaplin and Paulette Goddard always lunched in booth number one. Errol Flynn was a regular, usually in the company of his friend Freddie McEvoy. McEvoy, a playboy, rarely traveled without his butler, George. In the Polo Lounge it was George's job to pour his master Russian vodka. Irene Dunne and Loretta Young, who owned stock in the hotel, were early patrons. And Gene Fowler, W. C. Fields, Wilson Mizner, John Barrymore, Sadakichi Hartmann, and George McManus, the creator of Maggie and Jiggs [characters in the comic *Bringing Up Father*], formed the nucleus of an eccentric group of drinkers. McManus once crashed a Polo Lounge party, posing as a newspaperman, with a button marked PRESS, which he had torn from one of the men's room urinals. Captain Horace Brown, Marion Davies's husband, once rode his trail bike into the Lounge and departed before he could be apprehended. In the '30s and the '40s, the Polo Lounge was fun—filled nightly with the stars and their hangers-on. Those were the good times.

During the '40s the Polo Lounge was enlarged several times to include the loggia and the patio, which is why today it has the feel of an exotic warren. To discourage oglers, the mirror behind the bar was replaced with a mural depicting an early Persian game of polo. But for that, the green-and-white Lounge, filled with fake ferns and potted plants, remains much as it was. During the '50s and '60s, a dress code continued to be enforced. No exceptions were made. Brigitte Bardot came for lunch in bare feet and was promptly dispatched; Anita Ekberg appeared in leopard-skin trousers and was given a white wraparound skirt to wear. "We used to have standards," Pancho Holguin recalls. But in 1970 the dress code was relaxed and the rock 'n' roll crowd began to trickle in. "We had no choice," says Pancho, "we had to bow to the times."

It is all a darkness now. Dino Borelli, the Polo Lounge's evening host for eighteen years, died last year. It is said that there was no longing known to man that he could not sense in twenty minutes and gratify in twenty-five. He was replaced by Antoine Lupi, a Frenchman, who runs the Polo Lounge like a lion tamer who has lost his nerve. There is in Antoine's eyes what can only be described as a wild surmise.

If the Polo Lounge has lost its style, it has lost none of its popularity.

The Polo Lounge is the mecca of the Beverly Hills Hotel, but between five and nine it is as though someone has poured weed killer on the shrine. Dark, and filled with smoke and noise, it is populated with an unspeakable motley—what appear to be poachers and painted women, lamsters, fadmongers, wetbacks, and penny-ante pinochle players. The place creates an instant and malign impression on the mind and one turns away as from a lazaretto. Even so, if the Polo Lounge has lost its style, it has lost none of its popularity.

* * * * *

Wherever pleasure is to be found, one can be sure that business will not be far behind. Scattered here and there among the motley are the jades, or "actresses," as they often call themselves, sitting two by two looking hopefully, but discreetly, around the room. Despite the gloom, they are not difficult to isolate. As a local sage pointed out to me, "They're better dressed than the rest of the girls and they act more ladylike." Unaccompanied women are not permitted at the bar, but Antoine permits it, providing they are guests of the hotel and insist on sitting there. He will even allow suspected hookers in "if they behave discreetly and don't make a nuisance of themselves." The hotel management, of course, is horrified, but because it is difficult, if not impossible, to control, the trollops range at will.

This results in certain amusing difficulties. One night some weeks ago, Miss Carol Kane and two girlfriends were having drinks in the Polo Lounge. After some minutes, Miss Kane noticed a man across the room staring openly at her. Thinking possibly she might have met him before and not wishing to seem rude, she asked Antoine for his name. Leering, Antoine said, "Lady, why don't you just go back to your table and get on with your job." Miss Kane returned to her table and told her friends they were leaving. As she passed Antoine at the door, she said in a loud voice, "I don't know who you are, but my name is Carol Kane and I starred in *Hester Street*, not *Hooker Street*."

Toward the end of my stay at the Beverly Hills, I was leaving the hotel for a six o'clock appointment. Walking down beneath the porte cochere, I saw a beautiful girl with long dark hair and a mink coat coming toward me. She smiled, I smiled, and I continued on my way. Some two hours later, I returned. Leaving my car with the doorman, I saw her again coming out of the hotel. She smiled, I smiled, and she said, "*Surely* we've met before?"

Introductions were hastily effected and we retired to drink in the Polo Lounge. Her name was Penelope and she liked to drink margaritas. She had been having a drink with a friend, she said, and had been going home when we met. Other than requesting minor details concerning my marital state and occupation, she seemed curiously unconcerned about the really outrageous portions of my life. Many margaritas later, I learned she had had a brief but bawdy history, which, as one might expect, was a variation on the same sad tale. Penelope was twenty-six and, following a tiresome marriage, had come to California two years before. She had worked at many trades, she said with a smile, and was currently employed as a sales representative for a pharmaceuticals firm. In order to make ends meet, she modeled occasionally and moonlighted in such elegant groggeries as the

Polo Lounge. She rarely worked more than two evenings a week, charging $50 an hour and $150 for the entire night. Given my purely professional interest in her activities, Penelope said, she might be persuaded to give me a token rate. She worked for herself, and though she recognized the regular girls in the Polo Lounge, she had never tried to talk to them. "Baby, there's a lot of truckin' going on in here," she said. But when it came to business, Penelope minded her own affairs.

She wasn't hungry, she said, and shortly after ten o'clock, we adjourned to my room to continue the interview in seclusion. I ordered six margaritas from room service and searched through my clutter for a notebook. When I turned around, Penelope had undone her blouse. She wasn't wearing a bra. "Penelope," I cautioned, "we haven't *finished* yet. I have a few more questions."

"The Polo Lounge has turned into a singles bar at night. The women's movement and this whole sexual liberation thing have fucked the apple cart. I mean, it's *warped* the trade. These days, girls are giving it away for *nothing*."

Penelope seemed satisfied but did not rebutton her blouse. She sat on the sofa, pulled her skirt across her knees, and began to eat an apple. To begin with, she seemed hesitant and did not have much to say, but shortly after the margaritas arrived, she became quite voluble.

"Baby, *everybody* knows there are truckers in the Polo Lounge," she said. "Everybody *knows* that. It's been going on forever. It's changed a lot in the last few years, though. I have a girlfriend who worked the Lounge a lot eight, nine years ago. It was a different gig then. My girlfriend called it 'playing polo.' There were a lot of starlets. Yeah, one more beautiful than the other. The place was packed with them, I guess. And who do you see now? Beauticians, nobodies. The place is jammed with beauticians and cheap swingers." She took a bite of her apple. "Still, it's a place to get your kicks," she said. "I go into the Lounge 'cause it's easier to find the live ones there. You know? I mean, you can find them at Scandia or at the Luau on Rodeo, but they're a different class. Cheap and sweaty. You get a lot of lonelies in the Polo Lounge, a lot of out-of-towners with time on their hands. But you've got to be discreet, baby. I mean, knowing the maître d' helps a lot.

"The Polo Lounge has turned into a singles bar at night," she said. "That's one of the hang-ups. The women's movement and this whole sexual liberation thing have fucked the apple cart. I mean, it's *warped* the trade. These days, girls are giving it away for *nothing*. Giving it away for nothing is just screwing around. Listen, I'm no different from any other girl. I don't want one-night stands. I'm looking for the big score too.

"But I'm choosy and I like to play. And sex is the only thing that doesn't give you a hangover. Nowadays, sex is a toy that everybody seems to have discovered *yesterday*. They can't leave it alone. That's what the Polo Lounge is all about. It's out in the open now. You can smell it."

Penelope took another bite of the apple. "Okay, baby? Is that it?" she said. Crawling across the sofa, she began to undo my shirt.

"Penelope," I said, gently pushing her away, "there are only one or two more questions."

"Jesus," she said, "if I didn't know you were a bona fide writer, I'd think you had a fetish." Pouting, Penelope withdrew to the end of the sofa and finished her margarita.

"What about pimps?" I asked.

"Pimps?" she snapped. "I've got a good mind to take a hike. What do you think I am? A prostitute? Only prostitutes have pimps. You don't know *anything*, do you? Jesus, they're the lowest. Listen, you got prostitutes, right? Then you got call girls. A call girl is more of a businesswoman. She really digs the dollars and cents. Then you got the courtesans, you know? The mistresses. They're in for the long haul, they're lifers."

"And what are you, Penelope?"

"Me?" She laughed. "Well, I guess some would call me a call girl, and I was more of a mistress when I was married. But now, I guess you'd call me a sex counselor."

"A sex counselor?"

"Yeah. I mean, men have a sexual problem and I solve it, that's all. It's legitimate. And I don't charge a lot, y'know. The amazing thing is that men just love to pay. That's the turn-on. They really dig the cash transaction. That's how they get their thrills." She laughed.

"*Some* thrill, hunh?"

Getting up from the sofa, Penelope began to move around the room, her breasts darting in and out of her blouse. She continued to eat her apple. "Do you mind if I watch TV while we talk, baby?" She turned it on. "The Beverly Hills is a very homey sort of place, don't you think? I really like it. I've been really comfortable here. It's got class." She fell back on the bed. And then an odd thing happened. Tears suddenly welled up in her eyes. She didn't say anything. She just wiped them away, ate her apple, and began to watch Marilyn Monroe playing a ukulele.

Somewhat later we returned to the Polo Lounge.

As Penelope had pointed out she was a working girl. Antoine showed us to a corner table. Although it was past midnight, the Lounge was still crowded, for the most part with men. The kitchen would not close till one A.M., and after ten a late supper—steak sandwiches and such—would be served. The bar would remain open till two, by which time all the customers and most of the staff would have left. Only a houseman, an assistant manager, a bellman, a cashier, and a security man remained in the hotel throughout the night.

"Well, how will you do it?" I said.

Penelope laughed. "It's easy, the easiest thing in the world, baby. I've already got my man. Don't look, but there's a blond guy in the corner booth. He's got his eye on me."

Getting up suddenly from her chair, Penelope ambled from the room. I couldn't see whether she looked at the blond man or not, but moments after, he rose and followed her. Less than five minutes later, Penelope returned. She finished her margarita. "I told him you were my ex-husband," she said.

In a matter of minutes, the blond had paid his bill and left. He didn't look at our table.

"Well, I guess I'd better split," said Penelope. "Wish me luck." She kissed me on the cheek. "And remember," she said. "No names."

I nodded and watched her leave. At the door, she waved. She was a very beautiful girl. She didn't chew gum or bite her nails, and she had a way of bringing tears to her eyes that was particularly admirable. Antoine sent over another margarita. It tasted sour. I walked out into the patio, closing the door to lock the noise in the Polo Lounge. It was one o'clock in the morning and there were still a hundred people there.

I was drunk. I sat down under the Brazilian pepper tree. The dark hotel rose up around me. From one of the bungalows came the sound of low laughter. A couple, whom I had seen in the Polo Lounge, walked arm in arm to bungalow one. It was cold. The sedge had withered from the patio wall. And no birds sang.

The Beverly Hills Hotel of this period is preserved in movies such as Shampoo, American Gigolo, *and* California Suite. *The hotel changed hands several times over the ensuing decades, had an enormous renovation in the mid-'90s, and later endured much controversy due to a stake of the ownership belonging to the Sultan of Brunei, whose anti-LGBT sensibilities led to a boycott by some famous guests.*

Bradshaw could laugh at himself. He wasn't completely swept away in the idealistic version he presented of himself, he was way too smart for that. But he was very aware of how good-looking he was and how women liked him, and he played into all of that.

Anna Wintour

"You Used to Be Very Big." "I Am Big. It's the Pictures That Got Small."

New York, November 22, 1976

"I did not suddenly become an idiot. I did not suddenly unlearn my craft."

The old man hurried up and down the room, stopping abruptly at either end so he would not walk into the wall. He wore horn-rimmed glasses and a trilby hat. He held a regimental swagger stick which he snapped in the air to emphasize his arguments. "What did you expect to find when you came out here?" he said. "A broken-down director? A wizened, myopic boob in his dotage? Is that what you expected?" He spoke contorted English fluently—with a Viennese accent and a Viennese stutter. "I guess you thought you'd find me playing with my old Oscars? In a wheelchair maybe. Poor old Billy Wilder. The great director. Christ, you should see him now. A wreck. A ruin. A hole in the wall. Is that what they told you?" He snapped his swagger stick again. "Well, they told you wrong. I'm not just functioning in the motion-picture relief home, y'know. I feel just as confident and virile as I did thirty years ago." He paused for a moment and then he said, "I can still hit home runs, y'know." And he continued to move lightly about the room like a dance master.

He looks younger than his sixty-nine years, affecting a kind of opulent casual dress—loafers, slacks, a pullover, an open shirt. He rarely wears a tie to the studio. He has been in this office at Universal Studios for nearly two years. He is not under contract to Universal and sees himself in the role of visiting professor. His office had once been Lucille Ball's dressing room. The walls are cluttered with framed posters of art exhibitions in Berlin, Paris, and New York. Over his desk is an Oriental design of an elongated carp, a Japanese emblem of good luck. The bookshelves, which occupy an entire wall, are filled with books, his six Oscars standing like sentries to one side, the leather-bound collection of his twenty-eight scripts, and signed photographs of Agatha Christie, Noël Coward, Groucho Marx, and Shirley MacLaine. There is a Richard Avedon series of photographs showing Wilder in various poses with Marilyn Monroe. There is a black leather chair designed by his friend Charles Eames. Everything is in its place, neatly arranged. It is the office of a very fastidious man.

As he walked, he talked. He talked somewhat faster than he walked—a high stuttering monologue, filled with guttural embellishments, quaint colloquialisms, and oaths. "I am, I trust, only off the hit parade temporarily," he said. "I'm going through a dry spell, that's all. A slump. I've had them before, y'know. You can't figure it. It's element X, I don't know. I did not suddenly become an idiot. I did not suddenly unlearn my craft. It's a dry spell. Occasionally the vineyards produce a bad vintage." He stopped pacing, having reached a wall. Looking over his shoulder, he said, "But there will always be another harvest. I am the youngest of my generation of directors. My generation included Ford, Stevens, Hawks, Wyler, Cukor, and Hitchcock. My immediate contemporaries are Zinnemann, Mankiewicz, and Huston. They had their dry spells too, y'know. They had slumps. They had bad seasons."

Billy Wilder's slump has lasted for more than a single season. He has been in Hollywood since 1934. During that time, he has been nominated for twenty-one Academy Awards, winning six—three for writing, two for directing, and one for producing. He has both written and directed some twenty-three films, including *Double Indemnity*, *The Lost Weekend*, *Sunset Boulevard*, *Some Like It Hot*, and *The Apartment*. His films grossed something in excess of $150 million. Up until 1964, he had had only two commercial failures—*Ace in the Hole* in 1951 and *The Spirit of St. Louis* in 1957. But during the last eleven years, he has had five successive flops—*Kiss Me, Stupid* (1964), *The Fortune Cookie* (1966), *The Private Life of Sherlock Holmes* (1970), *Avanti!* (1972), and *The Front Page* (1974). *The Front Page* had actually made money, but Wilder considered it one of his lesser efforts.

"Listen," he said, continuing his restless prowl about the office, "every career has its ups and downs. It's just that in our business it goes a little faster. One year you're on the *New York Times* Ten Best Pictures list and the next year you're one of the Hundred Neediest Cases. Sure, you notice it when things go sour. When you're in a slump, you go for the fences. You want a home run. You're pressing. Striking out. What's so sad is that Tony Pérez comes to bat four times in an afternoon and eight times on Sunday if it's a doubleheader. I come to bat once every eighteen months.

"It's not that I'm not in demand anymore. There are all kinds of propositions. The telephone keeps ringing. Look at all that stuff on my desk. Some stuff. Somebody sent me a script about a rabbi who kicks field goals for the New York Jets. Then I was asked to do a movie of the English play about a scientist who has a formula for blowing up the whole world. The formula is tattooed on his penis and it can only be read when it's erect. Since the scientist is gay, the government has to train heterosexual agents to become homosexuals. How does that grab you?

"It's a bitch to find a project these days that would both interest me and have a chance in today's market. Though, if someone had asked me to do *Fear of Flying*, I'd've jumped at it. Today, we are dealing with an audience that is primarily under twenty-five and divorced from any literary tradition. They prefer mindless violence to solid plotting, four-letter words to intelligent dialogue, pectoral development to character development. Nobody *listens* anymore. They just sit there, y'know, waiting to be assaulted by a series of shocks and sensations.

"It's not only me, y'know. It's not only the older directors who face this problem. Mike Nichols, Arthur Penn, and other first-class younger directors have had miscarriages lately. It's a difficult time. Ernst Lubitsch, who could do more with a closed door than most of today's directors can do with an open fly, would have had big problems in this market." Adjusting his glasses, he pointed his swagger stick in the general direction of the Universal lot. "Y'hear all those typewriters going out there? What do you think they're up to? I'll tell you. *Jaws II*, French *Connection III*, *Airport* '77, and *The Return of the Exorcist*. We used to have cycles. Now everything is recycled."

He continued to pace about the room. At one point, he must have miscalculated, since he walked out of the room and disappeared. A moment later, he returned, laughing loudly. He looked like an elderly leprechaun. "I've often thought I would do a porno-horror movie," he said, "and capitalize on two of the going trends. The plot would have a sloppy hooker who gives all of her innocent customers crabs. The crabs grow into giant octopuses and eat New Orleans. Do you see the beauty in that? You get both nudity and animal horror in the same picture. I might call it *Deep Jaws*."

He looked round the room and brandished his swagger stick. "It's no wonder they say Wilder is out of touch with the times," he shouted. "Frankly, I regard it as a compliment. Who the hell wants to be in touch with *these* times?"

At noon, Wilder's secretary, Kay Taylor, who has been with him for two years, brought in a tray on which there were two containers of sake—Ozeki sake, Japan's finest in Wilder's view—served lukewarm the way he likes it. "Hah!" he shouted. "You thought we were all uncivilized out here, didn't you? You thought we all fell off a turnip truck." He looked at his secretary. "Well, some of us are civilized," he said.

Wilder suggested we drive to his apartment in order to see his art collection. Driving down the gaudy sprawl of Ventura Boulevard, he pointed out Art's, one of his favorite hostelries. A large sign ran the length of the restaurant. It said ART'S DELICATESSEN. EVERY SANDWICH IS A WORK OF ART. "I forgave Art for that a long time ago," said Wilder.

* * * * *

Hurrying out of the elevator, Wilder let himself into his twelfth-floor cooperative apartment and called immediately for his wife. Audrey Wilder, a trim, attractive woman in her early fifties, was setting the table for a dinner party that evening. Formerly a Goldwyn girl and a singer with the Tommy Dorsey band, she and Wilder have been married for twenty-five years. Wilder never tires of telling the story of their courtship. When she and Wilder met, Audrey Young lived in the shabby Pico–La Brea area of Los Angeles, a section she preferred to call "East Beverly Hills." When Wilder discovered where she lived, he said to her, "Darling, I'd worship the ground you walked on, if you lived in a better neighborhood."

"It's no wonder they say Wilder is out of touch with the times," he shouted. "Frankly, I regard it as a compliment. Who the hell wants to be in touch with *these* times?"

They have lived here for twelve years, and during that time Wilder has packed the apartment with paintings. The walls are covered with Mirós, Picassos, Dufys, Braques, Rouaults, Renoirs, Klees, Chagalls, a Fernando Botero, and innumerable French primitives. There are three Calder mobiles, and dotted here and there on shelves and pedestals are pre-Columbian figurines, the Maillols, and the Henry Moores. Beyond the main room, overlooking Century City, is the large terrace containing Wilder's bonsai trees, the ferns, the laurel, the ficus, and the Ming Aralia trees. The apartment has the neat and polished look of a provincial museum.

Taking off his trilby, Wilder offered a drink, insisting on aquavit. Not your ordinary, run-of-the-mill *Danish* aquavit. No, this was Linie, Norwegian aquavit, the best there is. Pulling a bottle from the freezer, the bottom of which was encased in a block of ice, he said, "I'll make an alcoholic gourmet of you yet." He called for his wife. "Aud, where do you keep the cheese?" His wife said there was no cheese. "No cheese?" shouted Wilder. "What do you mean there's no cheese? This man's come all the way from New York and you tell me there's no cheese. He'll crucify me. He'll think we're all barbarians. He'll think we fell off a turnip truck. What do you mean there's no cheese?" "There's no cheese," said his wife.

We moved to the terrace, Wilder skipping ahead. Looking out over the sprawling city, he shook his head and said, "Hollywood has changed a lot in the last ten years. It's a whole different ball game now. What used to be mah-jongg is now backgammon. The studios used to have more stars than there were in heaven. It's all a darkness now. In the old days, the studio heads were former scrap-iron dealers, butchers, traveling salesmen in ladies' underwear. Now, 80 percent of our executives are former agents. They used to be dealers and now they want to play. It is they who decide on that ugly word 'bankable.' It is they who have decreed that Miss Barbra Streisand is irresistible, that Mr. Howard Cosell is a living doll, that Mr. Rod McKuen is a poet." He smiled and, holding his hands up in the air, intoned, "O tempora. O William Morris.

"Even today's critics are not up to the standard of, let us say, James Agee. Y'know? Only a handful of critics really matter. They can't make or break a picture—look at *Mahogany*—but they can sure bolster or dampen your spirits. I mean, the ladies on the *New Yorker* write like angels—with diarrhea. The only thing longer than *Nashville* was Miss Kael's review of *Nashville*. I found it strange that *New York* replaced Christ with Judas. After all those legitimate-theater corpses John Simon left strewn around New York, he had to find a new neighborhood for his night of the long knives, so he went into movies. Simon is an irritant, but not deadly. Like hemorrhoids, he's not going to kill you, but he's very unpleasant. The only word I can use to describe him is *ekelhaft* [nauseating, loathsome]. *Time* and *Newsweek* are impish and vinegary and see things with a jaundiced eye. They review with karate chops, with kung fu and judo, and then they garrote you with a string of puns. They never bring themselves to suppress a particularly nasty witticism, even if they like the movie. And as for Rex Reed, that cultural oracle of the *Daily News*, he's a dilettante. It is fitting, don't you think, that he chose to make his acting debut in that masterpiece *Myra Breckinridge*."

Wilder walked into the study. Here again the walls were covered with paintings, including several of Picasso's early pornographic studies. A table was piled with old copies of *Gourmet*, Wilder's favorite magazine.

"It's a curious thing, a loss of reputation," he said. "It hasn't happened to me exactly, but I know that it becomes much more difficult to reach your agent. There is even a difference in the hello you get from the doorman at the studio gate. Or you're asked to be a judge at the San Sebastián Film Festival, because they know you're not working. When you strike out two or three times, you're not asked to be a pallbearer anymore. That's one of the first signs of decay. I used to be asked all the time. Can you believe I've only been asked *once* in the last two years? You also discover that you weren't the first or even the second directorial choice. But the high point of triumph in this highly competitive community in which we live is not only that you must have a smash, but that the director you're competing against must have a failure. Now, that's a great parlay." He grimaced. "There's a canard that the Hollywood community is full of bitterness, dissension, envy, and hostility. It's just not true. I've lived here for forty years and I can tell you it took one simple event to bring all the factions together—a flop by Peter Bogdanovich. The news swept Tinseltown like wildfire. Champagne corks were popping, flags were waving. The guru had laid an egg and Hollywood was united.

"Making pictures," he said, "is a bit like walking into a darkroom. Some people stumble across pieces of furniture, others break their legs, but some of us see better in the dark than others. The ultimate trick is to convince, persuade. Every single person out there in that audience is an idiot, but collectively they're a genius. There are moments when I get a little nervous. Am I doing the wrong thing, will it work?

"Making pictures is a bit like walking into a darkroom. Some people stumble across pieces of furniture, others break their legs, but some of us see better in the dark than others."

"But I've not been turned down on a project yet. Not being hot affects an actor or a director much more than it affects a writer. The actor and director have to sit at home and wait for the phone to ring. A writer still functions. Not being hot has affected my ego somewhat, disturbed my confidence. But one hit and that will change.

"I don't know. I've been doing a lot of bunting lately. I've been getting a lot of scratch hits, nothing very solid. I've not hit a home run in a long time. *Irma la Douce* was a home run, but that was during the 1963 season. *Kiss Me, Stupid* was a strikeout on three straight strikes. After that, Izzy Diamond and I felt like parents who had produced a mongoloid and didn't care to have sexual intercourse anymore. *The Fortune Cookie* was a scratch bunt. I just got on. *Sherlock Holmes* was a strike-out, an expensive error. *Avanti!* was a strikeout too, though it was a double in Europe. My last film, *The Front Page*, was a single. It was a nice hit and drove in a run or two, but that was all. It was solid, but hell, I used to hit the solid stuff over the fences."

He looked around the room and adjusted the angle of his glasses. "Listen, when Mickey Mantle bats .350, that's terrific. But if a director bats .350, he better change professions. He'd better start looking for another job.

"Well," he sighed, "it's hurt my ego, I suppose, but it hasn't hurt me financially. I was never given to mansions and yachts. I never played the market or had racehorses or expensive mistresses. My *life* has not been affected. It remains the same.

"It's just possible that I've been designing clothes which by the time the show comes round people are not wearing anymore. But I thrive on reverses. It makes me more determined, more ambitious. It doesn't paralyze me. I've always thought that you are as good as the best you've ever been. In Europe, they recognize that. In Europe, people have some sort of respect for what you have done, as opposed to what you have done lately."

He looked around the room again. "That doesn't mean that I look at my old films, y'know. That's like meeting a girl you slept with fifteen years ago. You look at her and you think, 'My God, did I go to bed with that?'"

Wilder got up and began to walk hurriedly around the room, walking nimbly between the tables and the chairs with the confidence of one who had done it many times before. "I'm getting old, I guess," he said. "Anybody who says to you when you reach your sixties, 'Welcome to the golden decade,' as Justice Frankfurter once said, I say to him, 'Bullshit.' It's like finding beauty in arthritis. You lose mobility, flexibility. The steps get steeper, though I myself still feel young and sprightly." And, as if to emphasize the point, he moved even more speedily. The movement was something between a pas de bourrée and the bunny hop. "To paraphrase the guy in *Fiddler on the Roof*," he continued, "it's no disgrace to be old, but it's no great honor either. In terms of directing, it's a tremendous physical ordeal. I mean, even if the movie's lousy, you still have to get up at five A.M. It's not like wine and violins, y'know. You don't get better simply because you get older. But I remain undismayed. It's gratifying to make it, but it's positively thrilling to make a comeback. A comeback is making it in spades.

"I'm working on something completely new now," he said. "Izzy and I have been wrestling with an idea about Hollywood for the past five months. I haven't made one since *Sunset Boulevard*, y'know. But there are too many pictures with a Hollywood background in the works right now. Sixteen or so. So we shelved it temporarily and are now tackling a completely different subject. I can't tell you what it is. It might be in the wastebasket by next Friday. Right now, I'm in a state of flux and indecision."

He was quiet for a time. He stopped pacing, leaned over the table, and tidied up the magazines. And then he laughed. "In the old days, I was a good ball player," he said. "What they called an untouchable. No team would have dared to trade me. Not under any circumstances. Today, I guess you could call me a free agent. I'm looking for the big hit. It's going to be a home run and the bases will be loaded. You can bank on it. Next time up," he said, "I'm hitting for the fences."

*Wilder never got to savor the thrill of another comeback—his final two movies were not successful. But in the end, he came out on top. Thanks to Turner Classic Movies alone, his enduring hits—*Double Indemnity, Sunset Boulevard, Some Like It Hot, The Apartment*—are always in heavy rotation, securing Wilder's place in the pantheon of great Hollywood talents long after his death, in 2002, at the age of ninety-five.*

THE CONNAUGHT LONDON

TELEPHONE 01-499 7070 TELEGRAMS CHATAIGNE, LONDON W.1.

Dear J.,

My scrawl is clear to the initiate (not only clear but clear) — No, there is no rewriter yet — Roz wants me back — I won't come without a director — He won't take Rydell — So there we are — I told him to wait for Sy. back — Then all the dummies would want to do the pic — Kael was absolutely right about the Water-torture of the Studios — first A of 10 directors: Send script to each — They read slowly, if at all — A year passes — They say no — Get another script — Then: ditto — Did you see my little friend Renata's piece on Kael? True but one-sided — The Morris office is making a concerted pitch to get Ray to take Rydell — If.... I'm back October 1 — I'd seen the Chandler Stuff — Ask Isherwood about R.C. G

Fast Company

Babe Bounces at Bergdorf's

New York, February 16, 1976

"Dear me. . . . You won't have time to clear my check this morning."

Late one wintry Saturday morning some years ago, a dapper little man in a wire mustache walked into the second floor of Bergdorf Goodman—the fur department. On his arm was a really exceptional blonde, a good head taller than he. The couple crossed the floor and the little man in the wire mustache summoned the manager. They wished, he said, to look at furs. While the little man sat down, crossed his legs, and lighted a cigarette, the manager escorted the stately blonde to the furs. The blonde seemed to know precisely what she wanted. Walking disdainfully past the foxes, the beavers, the lynxes, and the racoons, she paused only momentarily at the ermines and the seals and began to work her way through the minks, the chinchillas, and into the sables. Some thirty minutes later, she stood before the mirror in a dark Russian Crown sable. The fur fell just below her knees. The full collar fell half across her cheek, and, her mouth half open, she stared into the glass as though she had seen a miracle.

"Do you like it, darling?" said the little man in the wire mustache.

"It's the most beautiful thing I have ever seen in my life," said the blonde.

"Good, it suits you," said the man, and he snapped his fingers for the manager.

"May I ask," he said, putting out his cigarette, "how much you are charging for the fur?"

"Well, sir, it's the Russian Crown," said the manager. "It's $49,500."

"Do you really like it?" said the little man.

The blonde smiled and blinked her eyes.

Reaching into his inside suit pocket, the little man extracted his checkbook and a pen. Beginning to write, he looked at his watch, stopped, and looked up at the manager.

"Dear me," he said. "It's after twelve." (In those days, the banks closed at twelve on Saturday mornings.) "You won't have time to clear my check this morning." He hesitated. "Listen," he said. "I'll give you my check for the fur. You keep the fur, and on Monday morning when the check clears, I'll stop back and pick up the fur."

"That's really very considerate of you," said the manager, "very considerate. Yes, that would be just fine."

The little man wrote out the check, gave it to the manager, and out of the fur department of Bergdorf Goodman walked what appeared to be the happiest couple in the world.

On Monday morning, the check bounced. The manager, though not a little peeved, was secure. He still had the fur, after all. Putting the sable back in its place, he went about his duties and, by ten o'clock, had put the unfortunate matter from his mind.

Toward noon that Monday morning, into the fur department of Bergdorf Goodman came the little man with the wire mustache. The manager was amazed to see him again, but before he could begin his sharp complaint, the little man held up his hand, stroked his mustache, and said, "Obviously, you know that my check has bounced, and I know how surprised you must be to see me again. I have only stopped back to thank you for one of the most wonderful weekends of my life."

The Carter Presidency, by Richard Reeves
Rating the Top-Selling Yogurts
A Guide to Private-School Admissions

75 CENTS NOVEMBER 1, 1976

NEW YORK

Lottery Fever

"I've been a gambler all my life. Last week I bought $1,000 worth of lottery tickets..."

By Jon Bradshaw

Bradshaw on the cover of *New York* Magazine

Backgammon—Polite Cruelties

Harper's, June 1972

"You've got to learn when to give in, which in America is a difficult thing in any game, given the 'never say uncle, never say die' mystique most children are raised with. But in backgammon, that's of no use."

I remember a time, not long ago, when I had never heard of the game. Now and again, I look back on that time—in much the way nostalgic parents do when speaking of life before the war—as riskless, sedate, somehow undefinably benign. But only now and again. In fact, it is hard to recall what life *was* like before backgammon ruled one's leisure time. Did one frequent concerts and circuses then? Attend one's wife or lover? Did one play for sensible stakes and think of other things? Memory fails me. But I recall the very morning backgammon came up my drive in the person of a young man with a beard, carrying what *The Penguin Dictionary of English* innocently defines as "a hinged board with draughtsmen and dice."

From such inconspicuous beginnings obsessions are born. Since then, I have studied the game with a diligence that sometimes frightens me, and I have heard credible tales of fortunes won and lost, of losers threatening to throw themselves from the fortieth floor unless the game went on. I have seen the players leaving the gaming parlors at 5:00 A.M., humping heavily home or hurrying down side streets toward the neighborhood brothel.

Traditionally, the game has been a pastime of the rich, once restricted to such clubs as White's in London, the Reading Room in Newport, and the old Whist Club of New York. And today, despite a growing network of international tournaments, the heavy action remains for the most part in such clubs as the Mayfair and the Racquet and Tennis Clubs in New York and the Clermont in London. Not until 1964, when the first international tournament was set up and sponsored by Prince Alexis Obolensky, did the game begin to attract people other than the odd earl, millionaire, or socialite.

Backgammon's apparent simplicity, of course, is the game's initial attraction. I know of almost no one who has not learned 60 percent of the moves in a week; I know of no one who did not believe he actually understood the game the following day. But backgammon is so subtle that it is impossible to learn all there is to know about it. One acknowledged expert, who has played for thirty years, told me he probably understood only 90 percent of the game. Because of the skills involved (most average players believe players better than themselves are lucky), and because most players tend to rationalize the dice, blaming their misfortunes on "bad luck," it is difficult not only to recognize your own mistakes, but also to evaluate your own abilities. The game is usually played for high stakes, and self-deception can be very expensive. It is for this reason that Barclay Cooke, one of the game's finest players, refers to backgammon as "the cruelest game."

Talent is just one of the prerequisites of backgammon,

and not the most important one. Tim Holland, who has won more major tournaments than anyone else, claims there are many talented players, but the best players, the winners, are those who are not influenced by adversity. "You must learn to divorce your feelings from the game," he says. "The good player is one who does not compound his losses with personal feelings. And yet 99 percent of the people who play double up when they're losing and draw back when they're ahead. Result? Disaster. You must look at losing in backgammon in the same way you would look at a business reversal over which you had no control." Paul Magriel, a twenty-five-year-old professor of mathematics and the best young player in the game, says that "you've got to learn when to give in, which in America is a difficult thing in any game, given the 'never say uncle, never say die' mystique most children are raised with. But in backgammon, that's of no use."

I remember, particularly, a game one night in a rather shabby East Side bar. There were four or five players at the back table and a group of drunken onlookers hanging round. The bar was crowded and noisy, but the players seemed unaware of the din. So engrossed were they that a stranger might have mistaken the play for the rites of some low Masonite order. There was something almost orgiastic in their play, and I remembered that Dostoevsky had reputedly achieved orgasm when he gambled—but only when he lost. As the game continued, three of the players fell behind and suggested to the fourth, an elderly man who had contented himself with soda water while the others had been drinking brandy, that the stakes be raised. The man agreed with a cursory nod. Toward 3:00 A.M., a girlfriend of one of the other players leaned over, and, following a tense exchange, she stalked away from the table and out of the bar. The player, a young man in a dinner jacket, shrugged and turned back to the game.

Just before dawn, the proprietress announced they would have to go. Indignantly, the players demanded three final games, but she would not be moved. The match was over. The elderly player pushed the scoresheet across the table. The others studied it as though it contained a riddle they couldn't solve.

Gathering their coats, they straggled one by one into the street. The player in the dinner jacket threw his umbrella, end over end, into the night. The elderly man thanked them for their contributions. The others exchanged the drawn farewells of truant boys. The man in the dinner jacket wandered south and east, reeling clumsily through the empty streets; he looked like a man attempting to learn the steps of a new dance.

PLAYBOY

HUGH M. HEFNER
Editor-Publisher

December 23, 1975

Mr. John Bradshaw
41 East 67st Street
New York, New York

Dear John:

It is difficult for me to express my disappointment in your behavior on your recent trip to Los Angeles. Disappearing without a word to anyone regarding the money you lost is certainly not what I would expect from a friend and from one who has, on a number of previous occasions, enjoyed the hospitality of my home.

Needless to say, this matter is a source of very real embarrassment to me, and I hope and assume that you will correct the situation as soon as possible. For the record, you owe $1019.

Sincerely,

Hugh M. Hefner

Hugh M. Hefner

PLAYBOY MAGAZINE · 8560 SUNSET BOULEVARD · LOS ANGELES, CALIFORNIA

10236 *West Charing Cross Road, Los Angeles, California* 90024

July 11, 1988

Carolyn Pfeiffer Bradshaw
ALIVE FILMS
8271 Melrose Avenue
Los Angeles, CA 90046

Dear Ms. Bradshaw:

In this time of cynicism and hypocrisy, I am truly touched by the moral message of your letter. The offer to repay a debt in the name of your deceased husband Jon Bradshaw from so very long ago reaffirms one's faith in the human spirit. My God, was it really 13 years ago.

The debt involved a group of friends who played Backgammon several times a week at Playboy Mansion West, so the money was owed, not to an individual, but to the ongoing game. The books I kept reflecting who owed what have, happily, been closed out long ago, because of the feeling that some of my friends were playing beyond their ability and taking losses they really could not afford.

Whoever the eventual winners were in that ongoing game were more than compensated at the time, I am sure. I accept your conclusion that Jon kept my letter, because he eventually intended to pay and I think your letter sets the matter right.

I was sorry to learn of Jon's passing and consider him a very fortunate man to have shared the love of someone as special as you.

Sincerely,

Hugh Hefner

Hugh M. Hefner

HMH/p
cc: Robert Abeloff

Fast Company

Son, no matter how far you travel, or how smart you get, always remember this: Some day, somewhere, a guy is going to come to you and show you a nice brand-new deck of cards on which the seal is never broken, and this guy is going to offer to bet you that the jack of spades will jump out of this deck and squirt cider in your ear. But, son, do not bet him, for as sure as you do you are going to get an earful of cider.
—Damon Runyon

It began, I suppose, with the tales—the tales of gambling for immoderate sums at craps and cards, at pool, at golf and backgammon. The old gamblers would talk into the night, recalling the days when for a bet of twenty thousand Titanic Thompson pitched a key into its lock or when Nick the Greek, on his final card, filled an inside straight and won a half a million. They cackled softly among themselves and now and then, as if to punctuate their point of view, spun one-hundred-dollar chips into the air. They liked to talk about the past and spoke of it in present tenses. Sitting in hotel lobbies, in clubs and coffee shops in one or another of those western towns, there would usually come a time toward dawn, when the gamblers frowned and shook their heads, agreeing that those had been fine days and that none of us would see their like again. Despite their age they were hard, shrewd men and put aside my claims that they, perhaps, were merely sentimental. No, the times had changed, they said, the country had aged, become somehow tame and uniform. Gambling was limited to Las Vegas, a town they likened to a zoo. In any case the great high rollers had passed away and few had come along to take their place. America, one of the old men said, was overrun by vulgar tribes of businessmen; the high wild players were now extinct or imprisoned in a zoo.

Only the heady tales remained. And for a time, for me, they had been enough. In the course of the next few months, however, I met more than a few of those gamblers to whom the old men had referred. Those first brief encounters were more by accident than aim and only tended to excite my weakened sensibilities. When I came to Las Vegas for the first time and heard the siren sounds of dice and cards on green felt tables, I experienced odd and almost credible sensations of invincibility; given luck and self-control, I too might make my fortune here. Clearly it was not a place in which I dared spend much time, lest I linger there forever.

In the beginning, I had had some indefinite plan to write an account of winners and losers and toward that end had come to Vegas in search of suitable candidates. But it soon became quite clear that while losers flourished everywhere, winners were a rare and reticent breed with preferences for camouflage and anonymity. After I talked to the bookmakers, the pit bosses, the shills, the dealers, the croupiers, all of whom professed intimate and accurate views on the matter, even then, a dark confusion continued to hobble through my mind. How could one be sure? What esoteric qualities actually separated a winner from a loser?

Taught from the start to believe in absolutes, I found myself still half in love with the lie that losers were unlucky, that winners were merely fortunate—privy to none of those sudden catastrophes that snap at the heels of lesser men. But the types are so familiar a part of our mythology, we feel their faces could be picked as easily as twins' from a crowd. One, a cocky fellow with a self-appointed air; the other, drawn and self-defeated, the look of a man who would pawn his soul if he could somehow ascertain its worth. We have come to see them as little more than trite and quintessential types. As a result, when someone points them out to me, I feel sure he is also trying to convey some flattering evaluation of himself—as if by naming them he has managed in some way to define himself. Nick the Greek, possibly the most notorious of American gamblers, claimed the only difference between winners and losers was one of character, which, he added, was about the only difference one could find between people anyway. But Nick held a rigid view of the world—heads or tails, win or lose, no two ways about it. He was a gambler and gamblers incline to unconditional views.

Understandably, it was the winner, the successful gambler, who came to intrigue me more and more. Seen in retrospect, there was a certain magic in their lives. They seemed somehow blessed to me, inhabiting some strange and utterly unknowable kingdom. Their casual command of dice and cards, of odds and probabilities; their puzzling immunity to lures of cash or high stacks of multicolored chips astonished me. And yet, when looked at logically—at play, in conversation—they appeared to be such ordinary men.

For more than a year, I consorted with six such men, not to define myself or them, but to understand that part of myself I believed we had in common. I am not a constant player and gambling does little more than occasionally appease the romantic excesses my gods demand of me. The games I prefer to play emanate a particularly heady form of *angstlust*, which has enticed me for the usual magnetic reasons. For me, however, gambling is more of a cold than a cancer—incurable, perhaps, but hesitantly held in check. But these men were professionals and I became obsessed with them—their lives, their games, the cold philosophies that seemed to orchestrate their play. In effect, I wished to know what kind of men they were, what it was like to win and win consistently.

It would be helpful to explain what a winner is not. It has long been fashionable in psychiatric circles to refer to gamblers as flagrant examples of a particular kind of neurotic behavior. According to the late Dr. Edward Bergler, all gamblers are, in varying degrees, compulsive losers. It is not therefore surprising that such groups as Gamblers Anonymous have used Bergler's texts to reinforce their own contention that gambling is not only morally indefensible, but the outward symptom of a diseased and crippled mind. As a proof of sorts, Dr. Bergler often referred to Freud's essay on the Russian novelist Dostoevsky, entitled "Dostoevski and Parricide." In this paper, Freud drew parallels between compulsive gambling and sexual behavior. He believed that the gambling passion was a substitute for the compulsion to masturbate and noted significant similarities in the two activities—the importance placed upon the hands, the fact that both were held to be vices, the irresistible nature of the two acts, which led their devotees to renounce them time and again, only to derive exquisite thrills and subsequent guilt when their resolutions were broken. Bergler popularized this theory of Freud's and it has now become generally accepted. Such views, of course, tend to fall in line with the traditional moral attitudes toward gambling, particularly in America. That is, that the gambler is a low jade, remotely romantic perhaps, but intimate with all the usual vices. One remembers that three of the most popular melodramas of the mid-nineteenth century in America were *The Sinner*, *The Drunkard*, and *The Gambler*. In America, the gambler, at least the serious gambler, has never been held in high esteem.

A more recent example of this cliché occurred in the 1961 film *The Hustler*. In a scene with George C. Scott as the moneyman and Paul Newman as the young pool hustler, the two men discussed why Newman had lost a crucial match to Minnesota Fats. Newman claimed to be a talented player and Scott conceded the point.

"Then what beat me?" Newman asked.

"Character," Scott replied. "You're a born loser. You have no trouble losing when you have a good excuse. It's one of the best indoor sports, feeling sorry for yourself. A sport enjoyed by all, especially the born loser."

Thus, a classic description of the gambler has come to be defined not only as that of a born loser, but a compulsive loser as well. And although we feel rather superior to the insolent upstart and not a little compassionate, since he is seriously disturbed after all, we cannot help expressing an instinctive romantic interest in his flamboyant lifestyle. I have few doubts that Dr. Bergler and his followers are reasonably accurate about the vast majority of gamblers. But I am

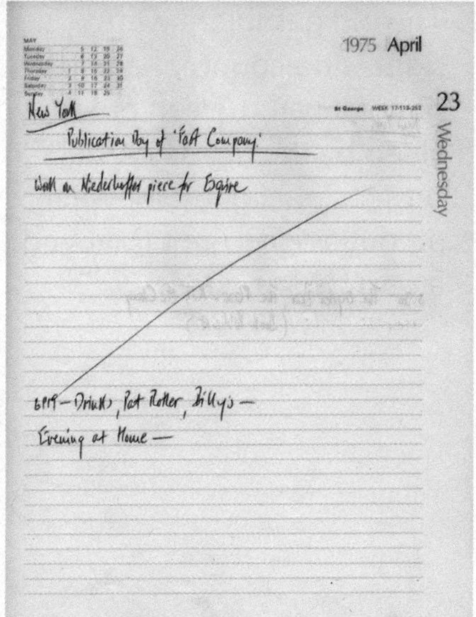
1975 April

23 Wednesday

New York

Publication Day of 'Fast Company'

Work on Niederhoffer piece for Esquire

6PM — Drinks, Pat Rotter, Billy's —

Evening at Home —

not concerned with them. I am more interested in a different species altogether—a small minority of men who are, if anything, compulsive winners. "Winning is my business," one of them said to me, but each of them might well have claimed that slogan as his own.

So much for what these men are not. In the strictest sense, they are not even gamblers. *The Penguin Dictionary of English* defines a gamble as a "risky venture, that which depends on chance." This alone would disqualify any of these six men as gamblers, since none of them believe in risky ventures or would be prepared to gamble on anything solely dependent on chance. Rather, they have devoted their efforts to games in which there is a direct relation between success and skill—tennis, golf, pool, backgammon, bowling, bridge, and poker. They are, in the best sense, gamesmen—experts at specific games. Gambling, however, invariably involves a certain risk, and the success or failure of that risk is rewarded or punished in terms of money. It is the greed and hence the fear of money that intoxicates most gamblers. With professionals, however, money is considered in another light and so acquires a different value. Most professionals would agree with Nick the Greek, who said that the majority of people share a common goal and a common failing: "They believe that money is something more than a handy scorekeeping device." By which he meant that the majority of gamblers develop a kind of love affair with the cash.

In those high-rolling circles of which I speak, money is a means of keeping score, nothing more. There is a case in point in the tale of the gambler who arrived at one of the larger eastern tracks some years ago with $5 in his pocket. He was a familiar figure in his rumpled suit and scuffed shoes, a punter down on his luck of late. In the first race of the afternoon he bet the $5 on the second favorite and the horse came in paying $30. In the second race he bet the $30 on a long shot going off at twelve-to-one. The horse won easily and the gambler collected $390. For the remainder of that afternoon, in each successive race, the gambler bet his total winnings on some previously selected choice. By the sixth race, he had amassed $4,000 and placed it all on the nose of a three-to-one shot. The horse, a tip from one of his friends in the paddock, spurted from behind to beat the favorite in a photo finish. The gambler now had $16,000 in his pocket. In the final race of the day he lost on the heavy favorite. The race began and the favorite, taking an early lead, held it into the top of the stretch. At this point, the horse was more than a length in the lead, but, tiring, she was nipped at the wire by a head. The gambler was broke. Buttoning his rumpled suit, he shuffled slowly from the track. At the main entrance he was hailed by an old acquaintance, who asked how he had fared that afternoon. Lighting a cigarette, the gambler shrugged and said, "Not bad, not bad. I lost five dollars."

In America, as short a time ago as the '30s, there existed an energetic society of professional players, road gamblers who hustled round the country in search of high action in the great midwestern pool palaces, the small-town poker halls, the plush coastal casinos, the southern country clubs. But because of innumerable economic factors and a burgeoning sense of bourgeois civic pride, most of these gathering places were forced to shut their doors. At one time or another, the gamblers depicted in the following pages worked what used to be the great American gambling towns—Hot Springs, Saratoga, New Orleans, Norfolk, French Lick, Miami, Chicago, San Francisco, New York, and, of course, Las Vegas. Today, all but one are gone, and in these tame times Las Vegas itself is a kind of museum, a place in which the tourist can bet his weekly salary and sense that he has somehow set himself in the company of Nick the Greek and Bet-a-Million Gates.

The old gamblers were right—the country has been domesticated, been put to sleep by the fire. The true profes-

> **The old gamblers were right—the country has been domesticated, been put to sleep by the fire. The true professional gambler was an outlaw, a truant traveling along back roads.**

sional gambler was an outlaw, a truant traveling along back roads, but because so much has been softened, cleansed, or simply swept away, because so much has been homogenized in the land, the paths along which those men passed have disappeared, and such men will come no more.

In one sense that is of little consequence, since even the most successful gamblers will secretly explain that the risks are great, the rewards are few, that gambling is, in the end, an exercise in impotence. Still, they were, or seemed to me to be, splendid freebooters. They wished no more to conserve than they wished to acquire. And it is beyond the imagination of a true conservative, to comprehend men who feel no special allegiance to money, men who will risk all for the risk itself. Such men are confined to a special solitude of their own making. They are not prepared to pay the moral-social tax that society attempts to extract from the rest of us. They have no desire to do well, to get ahead, to set a good example, and they remained, for the most part, undefeated. There was about them a superb and enviable insouciance. When they have gone, something important, some last fine flamboyant gesture, will have vanished with them.

These men shared that passion which someone once called the joyful acceptance of risk. Beyond that there was little they had in common. It was only in the pursuit of their passion that they could be said to have been alike. That pursuit was more important to them than God or love or money even. They were excessive men, and now and then they overreached themselves; but these were trifling retrogressions. From the beginning, each of them believed that the force of passion would somehow see him through. Much later, when I first encountered them, these six men, the separate sons of a telephone repairman, a bootlegger, a gambler, an oil executive, an evangelist, and a soldier of fortune, continued to believe with some queer unquenchable conviction that given time and talent and happy odds all things were possible.

They have no desire to do well, to get ahead, to set a good example and they remained, for the most part, undefeated. There was about them a superb and enviable insouciance.

In characters such as Bobby Riggs and Minnesota Fats, Bradshaw came up against verbal bunko artists who made he himself seem understated: talkers, in fact, who enjoyed freedom from restraints that he craved and could never achieve. As a journalist, however highly colored, he was forced forever to walk the wire between style and sense. But the members of a fast company could jump that wire, and did. For them, it did not even exist. Something in their very blood and marrow exempted them. Money, status, the respect of peers, meant nothing to them except as a parlay, the leverage with which to swing their next and positively most stupendiforous scam of all time. For Bradshaw, profoundly torn between the daily humdrum of his reality and the zipless buccaneering of his imagination, they made for perfect alter egos. And somehow, by chronicling their extravagances, he took on their release for his own.
—Nik Cohn

FAST COMPANY

How six master gamblers constantly defy the odds and always come out winners

JON BRADSHAW

British first edition of *Fast Company*

Bobby Riggs

He was what is known in the trade as a conniver—the sort of man who ostentatiously juggles a kind of charming conceit with sharp self-deprecation, in order, it happens, to keep his options open.

Currently I am less than ten miles beyond the small town of Ramona, temporarily detained in the lunar wastes of the Southern California desert. It is not the best place to begin, nor even the most convenient, but since this absurd charade has ended here, it will give a neat and cyclical turn to the tale. And besides, the place could do with a bit of form.

Today began as spring days do in this particular desert. The wind broke and fell away before first light, the skies are gray and drawn with underlying fog—the kind of fog that gums the windshield of the car with odd curlicues of oil. Earlier in the day, when I asked a gas station attendant about it, he laughed and said, "That's not oil, it's Southern California." That kind of fog, trite and commonplace. In the desert beyond Ramona one merely senses the presence of the sun; it is impossible to see. Already the heat is thick and motionless in the canyons, and down on the canyon floor, among the spiraling piles of awkwardly balanced stone, the silence is immense, indomitable. Should those three-hundred-foot-high stone totems collapse, the silence would muffle the sound of their fall—as in some early film. In such a place one's sense of reality is dulled and disconnected.

Only the road, twisting high above along the canyon's rim, indicated the presence of some separate and recognizable reality. And by ten in the morning it was glutted with hundreds of cars, buses, and limousines pushing down from Ramona, Escondido, San Luis Obispo, and from as far north as Carmel. Ramona had not been so perturbed since the summer of '72, when the temperature soared to 117 degrees and all the chickens died. Ramona is not accustomed to a tourist trade, which helped explain why signs to the town were so haphazardly marked. Today, however, May 13, 1973, very little had been left to chance. Every thousand yards along the road, beginning on the outskirts of the town, on linden trees in the Cuyamaca Mountains, on telephone poles on the Barona Indian Reservation, or on overhanging rocks down through Wildcat Canyon, large colored posters proclaimed that the Riggs-Court tennis match was at hand and immediately ahead.

Their destination was a still incomplete desert development called the San Diego Country Estates—a man-made oasis some thirty miles north of San Diego. At first glance the resort appeared to be a failed promoter's final fling at a moneymaking proposition. True, there was a golf course out there among the craters, three tennis courts, and a swimming pool, but the heat and the eerie lunar spaces prevailed. Nonetheless, it was here, on what might have been the moon, that this large crowd had gathered. Having heard the shrill, relentless prophecies of an old, forgotten athlete, and traveling, in some cases, for thousands of miles, they had trooped into the desert to see if the prophet would eat his words.

* * * * *

Down on the sidelines of what would become the center court, the CBS electricians and carpenters scuttled to and fro, tampering with wires, adjusting dollies and microphones. A high platform had been raised at the rear of the court, on top of which the four cameras would rest. A scoreboard had been erected opposite. Workers hung colored banners around the stands while others set the wind barriers in place. Out on the red-and-green cement court Bobby Riggs plodded through his morning practice with Lornie Kuhle, a Las Vegas tennis pro. Moving lethargically about the court, bandy-legged, bespectacled, and partially deaf, Riggs looked like an account executive who had been advised by his doctor to take some exercise once in a while. Rather than hitting out, he tried to intimidate the younger Kuhle with an assortment of junk shots—chips and dinks, slices and spins, and high topspin cross-court lobs—but most of them were off the mark. Between shots Riggs muttered to himself or complained out loud, reciting the grim list of his deficiencies: his overhead lacked power, his serve lacked speed, his lobs lacked depth and accuracy, his groundstrokes had no pace, his volleys were forced, the balls were too heavy, his legs too old, and his elbow, he feared, would never loosen in time for the match. All of which the reporters in the stands recorded faithfully and would, that afternoon, transmit to every major newspaper in the land. Unquestionably Riggs looked like a man past his prime, flat, dispirited. Serving again, he drove the ball into the net, and, adjusting his glasses and shaking his head, he shuffled to the sidelines. "Hey, how do I look?" he said to no one in particular.

"Terrible."

"Terrible, huh?"

"Clapped out."

"As bad as that?"

"Worse."

Riggs toweled his face and grinned. "Heck, I'm fifty-five years old. I've got one foot in the grave."

"Which one, Bobby?"

He looked around. "The one I'm not going to need," he said.

He grinned again and walked away.

Bobby Riggs had the face of a man who sold encyclopedias from door to door; one was suspicious, but never offended. There was always a sense of sincerity in his pronouncements. And so, at first, there was no way of knowing just how serious he was or how seriously he meant his inquisitors to take him. He was what is known in the trade as a conniver—the sort of man who ostentatiously juggles a kind of charming conceit with sharp self-deprecation, in order, it happens, to keep his options open. He had, in fact, only one straightforward role to play—that of the evasive innocent. "Do you think you will win, Bobby?" was the question reporters asked most often, expecting, I suppose, some simple positive or negative reply, or, at worst, some modest avowal of affirmation. But his reply was always a variant of the same equivocal theme: "Well," he would say, looking perfectly confounded, "she's the best woman player in the world, y'know, and gosh, I'm an old has-been with one foot in the grave, but if I can get a few breaks here and there, I think I'm in with an even chance." His lackluster practices on the court, however, indicated that his chances were less than that. The next day, in the tennis writers' private pool, eighteen out of twenty-four experts picked Margaret Court to win and most of them in straight sets.

When news of their verdict reached Riggs, he said, "You don't say?" and smiled with a barely perceptible shrug. He had the air of a small-town mayor seeking reelection. Polls? What did polls have to do with him? Full of impulsive promises and braggadocio, he reminded me . . . well, if a film had been made of this charade, Mickey Rooney would have played the part of Bobby Riggs—the artful, buoyant, cocky underdog. His euphoric chatter and adolescent exaggerations were reminiscent of *Boys Town* and *A Yank*

Bobby Riggs had the face of a man who sold encyclopedias from door to door; one was suspicious, but never offended.

at Eton. He had that habit of referring to himself in the third person, as if he were talking of his fondest invention. Garrulous and completely self-possessed, his head or his hands orchestrated his every word. He talked endlessly and brokenly, a sentence often left unfinished as he rushed into the next one. It was as though the manic flood of his words swelled, only to crash against some invisible reef in his mind, before gathering speed again.

"You don't say?" he said. "What experts? Those reporters out there? Those guys? Those guys from papers I never heard of? Those experts? Let me tell ya. I'll tell ya about experts. They've been saying that all my life. Right from the start. All the way back. Riggs is gonna lose, he's gonna lose. The loudmouth's gonna get what he deserves. They take one look at me out there, those guys, and whatta they see? I'll tell ya what they see. See what I want 'em to see. A tired old man who's past it, dead 'n' gone, always moaning and groaning; they see an old guy living in the past, who can't serve, can't volley, can't even see the ball without glasses, much less get it across the net. And what does he do? He keeps on talking and boasting and bragging, he keeps on. . . . Sure. They wanna see me get my brains beat in, served up like a pig with a tennis ball in his mouth. That's what they want. Heck, I *am* old, I'm practically a grandfather, maybe several times over, and sometimes the flesh won't do what the mind tells it to. And maybe it won't. Who knows? Experts. What can I tell ya? It's even money. You can cut it both ways. What a beautiful deal. Beautiful. You can see for yourself, day after tomorrow, right here. You watch. You'll see. Sure, the old skippiness is gone, the old zing. The way of all flesh, right? But I always rise for the big occasion. I get right up there for it. Heck, you know that, you know that. You know that much."

His tennis match with Margaret Court had become his chief obsession. And yet, for all his talk, he seemed like a man who had gone too far, as though, by accident, he had unleashed a monster he could neither explain, control, nor comprehend. For the moment, however, the attendant publicity seemed to appease the majority of his fears.

In the beginning Riggs had issued a lighthearted challenge to Billie Jean King. He had offered to bet $5,000 of his own money (added to a $5,000 offer from San Diego Country Estates) for a best-of-three-set challenge match. Miss King, whom Riggs called "the real sex leader of the revolutionary pack," had long insisted that because the women players provided a kind of tennis comparable to men's and because they drew an equal percentage of the crowd, they should also receive an equal share of the rewards. It was a just complaint, but, as in other areas of the women's movement, the men saw sexual rather than economic threats lurking in the tide. In his challenge Riggs claimed not only that she could not beat a top male player, but that she could not even beat him—"an old man of fifty-five." For reasons best known to herself, Miss King declined and, following a flurry of negotiations, Mrs. Court accepted.

"Heck, I haven't had any attention for twenty-five years. And I love the limelight, an old ham like me, I really love it."

Now, two days before the match, it had become, next to Watergate, the most fascinating affair in the land. The press boys in the backroom called it "a very important phenomenon," and nearly a hundred tennis writers and women's lib columnists had flocked to Southern California to be on hand. Riggs had not had so much notoriety since he had thrashed Don Budge for the world professional championship in 1949. Or, as he had said to me on the drive down to Ramona from his home in Newport Beach, the large Lincoln Continental (license plate: R. RIGGS) cruising confidently at seventy-five, "Heck, I haven't had any attention for twenty-five years. And I love the limelight, an old ham like me, I really love it." Little wonder then that he continually referred to the confrontation as "the match of the century between the battle of the sexes." Little wonder that he put himself forward as the man who could throw back the advancing female hordes. As Graham Greene said, "Fame is a powerful aphrodisiac."

"The '30s were the golden age of tennis hustling," he said. "Money was tighter and the professional game was not taken seriously anywhere. The basic hustle in tennis is the handicap. Thirty points a game or 5–0 leads in the set. You'd be amazed how many people think a lead like that is insurmountable. It's only when the score is 5–5 that that crazed look comes across their faces, when they realize that they're never going to win." While still in his teens Bobby knew that whatever edge he gave it was not going to be enough to beat him.

"I always rise to the occasion for that big bet," he said. "Pressure makes me produce. Kills most guys. Mortifies 'em. I love a contest, a game, a challenge. To be a winner, you've got to be an appraiser. You've got to be able to play at your best under pressure. And more money creates more pressure. Money is the finest fuel in the world."

His whole life seemed capsuled for him now, miraculously foreshortened, so that this current match with Court seemed to follow in some kind of consecutive sequences, as though it were still 1947.

But twenty-five years had passed. He had gone straight, more or less, he had divorced and remarried, he had gone into business, he had played the other guys' game and observed the rules, he had been a good boy, a kind husband, an indulgent father—and what did he have to show for it? One day, he had gone to a party or walked into a bar—he couldn't quite remember—and no one, not one of them, remembered his name. "Heck," he thought, "gosh, you mean? Gosh, I'm Bobby Riggs, god-damn it," and they had given him those infinitely polite but quizzical looks, as though he had said something they had not quite understood. Like all men, particularly athletes, who reach the peak of their lives at thirty, the rest was anticlimactic, a dull addendum to what had gone before. But that was no longer true. Bobby had been given one further game to play; the crowds would come, there would be apposite applause, and his name would be in the headlines again. And this time it would be even better, since nearly sixty million people would watch his act on television. Sixty million converts. Gosh. Bobby couldn't wait. He believed in an immediate immortality.

Riggs pulled off the improbable when he easily defeated Margaret Court in their exhibition match. This would end up being a footnote to the real "Battle of the Sexes" match that ensued against Billie Jean King. Riggs lost that one, of course, but was a winner just the same, as that match kept him in the public consciousness long after his death in 1995 at the age of seventy-seven.

It's just . . . you'd rather him around, that's all. By a large margin.

Martin Amis on Bradshaw

Minnesota Fats

"Putting a tuxedo on a hustler is like putting whipped cream on a hot dog."

The shot appeared to be impossible.

Telling a story of how he had once whacked out Zsa Zsa Gabor, the Fat Man circled the table chalking his cue. He talked loudly; he had the voice of a deaf man. Now and again he peered down at the pack of balls; interrupting himself, he explained to the crowd that the five ball, which appeared to be firmly lodged in the pack, would soon inhabit the corner pocket. The Fat Man was giving an exhibition of his skills to mark the opening of the new Gimbels department store in the Yorkville section of New York.

Leaning over the table, the Fat Man aimed and drove the cue ball toward the far rail. He continued to talk of Zsa Zsa Gabor. The cue ball sped down the bright green table; banking off the rail and swerving, it shot back up the table, skirting the pack to strike the near rail and bouncing back into the pack to nudge the five ball so that it rolled slowly but directly toward the corner pocket. When it fell the crowd applauded loudly. The Fat Man grinned and wiped his face with a handkerchief.

Turning round, he said to me in a vibrant undertone, "Listen to that. I've had ovations all my life. Ovations beyond compare. Most of them hustlers are nobodies. You could write their life stories on a matchbox. Most of them two-bit mooches don't even know the war's over. They don't even know they're alive. They couldn't beat nobody. And that Allen guy you mentioned that calls himself Fast Eddie? That guy I never heard of? That Allen couldn't beat a drum. He ain't never won enough to keep him in chewin' gum."

The crowd continued to applaud. The Fat Man stepped back to the table and began to demonstrate a series of intricate trick shots—hitting the ball on the wing, causing a ball to reverse direction unexpectedly, or knocking five balls into separate pockets on the same shot. Like any conjurer, Fats worked economically and with almost glib assurance. That which to the crowd appeared impossible was mere routine to him.

Fats looked like a man more used to the confines of an easy chair than to strutting back and forth before a table. And yet, despite his bulk, he had the movements of a thin and nimble man; he was always in transit, forever en route. His heavily jowled face somehow emphasized his small, bright eyes, eyes which invited trust, and more, belief. He had the accomplished charm of an old successful trouper, but there was about the Fat Man a sense of lingering regret, as though certain of his youthful dreams had not come true.

When the exhibition ended, the kids swarmed round the table thrusting out programs and scraps of paper and shouting for autographs. Reaching into the jacket pocket of his beige silk suit, the Fat Man extracted an ink pad and a little silver stamp. He began stamping his signature—"Minnesota Fats"—on every paper and program in reach. "I've got sixty million fans in this country," he said. "I know, 'cause I've signed at least sixty million autographs."

The next day we flew to St. Louis, the nearest major airport to the Fat Man's home in Dowell, Illinois, some hundred miles to the southeast. He more than justified his name. Of average height, he weighed about 260 pounds. He required two adjoining seats for the flight and demanded that the stewardess produce an emergency belt extension to accommodate his fifty-one-inch waist. His right shoulder twitched continuously, and he had a habit of wiping his forehead with his handkerchief. For the trip home he had changed into a silk suit of another color. His alligator cue case matched his alligator shoes. On his left hand he wore a ring of green diamonds—"a high-class ring, that's all"—and a silver diamond-studded watch, "which I beat a guy out of once."

Between snacks and constant Coca-Colas, he continued his rich harangue against his fellow hustlers. He talked swiftly, immoderately, in the way a hungry man eats. He wanted, he said, to relieve the public of wrong impressions. He did not want them nurturing misguided notions of the Fat Man's place in the nature of things.

"Why should I enter them tournaments?" he said. "I don't play for trophies. I don't play for bubble gum. If I want a trophy, I'll go out and buy one. It's ridiculous, ridiculous beyond compare, for them pool hustlers getting dressed up just because it's a tournament. Putting a tuxedo on a hustler is like putting whipped cream on a hot dog. You better believe it. What I tell you now, you could bet your life on.

"I've had the world by the nuts for fifty years and people are jealous of that sometimes. They all tell these elegant lies about me. Some of them hustlers are fabulous liars, really fabulous, when it comes to talkin' about who they beat and for how much cash. It's a congenital disease. Some of them guys would derange a lie detector, drive it stark raving mad. That Allen couldn't break an egg. I recently turned down $180,000 for a ninety-minute special on television. What do I want to play Allen for $6,000 for? Y'unnerstand?

"They all like to talk about me losin' all the time. That'll be the day. I can't give you any firsthand information on the subject, 'cause I ain't never had any experience in that line. Any information about losin' I give you would be outright lies, would be hearsay, just what I hear round and about. When I play pool, there's only one beneficiary."

He paused and wiped his forehead. "I came close once," he said, and he closed his eyes, as though trying to recall some obscure childhood memory. "I came close, I remember, about thirty years ago, yeah, about thirty years ago, I guess. I had to call on the patron saint of impossible propositions. I was even heavier than I am now. Must've weighed in around two seventy-five. I was heavy. I remember whenever I walked around that pool table, the floor took to creakin' and groanin' same as if it was haunted.

"Anyhow, to make a long story short, y'unnerstand, I am playin' banks with a guy called Lou Russo, a real good player outta Port Reading, New Jersey. We are playin' for some big money and the action finally winds down to this last shot. Everything in the world is ridin' on this shot. Russo's pretty confident, pretty cocky. He thinks he left me with nothin' to play with. He thinks he left me beat. I look over the situation and I see that there is just no way I'm not gonna sink that ball and take all of Russo's gold. I line up, say, 'One ball, cross-side,' let go, and whatta ya think happens? The floor falls in and I drop like a boulder. I am going right through the floor.

"Now, you can never trust them pool hustlers. Not even in emergencies. Y'unnerstand? It's automatic. So, as I am goin' down, I look over the lip of the table, and whatta ya think I see? I see that cue ball comin' off the rail like Citation on a good day, hit two cushions, and then just nudge that one ball toward the appointed pocket. Like I knew it would. Some of my bank shots are so accurate

FRIDAY 16 SEPTEMBER

1977 259th day – 106 days follow

Los Angeles

12 – Vidal Sassoon's – (Anthony)

1:15 – Lunch – Fiona Lewis, La Scala

Langusti's –

Alice Cooper's –

'The Harder They Come' –

they look like they're on automatic pilot. That's on the square. I probably fall ten, twelve feet, but right away I shout up I don't wanna hear no stories when I come up outta that cellar. And I don't get none. When I come up I collect the gold, and that's the closest I ever come to losin'. Some guys gotta tear the house down to try and stop the Fat Man."

In St. Louis at the airport garage, Fats introduced me to his car. MF 1, he explained, was a custom-built Fleetwood Cadillac costing $13,500. The interior was decorated in velvet. Fats claimed to own MF 1 through MF 9. Unlocking the trunk, he pointed out a few of the awards, trophies, citations, and plaques he had received over the years. There were also two pistols on the right-hand side—unlikely accessories, but Fats spluttered at my surprise. "Sure, I carry a gun," he said. "These days you need a gun in church. They've tried to heist me a dozen times."

The trunk of the Cadillac also contained four cue cases—in alligator, lizard, crocodile, and python. He had, he said, shoes to match each case and his wife had shoes to match his own. But these were incidental bric-a-brac. Most of the trunk was filled with neat piles of personal newspaper and magazine clippings and a book or two, including his autobiography. The Fat Man never traveled without them, presumably in order to educate the ignorant along the way. "Take whatever you need," he said magnanimously. "I'll give you whatever you need and you can change 'em around as you please. Y'unnerstand? I've been tellin' the exact same stories for forty years. I never change a word.

You don't have to talk to me and waste your time. I don't like wastin' time. I believe in killin' three, four birds with one stone."

The Fat Man seemed genuinely perplexed that I should wish to accompany him to Dowell. Indicating the trunk of MF 1, he seemed to say, *But it's all here. I've already made my statement. It's right there in black and white. There's nothing more to say. I've said it all before*. And to some extent he was right. In the course of the next few days, hearing his buoyant tales of his vagabond life was like listening to a man who had memorized long passages from some rags-to-riches melodrama. The Fat Man remembered too much and he remembered it too well.

Dowell is a town of about three hundred people in that part of southern Illinois called Little Egypt—where pyramid-shaped mounds of coal used to dot the countryside. The Fat Man has lived here since 1941. Dowell is a ramshackle town highlighted by the Kathleen Mine, formerly the largest strip mine in the world, and now the site of an abandoned junkyard. The town contains a post office, two taverns, a bait shop, the dilapidated quarters of the local branch of the American Legion, and the cheap and cheerless homes of its residents. Most of them are out-of-work miners, and those who are not unemployed have to drive nearly forty miles to the nearest mine. The land beneath Dowell is riddled with abandoned shafts and tunnels. "Everybody here is on relief," said Fats. "They wouldn't do nothin', these people, they wouldn't turn on the tap for you."

According to Fats the area had once been a popular gambling center, "Las Vegas without the ballyhoo," but obviously nothing happened now. The dominant noise was the shrill whistle of passing trains speeding west to St. Louis or north via Springfield to Chicago. "There used to be about eight hundred people here," said Fats, "but they've gone away. Everybody would've gone away if I hadn't stayed. I saved this cocksucker of a town. Could've bought the whole jurnt for $300 at one time."

When Fats was not away on business, selling personalized pool equipment or giving exhibitions, he liked to hibernate in Dowell with his wife, Evelyn, which he pronounced *Evaleen*, and Orbie, his mother-in-law. Given the drabness of the town, the Fat Man's house announced itself like some loud and unexpected gaucherie; it was too obviously the seat of the resident potentate. Not that there was anything architecturally remarkable about the house; it was little more than an outsized tinder box, but it loomed over Dowell like an exclamation mark. There was only one approach—an unpaved, cratered road that skirted an empty field. "I stopped them from paving the roads," said Fats. "It'd be too easy for the tourists to find me then. Dowell was always a good place to lie around in and hide."

Inside there was an odd air of abandonment, as though the occupant had died some years before and everything had been left just as it was at the time. It was as sparse and tidy as a museum. The large main drawing room was dominated by four objects. A large color television, on which a bouquet of multicolored plastic flowers had been arranged, occupied one corner; a "Minnesota Fats" pool table commanded the center of the room like a shrine; and in the opposite corner were two giant refrigerators containing the Fat Man's chocolates and his ice cream. The Fat Man claimed to eat about a hundred dollars' worth of candy every day. "At one time," he said, "I could eat eight gallons of ice cream without batting an eye. But you cut down when you get older."

There were no books anywhere, a fact that called attention to itself because of the prominence given his autobiography. This book, *The Bank Shot and Other Great Robberies*, was mounted on a gilded easel on a corner table, like a small but rare incunabulum.

The Fat Man was proud of his possessions and insisted on showing me his vast collection of clothes. He was particularly pleased with his wardrobe of silk suits, the cheapest of which cost $450. There were the dozens of Italian shirts at $45 apiece, the expensive slacks and overcoats, the python, lizard, and crocodile shoes. He also displayed his wife's fur coats and evening gowns, ticking off the sums as he pulled them from the closet. Plainly, prosperity pleased him. Yet, whenever he referred to it, he spoke loudly and with a certain flimsy familiarity, as he might have referred to some celebrity, a starlet perhaps, to whom he had once been introduced but had never seen again.

Although he and his wife had no children, some forty vagrant cats and dogs lurked round the place. A tall birdhouse stood on the front lawn, which Fats called "a thirty-room hotel." But what kind of birds made use of it he could not say. "They're high-class birds, that's all. My animals live like the King and Queen of England. Every one of them." At the back of the house a small cement blockhouse had been converted into a communal dormitory. "Let me show you," said Fats with the air of a man who is about to give you a tour of the east wing. He threw back the door. "Look at that. A palace beyond compare, the lap of luxury. These cats and dogs play together. They even sleep together," a fact he explained by adding, "Animals surpass humans on all counts."

When the Fat Man first came to Little Egypt the area was fairly prosperous. It was here he met his wife, a waitress in one of the local eateries. Fats had been told that she was "about the best looker in the whole of Little Egypt," and two months after meeting they were married and settled down in Dowell. Before his marriage Fats had weighed about 260 pounds, but he soon shot above 280 and sported a waistline of fifty-five inches.

His obesity obsessed him. "It's no wonder I'm fat," he explained. "I eat enough for ten big eaters. I'm a world champion with a knife 'n' fork, in the Olympic class. I can eat whole chickens and hams. I used to eat thirty quails at a time, and when I was done with those birds there wasn't enough left for a ravenous dog. I'm the biggest eater the world has ever seen. I can still drink more Coca-Cola than any human alive. I remember once I was eatin' against this guy, a real big guy, must've weighed 450 pounds, in an eatin' competition, and before we got started I grab a ham when we sat down and swallow it whole. Told him I wouldn't count it, y'unnerstand? He takes one look, gulps, and quits right there.

"Right now I'm five-eight or so and weigh about two forty. I useter be five-ten, but I gained sixty or seventy pounds overnight, and as I spread out I came down in height. For sixty years I've eaten anything I felt like eatin' any time of the day and night I felt like eatin' and I ain't never been on any diet. I have a tremendous consumption rate, tremendous. I've ravaged tons of food in my time. Tons. I wouldn't know a calorie from a cantaloupe. I'm the only fat man in the history of the world who was completely perfect.

"I've always been eighty, a hundred pounds overweight. It don't mean nothin'. I remember about ten years ago in Hot Springs I had a physical checkup. That doctor couldn't believe his instruments. He was sure there were about a hundred and four things wrong with me, but when he put the joint on my heart, he was dumbfounded. Dumbfounded, y'hear? 'My God,' he says, 'your heart sounds like a Rolls-Royce.' The same thing happened in Chicago. They called in a jillion doctors and they all stood around looking dumbfounded. I was checked outta this world twice and made medical history. Ain't never been nothin' wrong with me that a lot of food and sleep wouldn't cure."

The Fat Man was proud of the fact that he neither smoked nor drank. "Every livin' human is disturbed," he said. "Everybody who smokes and drinks is a disturbed person. A sucker needs them props. Not me."

The Fat Man liked to imply that he was perfect in every way. He spoke of it with perfect assurance, perfect certainty. Only his reputation seemed less perfect than it might have been, less generally upheld, and it nagged at him accordingly. He was the greatest money player in the world, after all. That much was clear. Yet he was still set upon by lesser men—him, the Fat Man, subjected to scorn and snickering contempt by players he had murdered a million times before. News of each fresh insult struck him to the core. It was amazing, amazing beyond compare. He nursed his reputation like a sore tooth.

"I've turned men gray before their time, put 'em in a state of permanent grief. I was a deadly killer. When it came to pool, Dillinger had nothin' on me. But there's nobody left now. Who's left? Nobody. All the great players have

The Fat Man liked to imply that he was perfect in every way. He spoke of it with perfect assurance, perfect certainty. Only his reputation seemed less perfect and it nagged at him accordingly.

given up for lack of competition or they died. All you got left are those mooches at the tournaments. Most of 'em aren't even included in the census. Strictly speaking, they don't exist. They might as well be in Timbuktu.

"And they say they wanna play me? You don't catch me goin' for that kind of dodge. Not for a whole barrel of gold. I'm wise to their skulduggery. Me play them? The king don't socialize with the mob. They want the gold and the glory, the glory and the gold. If they beat each other, all they get is a little gold. But if they beat me, they get a ton of gold and all the glory. Me play them? For what? They might get lucky and the news'd be in Zanzibar and even Timbuktu. It happens. Automatic. I'm the champion of the earth."

Minnesota Fats became famous by claiming to be the basis of the character played by Jackie Gleason in The Hustler *(1961). According to the* New York Times, *the movie made Fats "a celebrity, appearing on television, making nationwide tours and passing out stamped autograph cards proclaiming himself the greatest pool player ever." He died of congestive heart failure in 1996. He was either eighty-two or possibly ninety-five.*

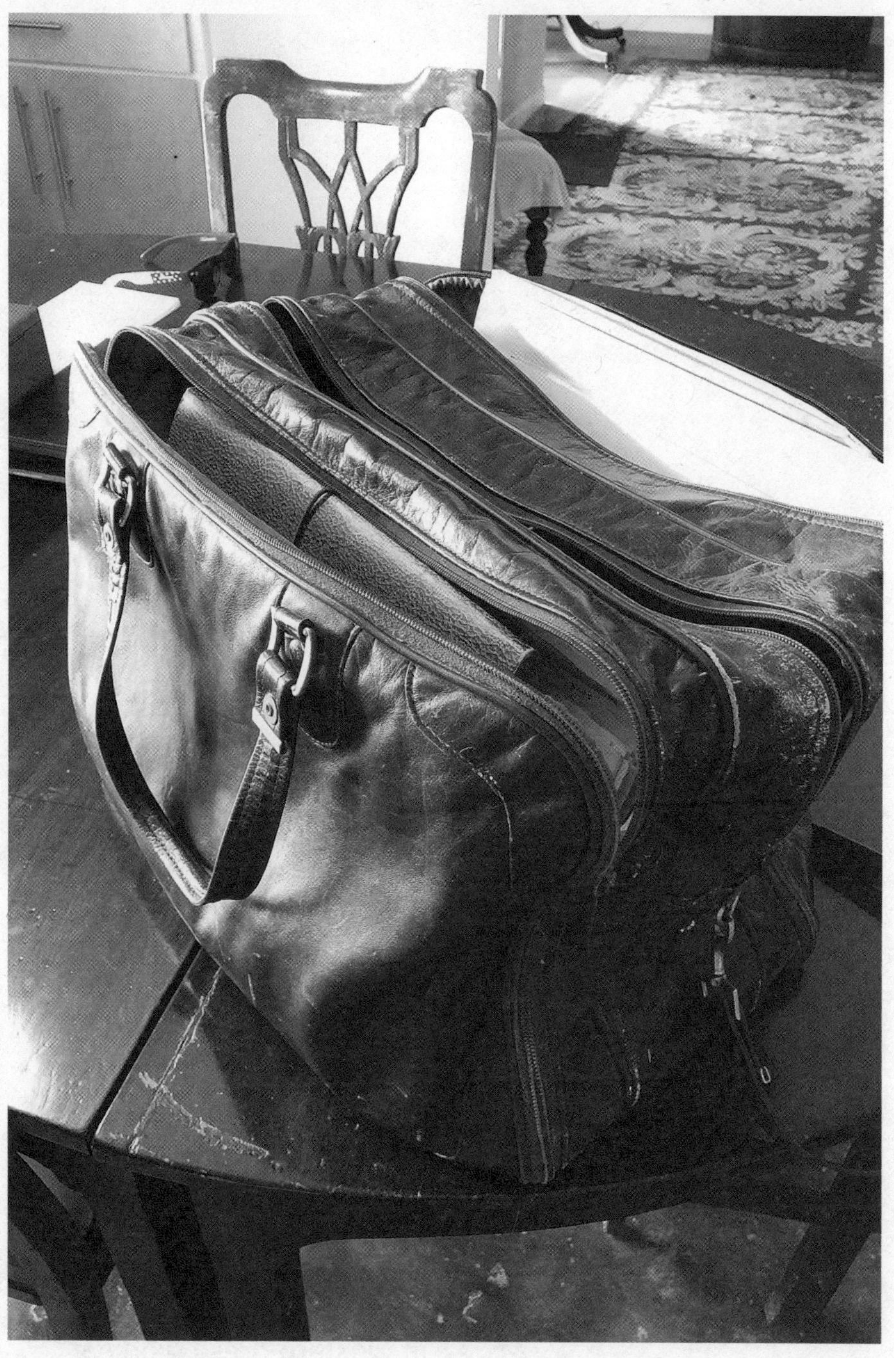

Bradshaw's travel bag

Johnny Moss

"I never choke . . . I play for the cash and you don't choke for the cash."

The card room in the Aladdin Hotel is in the hotel's large main room on the ground floor directly across from the Sinbad Lounge. On the wall behind the sea-green poker tables is a sign that says POKER—24 HOURS EVERY DAY. Above the sign is a spread royal heart flush and just below is the notation—*JOHNNY MOSS, MANAGER*. On this particular night the card room was crowded with loud flamboyant men in western dress who sat around or milled about the central poker table. There was a look of tense anticipation in their tanned and weathered faces. They looked like ranchers who had ridden into town for the annual rodeo. Large, brutish, heavy men, they might easily have come from central casting: they might, if appearances meant anything, have said such things as "Reach for the sky!" or "Saddle up!" or "Howdy, stranger!" but hunched around the poker table they talked instead of cards and propositions. Mainly Texans, they had come to Vegas to compete in the World Series of Poker, which was to begin the following day. Around the table were Pug Pearson, Texas Dolly Doyle, Treetop Jack Strauss, and Amarillo Slim. When Johnny Moss walked in they looked up from the table, greeting him with gruff and repetitious welcomes.

"Hey, Johnny."

"Hi, Johnny."

"Howdy, Johnny."

"It's sure good to see ya, ya son of a gun."

"Hullo, boys, hullo," said Moss. He nodded and smiled. The boys returned to their game. Ordering a drink, Moss sat on a chair against the wall and watched the others play. The poker limits in the Aladdin begin with a ten-cent ante and rise to the highest poker in the world. Moss obtained his license from the State of Nevada "because they know I don't do no business with nobody. I leased this card room just so me and the boys could play real high. I run it real well. I make the boys toe the line. I ain't a tough guy or anything. I couldn't lick a sick whore, don't misunnerstand me, but I'd take 'em outside anyway. They have to act like gentlemen in here," he said, "or at least as well as they know how."

He nodded toward the poker table. "These guys here is all high rollers," he said, "an' I got nothin' against 'em, y'unnerstand, but they don't play like the gamblers twenty, thirty years ago. See what I'm sayin'? There's poker players comin' up today that only have one game. Now when I'm playin' poker, I'd use to go to a place, they'd be aplayin' lowball. All right, I'd play along with 'em. I'd go to another place, they're playin' draw, I'd play draw; to another place, they're playin' stud, I'd play stud; go to another place, they're playin' hold 'em and I'd have to play hold 'em. And ace-to-the-five and deuce-to-the-seven and pitch and gin. You have to play all them games to be a *professional* gambler.

"Remember once when I first came to Vegas, for about forty straight days I flew from here to Los Angeles every day, hired a car and drove to Gardena to learn to play ace-to-the-five at the local joints. It was no higher than $20 limit. At five o'clock I'd fly back to Vegas, sleep for a few hours, and then go to the Flamingo for $6,400 limit ace-to-the-five. Takin' planes to Gardena to play with a lot of goddamn old men and women. But it was worth it. I learned the game at a tenth a the price.

"To be a professional gambler," he said, "not only means you have to know how to play all them games, you have to keep your eyes open for two dangers, the hijackers and the law, specially in the old days. They're both after the same thing, the cash, and they'll do almost anything underhanded to get their hands on it. You see what I'm sayin'? You got to learn to duck and dive, keep your ear to the ground and your eyes peeled. I'm tellin' you, it's like livin' in the jungle."

In 1956 Moss was subpoenaed for fraud and income-tax evasion and brought up before a federal grand jury hearing in Fort Worth. "It was a very confused and messy trial," he recalled. "Twenty-three jurors, the district attorney, and me. They wouldn't even let my lawyer in the courtroom. The trial went on for a long time, a two- or three-hour session, and that was after the jury had listened to several federal men for three weeks beforehand tellin' 'em what a bad man I was. I mean it was real boring, and by the time that attorney got around to questioning me, most of the jury had either fallen asleep or they were anoddin' and adozin'. Hot day too, a real hot day.

"Well, at one point during the proceedings that attorney, he asks me if it was true that I had played golf for $8,000 to $10,000 a hole, and a few of them golf-playing jurors begun to perk up. I guess he must a heard tall tales about that match I had at the Desert Inn a couple a years before, 'cause all the rest of them jurors woke up when he asks me if I had played a match for $100,000. They woke up. They were real interested now. Well then what happened, that attorney, he suddenly comes out with a putter. He wanted to learn how to putt, I guess. He got into a kind of putting stance and asks me how I had made that putt for so much money. He asks me to show him how I had done it. 'Well,' I says, 'I just sort of stand like this,' and I showed him. Now I had to be a dog, y'unnerstand, I had to be their dog. I had to put myself in the place of them jurors, just like they'd been there taking that putt, just like a sucker would feel about it. It was a ten-foot putt, but I told 'em it was five. I didn't want to seem supernatural or nothin'. I says to them, 'Up close the hole looks this big, but when I step back it looks this small. I know that even if I get that ball over there, the hole would be too small for that ball to get in.'

"Then one of the jurors says, 'But you made that putt?' And I says, 'Well, I was plain lucky, I guess. I had a good line, a good stroke, and I just shut my eyes, stroked it, and lucked it in, I guess.' And that juror says, 'I believe you, son.' All them jurors looked as though they did the same thing every day. Hell, I didn't want to tell 'em I was one of the best putters there is."

Moss laughed and looked around the room. "Then that attorney asks me if I choked, and I said sure I choked, sure, even the pros choke. The fear just grabs ahold of you. 'Listen,' I said, 'I once saw Ben Hogan miss a very important two-foot putt. Ben Hogan. Everybody chokes. It's only natural.' I didn't tell 'em I never choke, that I play for the cash and you don't choke for the cash. I wanted to be just like them suckers in the jury.

"Well, all along it looked like I was agoin' to get twenty years, five for sure. In the end I asked 'em if they would acquit me. A man could be in the corner about to cut off my head, I says to them, and I wouldn't ask him not to, but I asked 'em not to indict me. I said I never asked for nothin' in my life. This is the first thing I've ever asked for. I ain't exactly beggin' for mercy, but as far as I know I ain't guilty of what you say I am. And, y'know, they let me go."

The year after Bradshaw interviewed him, in June 1974, at the age of sixty-eight, Moss, against sixteen competitors, won the World Series of Poker and $160,000. Moss died in 1995 at the age of eighty-eight.

Pug Pearson

"Gambling isn't the money, you know. I've been broke lots of times. That don't mean nothin'. It's the competition. It's laying your ability on the line and invitin' challenge."

His name was Walter Clyde Pearson, but few of his friends or acquaintances knew it. For as long as he could remember, he had been called Pug—because of his nose, irrevocably flattened from a boyhood fall. Everyone called him Pug with what amounted to an implied familiarity—the doormen and carhops at the Strip hotels, the shills, the showgirls, the dealers and grifters, and all the hapless players who came to sit with him at poker. Only his mother, in keeping with the southern custom, called him Walter Clyde. He must have liked the nickname or had grown accustomed to it; when telling me comic tales of his early gambling days, he sometimes referred to *himself* as Pug—as though he were talking about someone else, a pigeon, some extravagant friend perhaps, whom, he implied, it might have amused me to know.

But that would have been unlike him; it would not have been in keeping with his homespun, southern style. He had a candid sense of humor, brusque and down-to-earth. He would not have noticed irony nor appreciated it if he had. He wasn't that kind of man, nor did he have that kind of circumambulatory mind. He saw things simply and then brought an inspired logic to bear. He once, for example, explained to me why there were so few good poker players in the country. "Poker," he said, "has a language all its own, but you don't expect most folks to understand it, any more than you expect 'em to understand Egyptian." His sense of humor was like that—shrewd and folksy and rooted in fact, since it was always related to the two subjects he knew best, himself and gambling. And blunt as he was, he was never offensive. Pug seemed to know that what one said was somehow unimportant, so long as one knew how to say it. I make a point of it, because it was his persuasive talents that I remember best about him.

Pug was good with people in the way some men are good with dogs. People responded to some quality of self-belief in him, which gave them an illusion of potential warmth and safety. It was the quality usually described as charm. Pug used it, as charming men do, to exert an influence in order to control. His voice, filled with unchallengeable assurance, simply extended and completed the illusion. But these were things I learned much later. In the beginning, when we first met in Tennessee, I remember thinking that I had come a long way to see a man whom, but for his name and heady tales of his prowess at cards, I knew nothing about at all.

I had been told I would have no difficulty recognizing him. "You'll know him," Jimmy the Greek had said. "Ain't but one nose like it in the world." Pug waited for me in the airport lounge, a tall, heavily built man in his early forties. He was almost completely bald. He had the round mischievous face of an elderly troll, a troll with a fondness for Cuban cigars. He had come to Nashville to compete in a golf tournament and to that end, I suppose, wore multicolored striped trousers, a lime-green shirt, green shoes, and a wide-brimmed plastic straw hat. There was an air of jauntiness about him and of inexhaustible good spirits, the air of a man who had had his share of passing pleasure.

"Good God," he said, when I had introduced myself. "I was lookin' out for a man of fifty. You sounded like that on the telephone. You've got the voice of an old man, son. Comes from wicked ways." He grinned, continuing to puff at his cigar. "That all you got? That little bag? Well, come on, let's go. I've got some golf to get to. And them old boys ain't much on waitin' around. You play golf? I'd rather play golf than breathe." He picked up my bag. "But there ain't no money in it."

Despite the way Pug immediately took one into his confidence, his accessibility, he had been a difficult man to meet, implying that it would detract from his anonymity. Nick the Greek had liked to say that in gambling "fame is usually followed by a jail sentence," and Pug, at least temporarily, had held some similar belief. "Son, you can't be too careful," he explained in the car. "The government is like the gestapo on gamblers. Like they was some kind of outlaws. But I'll tell you. Gamblers are the most broad-minded people in the world. If more folks were like 'em, there would be fewer laws. That's on the square. You've got to be sharp in this world, no matter what your business is, or the world is gonna gobble you up. That's what it's all about, son. That's what they call life."

Parking his Cadillac in the parking lot and taking his clubs and a handful of Cuban cigars, Pug hurried out to the course. Despite the early hour, the grassy area sloping down from the clubhouse to the first tee was crowded with nearly a hundred golfers. It was, Pug explained, the last day of a three-day tournament, held annually in memory of Teddy Rhodes, the first black [man] to break the color barrier in professional golf. Because Pug had helped to arrange the first of these tournaments, he was one of the few white golfers invited to play. During the rest of the year, this was just another municipal golf course in the black neighborhood of West Nashville. But Pug always used it when he was in town. He avoided the fashionable country clubs, which had better courses, because there was more action here than anywhere else in Nashville. Today, the players had come from all over the country. There were a few black professional golfers such as Lee Elder and a few black celebrities such as Don Newcombe in the tournament, but the majority were prominent black businessmen from the South or the Midwest and most of them, confided Pug, were connected in one way or another with the business of gambling. There, for example, in the purple blazer was the man who ran the numbers racket in Kansas City, and there in matching red was the most successful bookmaker in Detroit. All in all, it was the black golf tournament of the year.

Although Pug was officially competing, the tournament was of little consequence to him. He had, he knew, no hope of winning, and besides, he did not play for trophies. No, Pug had come for the side action, and to that end he had matched himself with three other players for sizable stakes. As golfers go, Pug was little better than average. He had taken up the game fifteen years before and only then because he had won a set of clubs in a poker game and had not known what else to do with

Despite the way Pug immediately took one into his confidence, his accessibility, he had been a difficult man to meet, implying that it would detract from his anonymity.

them. Pug had a handicap of about nine, though it fluctuated according to whom he was playing against and the stakes involved. He employed what politely might be described as an eccentric swing—a looping, half-jerked swing which would have repelled a novice. It was a swing which appeared to compensate for some physical deficiency—an arthritic shoulder, a withered arm—but, as Pug explained, it was merely the way he had learned to play, practicing day in and day out without professional advice, until he could drive a ball 250 yards with surprising accuracy. Pug also knew that his swing added a few strokes to his handicap, since it was improbable that anyone could hit the ball with such a motion, much less control its direction. But the swing was deceptive and Pug had worked hard at his game. "Hell," he said, as I watched him practice, "when I first won these here clubs, I went to a course to see how they played and I thought, hell, they put their britches on same as me. If they can play, I can play. It's a question of application."

The tournament had begun at eight o'clock that morning, and just before nine Pug's foursome was summoned to the first tee. Before setting out, Pug and his three black opponents sorted out their various wagers. This involved long and intricate negotiation—pained talk of handicaps, of colds and bad backs, off days, a lack of practice, and the difficulties of playing on a strange course. But the four men knew one another well, and after some minutes satisfactory and not altogether unexpected compromises were reached. Pug drove his first ball straight down the middle of the fairway; then, riding out in the golf cart, he attempted to explain the delicate art of negotiation to me. "Now, what does a politician do?" he said. "He projects himself in such a way as to capture the people's train of thought and turn 'em to his way of thinking, don't he? He's got to talk 'em into the bottom line. Well, in gambling, it's the same way. The con and the bullshit is very important. And in golf, which ain't the same as poker, you can't bluff. In golf, the bullshit has got to be backed up. Otherwise, you're a loser, son. A dead man."

Approaching the first green, Pug suggested that I bet a moderate amount on him for the eighteen holes.

"Well . . ." I hesitated. "What do you usually shoot, Pug?"

"Oh, about a seventy-seven, seventy-eight."

"And the others? What do they shoot?"

"Oh, them old boys'll shoot anywhere between seventy-two and seventy-five, depending on the day."

Pug looked surprised when I expressed what seemed a reasonable doubt that the odds against him appeared to be unfavorable. "Son," he said, "I don't think you understand the game. We bet by the hole, not on the total number of strokes." Even so, the mathematics seemed clear to me. Whether they bet by the hole or not, at the end of the match, Pug's opponents were going to be anywhere from two to six strokes ahead. Pug laughed loudly. "The percentages are all right," he said, "as far as they go. But I don't think you're takin' into account your human element. Hell, I know them old boys. I know 'em real well. And I know their chokin' points."

"Their choking points?"

"Their chokin' points," said Pug. "The point where they begin to cut their own throats." He looked at me out of the corner of his eye. "Where you been, boy? You don't know nothin'. I was only tryin' to help you, being a newcomer and all. And I'm tellin' you, a bet on me is a sure thing. Can't fail."

As I have said, it was Pug's persuasive talents that most impressed me, and by the time we had reached the first green I had bet three hundred on him at even money. Pug merely laughed and by way of assurance pointed out that two of his opponents had driven into the bunker.

The rest of the morning was spent in the golf cart in pursuit of Pug's eccentric drives. At the end of the first nine, Pug had somehow managed to remain even with one of his opponents and two holes up on each of the others. Chortling to himself, his cigar swiveling back and forth in his mouth, Pug scuttled off to the tenth tee. Within three holes, however, his good humor had been replaced with puzzled frowns and a garbled progression of low oaths. On the fourteenth tee they were all even, and during the next three holes Pug, in spite of singularly consistent drives into the rough, the water, or the sand traps, managed to produce those few, apparently lucky, last-minute shots that kept him out of serious trouble. When they reached the eighteenth tee, Pug was two holes up on one man, one hole up on another, and even with the last—a bad-tempered, burly man called Joe Louis.

On the eighteenth fairway, at the edge of the rough on the left-hand side, there was a tall linden tree. Pug teed off first and his drive, one of his longest that day, was traveling at great speed, when it hit a branch of the linden tree and bounced some forty or fifty yards back toward where we were standing. Staring in disbelief, Pug grabbed the cigar from his mouth, then swore and struck his club on the ground. Joe Louis, standing to one side, smiled broadly, but expressed his sympathies. Pug turned angrily round and, seeing Louis's smile, he seemed to lose his temper. He continued to strike his club on the ground while Louis waited patiently. At last Pug announced that he wished to press all bets. Louis and one of the other players promptly agreed. Pug stalked to his cart cursing all the way and, when he slid in next to me, winked and then relit his cigar. As Louis lined up to take his final drive of the day, Pug neglected even to turn around and watch him, continuing rather to light his already lighted cigar.

An extraordinary thing happened then. Joe Louis did something he hadn't done all day; he sliced his ball deep into the dense rough some 150 yards away. And the next player drove his ball very nearly into the same spot. Neither of them could believe it. They looked incredulously into the distance, as though they were seeing something they had never seen before. Pug accelerated his cart down the fairway and tried not to smile. As Pug's drive lay closest to the tee, he played first. It lay in the middle of the fairway, and, using his driver, Pug drove it to within fifty yards of the green. Getting back into the cart, he rode into the rough and stopped behind Joe Louis. His ball lay in six-inch-high grass just behind a small tree. It was practically unplayable. Pug studied it for a moment and said, "Now that's what I call real unlucky, Joe." He examined the ball again. "Damn, do you think you'll be able to play it from there? It's a bad break, Joe, real bad. Just ain't no justice in this world. None at all." Joe Louis looked over his shoulder at Pug. "You're a lucky son of a bitch," he said.

Riding up the fairway in the cart, Pug chuckled to himself. "Now, that's what I mean about a chokin' point, son," he said. "Old Joe couldn't keep his mind off the money." Despite his early error Pug parred the hole. It took Joe Louis three strokes just to get out of the rough. Pulling a wad of one-hundred-dollar bills from his pocket, he paid Pug on the green. Pug took the money, a big smile on his face. Joe Louis scowled. "You're a lucky son of a bitch, Pug," he said. "Real lucky."

Later, in the clubhouse, Pug said, "I'll tell you what luck is, son. It's a line which on one side is wrong and on the other side is right. Now, most folks try to keep as close to that line as they can. To be on that line always would be perfect and that's impossible. You keep on sliding back and forth across it. That line is what most people define as luck. And that's on the square. I know, 'cause I've been tucked in next to that line all my life."

Taking a roll of one-hundred-dollar bills from his pocket, Pug gave me my share of the winnings. Then, holding his roll in his hand, he said quite firmly, but as though he were trying to reassure himself of something, "I'll tell you one thing. Gambling isn't the money, you know. I've been broke lots of times. That don't mean nothin'. It's the competition. It's laying your ability on the line and invitin' challenge. That's all I can do. I do it for myself. That's what I take pride in—being a winner. That's what life's all about, ain't it? It's the satisfaction of performing well." He spread his hands about two feet apart. "You live from here to here, you understand? And, in between, that's all you ever get if you're smart. Just a little self-satisfaction and enjoyment. And that's enough. Why hell, there ain't a breeze in the sky floats freer than I do."

Pearson owned a $200,000, thirty-eight-foot diesel Holiday Rambler Imperial motor home that he called "Rovin' Gambler." Painted on the van: I'LL PLAY ANY MAN FROM ANY LAND ANY GAME THAT HE CAN NAME FOR ANY AMOUNT THAT I CAN COUNT. *In smaller letters:* PROVIDING I LIKE IT. *Pearson died at the age of seventy-seven in 2006.*

Titanic Thompson

To the end of his life Titanic remained a backwoods Southern boy. Even in what he liked to regard as his sophisticated days, when he favored yellow polo coats and drove nickel-plated limousines, he seemed somehow out of context, inconvenienced, like a farm boy made to slick his hair and wear his Sunday suit.

In what he liked to imagine were sweeter times, in the days before the action was monopolized by Las Vegas, gambling was as common a part of American life as jazz or Prohibition. Particularly in the South. During the '20s and early '30s there had been instant action in the most upright Southern towns. Before Las Vegas most gamblers were road gamblers, traveling from town to town with the confidence of men who knew there would always be another game a little farther down the line. The times, he remembered, were not so treacherous, so unreliable as now. Gambling was illegal of course; but most southern country towns had their clandestine back rooms, often concealed in the best hotel, in which games of craps and cards were run as regularly and efficiently as the trains that brought the boys to town. Rare dependable wells, they were, in otherwise dry and inauspicious country.

Those had been his dream decades, his fine high-rolling days, when, as a matter of course, he had risen late and read the morning line, practiced his propositions, backed a horse or bought a car, killing time till that day's play began. There were few games he would not play; and because he was one of the few really big high rollers, the sort of man who bet twenty thousand on the turn of a card, he was courted constantly by his fellow travelers—by those who hoped to get a piece of his play or, in a moment of folly, to break him altogether. Therefore, long before the action died in whatever town he happened to be in, he had received the news of other games in other places: in Hot Springs the hustlers were anxious to play some pool;

a millionaire in Lubbock had offered a lucrative golfing proposition; a high-stake poker game had started in Tulsa the day before; and, should he have cared to travel north, there were rumors of really serious action in Joplin and St. Jo.

Thus, in the late spring of 1932, Titanic Thompson, as he was known, motored down from Dallas to the boom town of Tyler in East Texas. Titanic had nothing particular in mind—that is, no definite wager had drawn him there—but he had a friend or two in town and Tyler had always been good for ready action. In 1932 Tyler was in the midst of a big oil boom. Between Tyler and the little towns of Longview and Gladewater and Kilgore, the derricks stretched across the open prairies as far as the eye could see. There was a lot of money around—Texas money—and the town had attracted the usual assortment of prospectors, speculators, oilmen, and gamblers. Everyone, it seemed, was rich or just about to be. It was the kind of town Titanic knew well and felt most at home in. Where there was oil there was loose money, and loose money meant action.

In the early part of the century the professional gambler was still a romantic figure—a fallen man, perhaps, and evil, if the melodramas of the period are to be believed. He was a freebooter, a man who took the long chance at a time when the country still believed in dark horses. Titanic Thompson was at the heart of that belief. In 1932 he was forty years old and had achieved a kind of mythical status in his profession. Reverent tales of his gambling prowess are still told along the Vegas Strip. He was a master of the cunning proposition, a crack shot, a scratch golfer, a champion bowler, a good pool player, and an expert at craps and all forms of cards, particularly poker. He had won more than a million dollars in places as far afield as San Francisco, Chicago, and New York. In the early '30s Titanic and Nick the Greek Dandolos were reputed to be the shrewdest gamblers in the country.

In a photograph of Titanic taken about that time, he is standing next to one of his favorite cars—a 1930 Pierce-Arrow. Posed languidly beside a robust girl, a rifle under his arm, he appears insouciant and boyish. They look as though they have just committed a particularly amusing crime. The girl wears a cardigan and long skirt, Titanic wears a double-breasted suit and hat; there is a more than passing resemblance to Bonnie and Clyde.

In the early part of the century the professional gambler was still a romantic figure—a fallen man, perhaps, and evil, if the melodramas of the period are to be believed.

He must have looked much the same when he drove into Tyler in 1932 with his third wife, Yvonne, and her sister Joanne, who would ultimately become his fourth. They put up at the main hotel and Ty went out to scout the action. He did not have far to look. At the local golf course the club professional, Jimmy Haines, wagered Ty that he could not shoot the front nine in fewer than thirty-five strokes. The bet was agreed at $500 and the stakes were held by the young caddy-master. Ty had been playing golf for only ten years. He had become an extraordinary golfer, though he liked to belittle the fact, claiming it was an impertinent rumor put about by his enemies. That afternoon in Tyler, he shot the front nine in thirty-four.

Ty had driven down to Tyler in a Lincoln Continental. It was a new car, and, as was his custom, he had fitted it with a special horn, a kind of early burglar alarm. Ty favored such precautions. That evening, while he was sitting in his hotel room with his wife and her sister, the alarm suddenly sounded. Pulling back the curtain, Ty peered out the window, but it was dusk and difficult to see. Only that afternoon he had heard rumors that out-of-state hijackers had come to town. Someone in a car had tried to hijack him two days before but had driven away when he pulled out his gun. Ty was an expert shot with both pistol and rifle and had killed five men in his time. Looking out the hotel window, he shrugged. He was used to these little interruptions. Ty carried a .45, the butt taped with adhesive to ensure a firmer grip. He had always favored a big gun. "Shoot a man with a .32," he said, "and he might get up and shoot back." Ty did not believe in second chances.

That evening, therefore, when he heard the alarm he picked up his .45 and slid it inside his belt. He checked with his wife to see if she had touched the gun. He did not want any accidents. He was wearing wide flannel golf trousers; slipping on a sports jacket to cover the gun, he went outside to investigate.

Ty walked cautiously down the path to his car. There was no one about. Except for the horn it was quiet and everything seemed in order. But as he approached the car a man jumped out from behind a tree to his left. Despite the semidarkness Ty could see that he wore a mask pulled down over his face. The man brandished a gun and shouted, "Throw up your hands, mister, or I'll shoot you down!" Ty did not hesitate. Dropping swiftly to his knee and pulling the .45 from his belt, he shot the man an inch or two above the heart. At twenty feet he was an easy target. As a boy Ty had hit washers thrown in the air at twenty feet. The masked man was thrown back against the tree. Taking no chances, Ty shot him again through the mouth. The figure crumpled to the ground. Ty walked slowly up to him and kicked away his gun. Shouting to his wife to telephone the police, he knelt down over the fallen man. He was still alive. His face twitched behind the mask. "Help me up. Help me up, Mr. Thompson," the man mumbled, "I think you've killed me." The voice was familiar and Ty pulled off the mask. In the darkness the face was very white. The jaw was slack and pulsed with broken teeth and blood. Ty recognized the young caddy-master who had held the stakes that afternoon. "Boy, I hope you'll be able to tell the police this was your idea," said Ty. The boy nodded. When the police arrived, he mumbled that he had tried to rob the older man. He was taken away. That night, in the hospital, he died.

"I was surprised he lived as long as he did," said Ty. "I really felt bad about that kid. If I'd've known it was a young boy like that I'd've given him the money. I hated to shoot a kid, but how could I know who it was with that mask on? Could've been anybody. It was just one of those things, I guess."

Next day it was agreed that he had shot the boy in self-defense. Nonetheless a young police lieutenant suggested that Ty might be happier in another town—in Hot Springs, perhaps, or Oklahoma City, in any town that was not in Texas. The young lieutenant looked smug. Ty smiled and said nothing. He had seen that look before. By nightfall he had disappeared.

* * * * *

To the end of his life Titanic remained a backwoods Southern boy. Even in what he liked to regard as his sophisticated days, when he favored yellow polo coats and drove nickel-plated limousines, he seemed somehow out of context, inconvenienced, like a farm boy made to slick his hair and wear his Sunday suit. Fashion was not Titanic's métier. Gambling had taken him off the farm and into some of the country's largest cities, but he rarely dallied in them. He disliked cities; he thought them stiff, uncomfortable, and cold. He preferred the slow country towns of the South—towns such as Grapevine, Texas; Lafayette, Louisiana; Marked Tree, Arkansas; or Monett, Missouri, where he was born in the winter of 1892.

"Every little town had a poker game or two," he recalled. "It was illegal, of course, a $20 fine if you was caught, but once you got to a town you always checked at the pool hall and chances were the game was being held in the backroom or down the street at the hotel." Before Ty turned nineteen he had picked up a sound if eccentric education.

"It used to be that people would bet anything on anything," he said. "They bet pitching half-dollars to the crack or put a dime down and pitched to that. They bet on pool and poker and dice and pitchin' horseshoes and on card games most people never heard of. It used to be that people really loved to bet. And so did I."

Thus, in one or another of those Southern towns, Ty learned to shoot craps, how to place the six and the ace in the middle, false shake them, and roll them straight out so that he could not crap. He learned the odds on every proposition—the true odds on how many coins will come up heads or tails should you throw a handful into the air at once, how many throws of the dice it takes to obtain a specific number, the odds on securing a pair in a five-card hand, on drawing the highest spade, or the price on getting aces back-to-back. He learned how to scuffle, how to cheat and to connive; learned all the card cons—playing to the light, how to mark cards or use spotted edges to change the suit, the art of signals, the use of pig-joints or thumpers, dealing seconds, cold-decking—anything that gave him "the advantage going in." He practiced such dodges by the hour. "I learned to beat people at their own game," he said. "And if I couldn't beat 'em, I'd find someone who could." He beat the checkers champion of Missouri, for example, by installing a better player in a peek hole in the ceiling, who signaled the correct moves to Ty through the use of the thumper wired to Ty's leg. And, should emergencies arise, he always carried a gun, which he kept on the floor next to his chair when playing.

"I learned to play any game you could name for any amount of money you could count. And I never made bets on even chances." To that end, he began carrying his own horseshoes, bowling ball, pool cue, throwing rock (made to order—beveled on top, flat on the bottom), his own rifle and pistol. "No sense takin' a chance on somebody else's," he said. "Might be rigged. I learned to do things pretty good or else I didn't do 'em. I aimed to do everything a little better'n the other fellow. And those were the things I bet on that's all." At eighteen, his apprenticeship was over. By the time he was twenty-five he had acquired a large bankroll—and a reputation.

In the period between 1912 and the end of the First World War, Ty became famous in the netherworld of gamblers and confidence men for the success of his improbable propositions. Not that he sought notoriety in any way, since it was "hard to get somebody to take your proposition," he said, "if they knew your reputation." But by changing the common hustle into a pure and elegantly constructed con, Ty earned an envious respect among his fellow gamblers. Tales of his feats were recounted so often they acquired the legitimacy of legend.

During the 1920s in New York, Damon Runyon, who had met Ty on many occasions, must have heard those tales in one or another of their fanciful forms, since he based one of his most famous characters on him—Sky Masterson, the gambler in "The Idyll of Miss Sarah Brown." "Of all the high players this country ever sees," wrote Runyon, "there is no doubt that the guy they call The Sky is the highest. He will bet all he has, and nobody can bet more than this. The Sky is a great hand for propositions, such as are always coming up among citizens who follow games of chance for a living. And no one ever sees The Sky when he does not have some proposition of his own."

A proposition, it should be explained, is a neat and often preposterous ploy to lure the innocent into parting with their cash. Thus the example given Sky Masterson by his father, prior to leaving home, that he should not bet a man who offers to make the jack of spades jump from behind a brand-new deck of cards and squirt cider in his ear. Does the jack of spades have hydraulic talents or not? Therein lies the wager. In "Sarah Brown," Runyon related several of Ty's cannier propositions. The reality, however, had a seductive and more complicated charm.

A proposition, it should be explained, is a neat and often preposterous ploy to lure the innocent into parting with their cash.

In the summer of 1917, for example, Ty was sitting on the porch of the Arlington hotel in Hot Springs, Arkansas, eating a bag of Danish walnuts. He still had that fresh, uplifted look that often passes for innocence. A local merchant walked onto the porch, said hello, and the two men fell into conversation. Ty continued to eat the walnuts, occasionally offering the merchant one. The merchant seemed to like the walnuts, since he asked for another and referred in passing to their light, piquant qualities. Ty offered him the bag and then, almost absentmindedly, he said, "I'll tell you what. I've got an interesting proposition for you, since I know how much you like them. What odds will you give that I can't throw one of those Danish walnuts over that hotel cross the street?"

The merchant smiled, looking across the street at the hotel. It was five stories high. "Ty," he said, "you're some thrower, I know that, but not even Ty Cobb could throw a nut over that hotel. Not on a good day with the wind behind him."

"Maybe not," said Ty, "but I'm willin' to bet I can. Shucks, I'm willin' to bet a hundred dollars if you could see your way to givin' me odds of, uh, say, three-to-one."

"One of *these* walnuts, Ty?" said the merchant, pointing to the bag.

"Yep. You can pick any walnut in this here bag." Ty cracked another, eating it noisily.

The merchant agreed to the odds and selected a walnut from the bottom of the bag. Balancing the walnut in the palm of his hand, Ty stepped off the porch and into the street. Cocking his arm and throwing effortlessly, he lofted the walnut over the hotel. He turned round and grinned. The merchant scratched his head, began to remonstrate, then reluctantly reached for his wallet. And he never discovered, as many others were not to do, that Ty had palmed the walnut for one of his own special nuts, which he carried with him everywhere—a Danish walnut filled with lead.

Another of Ty's propositions, which Runyon reworked in "Sarah Brown," occurred in Toledo, Ohio, in a club owned by Johnny "Get Rich Quick" Ryan. The club was in an old building in the center of the city. To reach the men's room, one descended a broken flight of stairs and crossed a darkened storeroom. One night, returning from the men's room to the poker game, Ty nearly stepped on a large rat scuttling between the packing cases and he instinctively knocked one of the heavy cases over, pinning the creature to the floor. Assuring himself the rat was secure, Ty hurried upstairs to the card room.

A few minutes later, in the middle of a hand, Ty turned to the player at his left, a mobster from Cicero, and said, "Say, why are there so many rats in this place? There are so many rats runnin' loose in that room down there, a man could shoot one of 'em between the eyes inside a minute."

The mobster continued to look at his hand. "I saw 'em, mister," he said. "But get this. It'd take a sharpshooter to hit a rat in a cage. To hit a runnin' rat in the eyes in the dark, guy'd need a machine gun at least."

"Hell," said Ty, "I used to pop rats when I was a kid. Ain't nothin' in that."

The mobster looked up at Ty. He took the cigar from his mouth. Turning, he looked around the table. "Boys," he said, "got a kid here thinks he's Buffalo Bill. Kid, I'll lay you five hundred says there's more to it than you think."

"You got five hundred," said Ty. He put down his cards and picked up his gun from the floor. "But I want odds. This ain't no ordinary proposition."

"I'll give you two-to-one. Can't give a great rat killer like you more'n that."

The game stopped and Ty covered an additional $500 in side bets. Checking his gun, he walked to the door.

"Hey, kid, wait a minute," said the mobster. "Don't get cute with me. That rat better be warm. I ain't bettin' money on a rat you knocked off day 'fore yesterday. And I'm timin' you. You got sixty seconds, kid."

Down in the storeroom the rat was still struggling to get out from under the packing case. Ty shot it in the head, upended the case, took the rodent by the tail, walked back upstairs, and dropped it on the poker table. The mobsters, Ty recalled, treated him with a certain reverence thereafter.

Another of Ty's stratagems occurred in Joplin before the war. Ty had become friendly with two gamblers called Hickory and Beanie. They were local boys, and when they were not gambling they took Ty around Joplin or to their fishing camp outside of town. Driving into town one day, Ty noticed some workmen putting up a signpost which said JOPLIN—20 MILES. That night he returned to the site, dug up the signpost, and planted it five miles nearer to Joplin, checking carefully on the way home that it was exactly fifteen miles to the city limits.

Next day, as the three men were driving back from the fishing camp, they passed the sign and Ty suggested they stop so that he could take a leak. Before getting back into the car he seemed to notice the sign for the first time and shook his head. "Hey, look at that sign," he said. "Those boys just don't know what they're talkin' about. That there sign is an outright lie. Couldn't be more than fifteen miles to Joplin from here."

"Oh, there're pretty careful about that sort of thing," said Beanie. "Check it real good. You better believe it."

"It ain't right, Beanie," said Ty. "I'd bet on it."

"How much?" said Hickory, nudging Beanie.

"Why, hell, I'd bet a hundred. That sign just couldn't be right. Only took me twenty minutes into Joplin from about here yesterday. I remember that. I'd bet a hundred it's no more'n fifteen miles from here to Joplin."

"Well, I'll bet you five hundred it's at least sixteen," said Hickory.

"And I'll take five hundred on that too," said Beanie.

"Well, okay, boys," said Ty, "but I'm tellin' you. That sign is wrong."

The three men drove back to town and, of course, it was exactly fifteen miles. "Christ," said Beanie. "I'm gonna raise hell with the road department. They don't have no right foolin' the public that way."

* * * * *

"Some folks," Ty recalled, "thought I bet too fast. They'd take me on because they reckoned I was bettin' without stoppin' to think. But I can't help thinkin' fast. These fellows who stroke their chins and say, 'Now, what was that proposition again?' are marks for me. I figured so far ahead of 'em that their money was gone before they knew they'd been bettin'.

"In poker," he said, "money is power. And I always made sure I had it. I not only played my own hand, I played everybody else's. I watched every card, every draw, every bet, every expression. I don't trust on luck. I am bettin' all around the table, on every card drawn by every player. I often have more on side bets than I have in the pot. I have to think fast and figure my percentages. I can't relax for a second. I treat everything like playin' roulette. And the only way to win at roulette is to own the wheel. I tell you, gambling is hard work."

"I can't relax for a second. I treat everything like playin' roulette. And the only way to win at roulette is to own the wheel. I tell you, gambling is hard work."

In San Francisco, Ty learned a new game—golf. He had just turned twenty-nine. Golf was to become his best game and his favorite, when he learned there were more ways to bet on golf than on cards or craps. It came naturally to him. The first time he ever hit a ball, he remembered, he drove it nearly three hundred yards. When the nightly poker sessions at the Kingston Club ended, Ty spent his mornings on a local course practicing golf. He told no one; he always practiced behind the bushes on the back nine, taking care to keep out of the sun. Since driving came easily to him, he concentrated on chipping and putting. In a matter of weeks he found he could almost always hole in two strokes and never in more than three from distances up to 150 yards. "It was the easiest thing you ever saw," he said. "I played golf almost as well as I breathed." However, he never actually played a round.

One of those who came to watch the late-night poker games at the Kingston Club was a local golf professional called Buddy Brent. One night he and Ty fell into conversation, and Ty, who liked to brag that he would bet on anything, told Brent that he could probably beat him at golf. "I hear golf is a child's game," said Ty, "pick it up in a morning." Brent knew that Ty had never played the game but condescended to compete with him for $10 a hole.

The following day Brent beat Ty on every hole and collected $90 for the nine-hole wager. Driving back into San Francisco, Ty sulked. He complained that nothing had gone right for him, that his luck had been atrocious, that his clubs were borrowed, that his back ached from all-night poker games, and that had he been fit he would have given a better account of himself. Brent smiled and sympathized; he could see, he said, that Ty was a natural golfer, that all he required was a little practice, but for the moment he should concentrate on playing poker. He said that Ty was a terrific poker player.

That night at the Kingston Club a few of the poker players, having heard the story, heckled Ty unmercifully. Ty glowered, insisting Brent had merely been lucky. Later that evening, when Brent dropped by the club, Ty challenged him to a match the next day; he would play, he said, for $1,000 a hole, but he had to have three shots a hole. Everyone laughed. The incredulous Brent agreed to the wager but would only concede one shot a hole. Ty insisted the cash be put up front. As always happened, a group of enthusiastic gamblers wanted as much side action as possible, and when the betting was concluded nearly $60,000 lay on the table. Ty covered the bets and went back to playing poker.

The next morning a little crowd of joyful gamblers gathered around the first tee. When Ty arrived, there was much sympathetic applause. Ty, driving first, hit his ball about 275 yards down the middle of the fairway. Brent blanched. The gamblers looked uneasily at one another. Ty never remembered what he shot that day, only that it was a stroke or two better than Brent. He won $56,000. "I never, ever shot more than a stroke or two bet-

The most fantastic thing about Titanic was his hands. He had the hands of an artist, which is as good a word to describe Ty as you can find. He could do almost anything with his hands, everything except play pool.

Minnesota Fats

ter'n the opposition," he said. "If a man shoots eighty-nine, I shoot eighty-eight. If a man shoots sixty-eight, I shoot sixty-seven. I never liked to add insult to injury."

It is inaccurate, of course, to give the impression that hustlers, even the best of them, never lose a bet. Ty himself lost dozens of wagers, but like most gamblers became wonderfully absent-minded when one referred to them. One bet, however, which rankled him for years was made in San Francisco in 1922. He was playing golf with Nick the Greek, and coming down to the last hole he had beaten him for $20,000. On the last green Nick was lying some twenty feet from the hole. Ty offered to bet him double-or-nothing on the $20,000 if he could sink the putt and Nick agreed. "It was four-to-one Nick couldn't make that putt," Ty recalled. "Hell, it was two-to-one against *me* making it and I was a great putter. Nick had five hundred grand in his pocket that day and I could have got it all if he'd missed. But the son of a bitch put it in."

* * * * *

In 1930 Ty was still only thirty-seven years old and had more than a few propositions left to perform. The Depression years were to coincide with some of his most extravagant hustles and the period of his greatest fame.

During the '30s Ty defeated the world champion horseshoe thrower by luring him into what he assumed was a regulation-length court, not knowing that Ty had extended it by a foot. The champion could not understand why his throws kept falling short. Ty beat Nick the Greek in a shooting contest—the bet being that Ty could not hit a stationary silver dollar eight out of ten times at ten feet. Nick, of course, did not know that Ty could hit a dime ten out of ten times at greater distances. Ty beat countless innocents at countless propositions. But through the '30s his favorite hustling game was golf.

Ty spent thirty years barely breaking one hundred in public, and he always ignored the official handicaps. Johnny Moss remembered seeing him take a thousand dollars from Byron Nelson over nine holes by shooting a twenty-nine. Ty often played with the young Ben Hogan. "I had to teach the kid how to play," said Ty. "We played a lot together and I took him to Shreveport to play some matches." In a Fort Worth newspaper, Lee Trevino acknowledged his debt to Ty's teaching skills.

In the '30s there was little point in turning professional, as there was no money in the game. And hustling, of course, was forbidden. In those days Ty contrived dozens of ingenious hustles. He would bet standers-by that a man in a wheelchair could beat them—previously having trained the man to play brilliantly from the chair. He challenged a Texas pro, who demanded a handicap. "All right," said Ty, "I'll let you hit three drives off each tee and you can play the best drive. Is that enough of a handicap?" The pro assented, for stakes of $1,000 a hole. Playing the best of three drives, the pro won the first seven holes, but on the eighth tee, he sliced all three drives into the rough; on the ninth, obviously fatigued, he missed one ball altogether. Ty swept the last eleven holes and won $4,000. "Course, he was tired," said Ty. "Hit three drives a hole and on a tough course you'll be lucky to break a hundred."

On another occasion, in the dead of winter, he was bragging in the clubhouse about how far he could drive the ball. The other golfers became exasperated. "On some days I'm so good," said Ty, "that I can drive a ball four hundred yards." Anxious to teach the braggart a lesson, one of the golfers took the bet. Selecting a tee on the downward side of a hill overlooking a lake, which given the season was frozen, Ty drove his ball. It was still rolling as he pocketed his winnings.

But Ty's most devious hustle, which he employed again and again throughout his career, first occurred in the little town of Ruidoso, New Mexico. Ty had arranged a match with the town millionaire. The millionaire, who believed himself to be the best golfer in the state, was left-handed and liked to gamble high. After protracted negotiations, Ty agreed to give him three strokes a side for a $25,000 wager. A little crowd of enthusiasts, including Johnny Moss, followed them around the course.

"Ty," Moss remembered, "always cut these things pretty close, but he hadn't meant to cut it as fine as this." Approaching the eighteenth green, the two men were even. The millionaire two-putted; but he was not particularly worried since Ty had hit a poor iron shot to the far side of the green, leaving himself a difficult, downhill twenty-foot putt to win the match. Ty lined it up carefully, stroked the ball, and it curved round the downward slope of the green and dropped into the hole. Ty looked up, his face expressionless. The millionaire was livid.

Ty looked blankly at the man. "You're lucky to have lost by one shot," he said. "I shoulda beat you by three or four. You're the worst golfer I've ever seen in my life. I know children that can beat you. Why, you're so bad I could beat your ass with your own clubs, those left-handed doodads you carry around with you. I could beat you using them."

The millionaire suddenly looked calm. "For double-or-nothing?" he said.

"Sure," said Ty, "double-or-nothing." He turned away.

"Okay, you're on," said the millionaire.

Ty looked surprised. He shrugged his shoulders. "A bet's a bet," he said.

The millionaire laughed. They walked to the first tee. Three hours later, Ty had beaten him by four strokes. He pocketed the millionaire's check and walked back to the clubhouse. The millionaire was in anguish. "I don't understand it," he mumbled, "I just don't understand it."

"You would, sir," said one of the attendant caddies, "if you knew Titanic was a natural-born left-hander."

* * * * *

In 1938 Ty turned up in Evansville, Indiana, where his old friend Hubert Cokes had settled. Outside of town the oil boom had just erupted, and word was out that the boys were playing higher in Evansville than anywhere else in the country. Ty remained there during the early war years, living with Joanne, his fourth wife.

"He didn't have a whole lot of cash when he first came," Coke remembered. "He put up at the McCurdy Hotel. There were more oil wells drilled in the lobby of the McCurdy Hotel than in the oilfields outside of town. I remember once, after Ty came, I heard about a big card game down in Charlotte and I staked Ty $2,500 and told him to go down and check the game out. And if there was no action to come back and tell me. The money was also supposed to cover his expenses. Ty came back after about a week and gave me $1,000. I said to him, 'Christ, Ty, what did you spend the money on? I could've taken three girls and spent a week at the Waldorf-Astoria and not spent that much.' Little did I know, that's just what he'd done. He was the limit, Ty. It wouldn't make no difference if Ty was married to the Queen of England, he'd still have two or three tramps around.

"Ty said there hadn't been no action, so the next week I send him down again. He comes back and says he won about fifty thousand. I ask him how much he thinks he owes me and he says about twenty grand. Well, I then sent one of my boys down to Charlotte to check out that game, run by a fellow called Slim. He hangs around down there and finds out they won ninety thousand and are owed twenty-six thousand more. When it came to cuttin' up money Ty always took care of Ty. He was staying at the McCurdy Hotel and that night I went up to his room. He was in bed and I stormed into his room and said, 'Ty, do you have a pistol? Because if you don't, I have two and you can use one of mine.' He said, all nice and meek, 'Hubert, would you kill your best friend while he's lyin' asleep in his bed?' He was always wily, Ty, but I confronted him and he finally paid me my money."

Ty spent much of his time in Evansville buying and selling oil leases, trading and promoting. "I made $740,000 out of oil wells on five acres out in Salem," he said. But he still found time to gamble at cards and at pool. Minnesota Fats was in Evansville at the time, and he and Ty and Hubert played a lot of cards. "Fats was only good at knock rummy," said Ty. "He was a terrible clabbiasch player. He'd play clabb, win two games, and quit."

The Fat Man, however, did beat Ty at pool. "He killed me at pool," Ty remembered. "At Adolf's Bowling Alley and Pool Hall. I'd been pitchin' to the crack of $50 a throw the night before the match and my arm just went dead when I came to play, but I didn't know it till too late. He beat me outta thirty thousand before I knew what was wrong. But, of course, the Fat Man says it was seventy-five thousand and claims he was playin' one-handed. That Fat Man. He was always windy."

In his autobiography the Fat Man describes one of Ty's favorite cons. "Ty was driving in from the oilfields outside of Evansville when he sees this farmer hauling a whole truckload of watermelons to market. So Ty stops the farmer and right away he buys the whole batch of watermelons for a very inflated sum. Then he pays the farmer to count each watermelon and pays him another tremendous price to drive past the old McCurdy Hotel in downtown Evansville at an appointed hour. "Now Ty hustles to the McCurdy, and all the high rollers are standing in the lobby and out on the sidewalk in front, and after a while here comes the farmer driving out First Street with the load of watermelons. So Ty gets the show on the road by allowing he will wager any amount that he can estimate exactly how many watermelons the farmer has on the truck. It looked like such a Hungarian lock that the high rollers all got down real heavy, and when they stopped the farmer to inquire about his inventory, Titanic just happened to have hit the precise number. He won a fabulous bundle on the watermelon con, but I obligingly relieved him of most of it on pool."

Toward the end of the war Ty moved to Virginia, where, again according to Fats, he was one of the leading luminaries around Norfolk in the middle '40s. "He had hit the gold roll in oil out around southern Indiana, and when he came to Norfolk, he moved in like a real sultan. He was on a brand-new wife, a gorgeous doll named Maxine. But he also brought along Maxine's sisters, Betty and Bonnie, who were even more fabulous-looking than Maxine.

"When Ty first came to Norfolk he couldn't find suitable housing for his ladies, so he moved out to Virginia Beach and took over one of those mansions the generals build right out on the oceanfront. It was a fabulous joint and Ty entertained the way Perle Mesta wished she could. All the high rollers would call a recess on the weekends and drive to Virginia Beach just to be on hand for Ty's soirees.

"Even though Ty was already in his fifties, he never looked a day over twenty-five, and when he entertained he loved to have young people around him, especially young tomatoes. He had a real tall, trim build and a full head of brown hair and dark, deep-set eyes that were always dancing.

"But the most fantastic thing about Titanic was his hands. He had the hands of an artist, which is as good a word to describe Ty as you can find. He could do almost anything with his hands, everything except play pool. . . . He could do all sorts of amazing card tricks and sleight-of-hand gimmicks on account of his fingers were long and agile. Just watching him perform was fascinating. The way he moved his eyes and his fingers at one and the same time was liable to hypnotize you on the spot. He was a regular Houdini."

And like Houdini, Ty seemed locked in a box from which, for once, he could not escape. His postwar activities became secretive and more and more obscure. Sometime in 1946 or 1947 he left Norfolk for Tucson, Arizona, where he remained until 1955. He seems not to have gambled a great deal. His only public activities were winning three consecutive Arizona State trapshooting contests and a party he gave in early 1954.

The party was held in his large home on the outskirts of Tucson. That night Ty may or may not have noticed a teenage girl roaming drunkenly from room to room. If so, he thought nothing of it. He had many other guests to attend to; he was good at giving parties. The next day Ty was arrested by the local constabulary. The girl claimed that she had been assaulted by one of Titanic's guest. Ty was charged with contributing to the delinquency of a minor. In efforts to circumvent any possible sentence, Ty contributed $35,000 to various police charities, but during the trial, when his background was recounted to the suburban jury, he was pronounced guilty and sentenced to two years in the state penitentiary at Florence. Eight months later he was paroled. He was sixty-two years old.

Ty drifted around the Southwest—from Arizona to California and New Mexico—and thence to smaller and smaller towns in Texas—Dallas, San Antonio, Corpus Christi, Colleyville, and finally to Hurst, an obscure suburb midway between Dallas and Fort Worth. For nearly twenty years there was only silence. In the summer of 1972, when I set out to find Titanic, I was told by an elderly gambler in Las Vegas, a man who concerned himself with such things: "Him? Old Ty? Why, hell, son, Ty's dead. Ain't no tellin' how long he's been gone. A long time. Years and years."

* * * * *

The little town of Hurst, divided by the main Dallas–Fort Worth highway, has all the stiff and stilted charm of a suburban shopping center. One of those instant modern towns, it might have been built yesterday and could well be gone tomorrow. It contains the usual array of supermarkets and gas stations, bars and bowling alleys, parking lots and five- and ten-cent stores. Out beyond the drab main plazas are the curled rows of suburban dwellings, as neat and normalized as soldiers on parade. It was to this remote and inconspicuous place that Titanic Thompson had come to die.

Ty had come to Hurst the year before from another suburb twenty miles away. Here he lived in a rented house with his sixth wife, Jeanette, their thirteen-year-old son, and his in-laws. He did not foresee further moves. Hurst was as good a place as any to while away what little time remained.

In the kitchen at the rear of the house, Titanic sat at the breakfast table playing blackjack with his son. He wore pajamas and a robe. His white hair fell in disarray about his head; it had not been cut for months, apparently, and lay thick at the back of his neck. He was unshaven. He was tall, though bent, and hard of hearing. He was plagued with arthritis in his left hand. His new set of teeth did not quite fit, causing crankiness and complaint. His eyes were dulled with resignation. He looked like a patient in a nursing home waiting for visitors who would never come. He would soon be eighty.

Ty rarely left the house anymore. He missed the action, but was not prepared to make the journey. Until the year before he played golf every day, pitching and putting on the local course, but arthritis had intervened. Jeanette tried to take him to the bowling alley each afternoon when she came home from work. Occasionally, when the weather was good, he pitched horseshoes in the backyard. He led an uneventful life. He had arrived, as Casanova said, at that age which chance despises. His wife went out to work, the little house was rented, the car was on the never-never. He had no possessions, no bank account, no insurance, none of the humdrum securities. All he had ever owned was his bankroll and now, old and out of favor, even that had gone. The game was over and only now and then did Ty pretend that he would play again.

During the long afternoons, waiting apprehensively for Jeanette to return, Ty talked of his life and showed me tricks and propositions. "One proposition's as good as another," he said in his clipped Southern monotone. "Depends on your advantage. I'd just as soon deal blackjack as play it." Ty always talked as though talent were an ability to get away with things. He showed me endless coin and match conundrums, betting small sums that I could not unravel them. And it was not the money (which I invariably lost) that excited him. It was the slow flush of amazement, the startled cry of comprehension, that brought a light to those sad eyes. Once cash had been enough; he now required applause.

Ty talked eventually of promises of money, of fame, of films of his life story. He had been, he said, the most colorful gambler of his time. He could do more things than any man he had known. Nick the Greek? Hah! Could only play cards and shoot craps. Nothin'. "The smartest gambler I ever knew was old Hubert Cokes. The best cheater and conniver was Bill Douglas till he was shot down in a poker game in Memphis two year ago. And Little Man from Alabama was the highest gambler I ever saw. Real high. Would bet everything on anything, that Little Man. But I could outsmart, outcheat, outconnive, and roll higher than 'em all in my day. And that's no lie."

He clicked his teeth. Looking out into the backyard, he fell silent, conjuring up the old high-rolling days again. Gambling was all he had ever known; it had been everything. Because he did not read, because he had not taken part in any of the events of his time—elections, wars, depressions—he seemed curiously remote, not merely outdated, but outcast, detached from life. He had spent a lifetime casting lots in back rooms, and the world, for what it was worth, had passed him by.

"My teeth. They still don't set right," he said to no one in particular. Jeanette said she would take him to the dentist after work the next day. He seemed not to hear, that odd vacant look coming into his eyes again. Standing up from the table and drawing his robe around him, he shuffled out of the room to bed.

The next day Titanic came into the kitchen just before noon. He had tried to shave the stubble from his face but most of it remained. He wore his best trousers, a plaid shirt, and a baggy jacket. He looked frail and vulnerable. Putting a little water in his hand from the kitchen tap, he smoothed down his rumpled hair. He took me into the backyard, betting he could ring seven out of ten horseshoes. His son's bicycle lay across the pitch. I moved it. Picking up the rusted horseshoes, he pitched them easily, but without enthusiasm. Only two of them curled round the stake. He could not seem to get his eye in, he said. It began to rain. We went inside.

In the kitchen Ty said that he would wager anything he could hit a target eight out of ten times with his .45. At twenty feet. With either hand. "I'll get my gun," he said. He shuffled from the room. Almost immediately he returned. "Can't find my gun," he said, scratching his head. "They're always movin' my things around." Just out of his sight in the next room, Jeanette's mother, the gun in her hand, shook her head at me and put a finger to her lips. Titanic sat down on the worn sofa and ground his teeth.

Outside the rain continued to fall, a thin enveloping rain, wrapping itself round the trees in the backyard, the bicycle, the rusty horseshoes, wrapping itself round the house like a winding sheet. A little later when Jeannette came home, she straightened Ty's collar and reminded him to bring his glasses. Looking into the distance, Ty ground his teeth. He placed a cheap fedora on his head. Taking his hand, Jeanette led him out of the house to the waiting car.

Thompson died at the age of eighty-one shortly after Bradshaw spent time with him. For Bradshaw, none of the old-timers matched the overall brilliance of Titanic Thompson.

Next:
On the road

Have Pen, Will Travel

Previous:
Contact Sheet.
Photograph by
Gene Moore

Haiti's Gingerbread Palace

Queen, March 1971

Staying at the Oloffson is like visiting the country home of rich relatives who have come down in the world. There is an air of ease and indulgence, the sort of place which grants full pardons and one wanders into dinner without shoes.

The summer sun rises early over Port-au-Prince. Then, from the main balcony of the Grand Hotel Oloffson—halfway up the mountain in the suburb of Petión-Ville—one looks down across the town to the harbor and watches the fishing boats trailing out to sea. In the very early morning, it is already hot and the waiters, ties askew, pad glumly along the balcony setting up the breakfast tables. By 7:30 the corner table overlooking the pool is usually filled with the Oloffson's permanent guests—two or three youngish men attached to various missions at the American embassy and a former mayor of Port-au-Prince, newly returned to politics as a country "MP." He scans the pages of the *Nouvelle Monde* to see whether his articles, usually pointedly anti-American, have been given the prominence he feels they deserve. The former mayor may read aloud from the current invective and the Americans may chuckle over their pawpaw and scrambled eggs. They are indulgent with one another, like old enemies. One of the Americans has lived at the Oloffson for eighteen months, the former mayor for many years. Men of the world, presumably, they converse with the guarded affability of diplomats who have participated at peace talks too long. There is no one else; it is much too early for any tourists who sleep, perchance, above. But the Oloffson, strictly speaking, is not a tourist hotel, and the men breakfasting below are unaccustomed to the clack of Instamatics or the loud acknowledgment of local color.

About eight o'clock, Al Seitz, the Oloffson's proprietor, pushes through the saloon doors of the kitchen and ambles down the balcony, nodding solemnly to attendant waiters. A large, somewhat burly gentleman of middle years, he is, by 8:00 A.M., well into his first cigar. He will pass the table and smile at the diplomats without removing the cigar from his mouth. He has so fashioned his smile that if he wishes to convey a friendly acknowledgment, while keeping himself aloof, he smiles with his eyes, the pupils actually jumping within their spheres, while his mouth remains uncommitted and dégagé. So he smiles with his eyes and passes into his office at the rear of the balcony.

The diplomats leave for work, the waiters clear up and reset, bill collectors begin to arrive, one of the local primitive painters arranges his salable canvases along the front steps, and by 8:15, the first tourist—a nurse from California who hadn't intended to stop in Haiti at all, but for mechanical reasons, forcibly deplaned in Port-au-Prince, arrives in time for breakfast. The regular morning flights from New York, San Juan, and Santo Domingo will touch down later that morning, depositing a few local Syrian businessmen, a journalist, a member of the Haitian Tourist Board, and a handful of tourists, only one of whom will direct herself toward the Grand Hotel Oloffson.

The Oloffson does not fit neatly into any architectural style; rather it seems the product of some eccentric artisan, permitted on this one occasion to gratify any or all of his most baroque caprices. Built in a manner known as "gingerbread," the Oloffson seems more perfectly suited to Hansel and Gretel than it does to the mid-twentieth-century tourist. Within this huge green-and-white construction—complete with towers and balconies, with scrolls, cupolas, dados, and assorted festoonery—there lurks, one suspects, mad, though affable, artistes reciting high-pitched poetry, or wizened, long-gowned women, slowly rocking, their vacant eyes upon the heavens. One senses the blur of pale faces pressed against dusty panes. One either is drawn in or turns away as from an asylum or a sanatorium. Seen from

"The Oloffson has always been like that, offbeat and slightly bizarre. It is not a halfway house, a place to stop along the way, but an end in itself, a destination."

the road through long-leaved palm trees and casuarinas, sweeping upward like gigantic horsetails, the effect is sad and shining and showy and unsubstantial, the corpse of some half-forgotten extravagance. And yet, the hotel is as thick and familiar as a child's toy, made out of fret and filigree. In Haiti it is known as the "gingerbread palace."

And thinking this was the oddest "palace" she had ever seen, the little white-haired lady hesitantly climbed the stairs of the Grand Hotel Oloffson. This was her first trip to Haiti, which a travel agent (one she had never used before and whom, by the look of this hotel, she would never use again) had recommended, and she moved down the balcony with obvious alarm. From behind his desk, Al Seitz, not altogether unamused, watched the lady approach. He waited. The white-haired lady spoke—almost blurted—first:

"I dunno, I have a reservation, but I dunno," she said anxiously. She looked nervously round the balcony. "I'm not artistic, y'know. I just dunno."

Al Seitz rose from behind the desk and, putting his arm round her, smiled and guided her back down the balcony. "I understand," he said. "Your first trip to Haiti? I understand. Now, I can recommend a very nice place further up the hill. All the modern conveniences. You'll be much happier there, I know. I'll phone ahead and let 'em know you're coming." Seitz spoke without surprise. He escorted her to the waiting taxi, gave the name of a large modern hotel to the driver, and smiled sympathetically at the lady, now ensconced in the back seat. She didn't say another word and didn't look around as the taxi drove away.

"Y'know," said Seitz, settling himself behind the desk again, "it's a funny thing, but y'know, three, four years ago, we had another guest, a colored lady, who arrived, went up to her room, and a few minutes later came storming down the stairs shouting, 'I have better rooms than this in my home back in Washington.' She went to another hotel too. It was beaut-ee-ful. Really beaut-ee-ful." Seitz chuckled and lit another cigar.

Opposite:
Assorted envelopes from Paul Bowles. Bradshaw befriended Bowles during his Libby Holman research

The Oloffson has always been like that, offbeat and slightly bizarre. It is not a halfway house,

Mr. Jon Bradshaw,
9806 Yoakum Drive,
Beverly Hills,
California 90210,
U. S. A.
(ETATS-UNIS D'AMERIQUE)
par avion
VIA-AEREA
PAR AVION
BY AIR MAIL
ROYAUME DU MAROC
1,00
0,40
0,10
TANGER M'SALLAH
TANGER PRINCIPAL
496
R
Mr. Jon Bradshaw,
9806 Yoakum Drive,
Beverly Hills,
California 90210,
U. S. A.
(ETATS-UNIS D'AMERIQUE.)
PAR AVION
Mr. Jon Bradshaw,
9806 Yoakum Drive,
Beverly Hills,
California 90210,
U. S. A.
(ETATS-UNIS D'AMERIQUE.)
Mr. John Bradshaw,
9806 Yoakum Drive,
Beverly Hills,
California 90210,
U. S. A.
(ETATS-UNIS D'AMERIQUE
0,50
1980
Mr. Jon Bradshaw,
9806 Yoakum Drive,
Beverly Hills,
California 90210,
U. S. A.
(ETATS-UNIS D'AMERIQUE.)

a place to stop along the way, but an end in itself, a destination. And it is inseparable from the character of its owners. Built in the latter part of the nineteenth century as a mansion for President Tirésias Simon Sam, it was taken over as a military hospital when the United States Marines occupied Haiti after President Vilbrun Guillaume Sam was killed in the 1915 revolution. The mansion had twelve large bedrooms and the Marines added a small surgery and a ten-room maternity wing, both of which are now part of the hotel. In 1935 it was bought by a Norwegian sea captain called Oloffson and became Haiti's first hotel.

In 1954 the hotel was bought by a Frenchman, Roger Coster, a voluble ex-photographer who began to refer to it as the "Greenwich Village of the Tropics." Coster set the tone of the Oloffson and it soon became a favorite of actors and writers and journalists and millionaires. Coster fell into the habit of naming the rooms after famous guests, so that the largest room became the "John Gielgud Suite," and when James Jones, the American novelist, was married in the small surgery building, the surgery was promptly renamed the "James Jones Chateau."

Al Seitz, an American, born in New York City, has lived in Haiti since 1949. He spent most of those years overlooking the management of a famous Haitian restaurant called the Pechoir (now closed) and running La Belle Creole, a luxury merchandise shop in downtown Port-au-Prince. During 1958–59, Roger Coster, afflicted with acute longings for Paris, the city of his birth, began to look round for a successor. He took to dropping into Seitz's shop for coffee each morning, mentioning casually the countless advantages of owning a hotel. Coster's visits became a normal part of the day; his descriptions of the hotelier's role became illuminating tales of joy and joie de vivre. For two years, Coster was punctual and persistent.

"To own an hotel wasn't a dream of mine or anything," said Seitz, "it just happened that way. I had only been to the Oloffson two or three times, but one morning in June of 1960 I got into a taxicab with Roger Coster and I never got out. Coster just couldn't unload this old maison, but that morning he brought his books with him and we got into that taxicab and went to the notary public, the lawyers, the bank, and the registry. By noon I was an hotelier and I'm still along for the ride. I didn't know anything about running an hotel. Coster promised to give me three weeks of instruction. Next day he was on the Paris plane with the loot.

"It was difficult at first," said Seitz, lighting a cigar, "but despite the difficulties and local events, the hotel pays its way." Tourism in Haiti was very good until 1963. Before 1950 there were almost no tourists, but it shot up to eighty thousand by 1953. Ten years later the figure suddenly fell to fifteen thousand and matters have not noticeably improved. The Oloffson attracts most of its guests through recommendations of those who have stayed before. During Seitz's tenure four men have returned requesting the rooms in which they were born. Sons of U.S. Marines, they were born in the maternity wing during the American occupation. Less than 10 percent of the Oloffson's business comes from travel agents, and many of those are just as likely to register at a grander hotel the following day. But those who stay remain for a long time. An average stay is about ten days, but the Oloffson has three or four guests every year who will stay for two months at a time. There is a staff of twenty-two, most of whom, including Cesar, the barman, C'est Dieu, a waiter, and Edmund, the headwaiter (and one of seventy-three children), have worked at the Oloffson for fifteen years or more.

"Y'know," Seitz continued, "it's beaut-ee-ful, it really is. Let me tell you about this hotel. We only paint the rooms every ten years. The balcony hasn't been painted in more than twenty. Try it and the guests would revolt. Most hotels, for example, pride themselves on their kitchens. So spic and span. In the Oloffson, the guests are simply told—you can't enter. Though the food's quite good. I don't think there's a bad cook in Haiti. There's no menu, but we try not to be repetitive. No one goes hungry. If they don't like what we serve, we can always rustle up a steak or a chicken. Despite its external appearance, the rooms are comfortable, air-conditioned, et cetera. But it's by no means a hotel. It's a sort of boardinghouse for friends. A shrine, if you like, and it belongs to the people who come. It's a great equalizer. It's so small that the bank president is often thrown together with the bank teller. If they're interesting, they'll talk. If not, not." Above all, the Oloffson is comfortable, even intimate, the sort of hotel Seitz refers to as being of low degree and high presumption. Staying at the Oloffson is like visiting the country home of rich relatives who have come down in the world. There is an air of ease and indulgence, the sort of place which grants full pardons and one wanders into dinner without shoes. "And money isn't the factor here," said Seitz. "One of the Rockefellers stays with me for three months a year. He could go anywhere. It's the atmosphere and the individuality of the guests. That's how I get my kicks—from the people. And the money."

His "kicks" come from such individuals as Mrs. Oscar Hammerstein, Anne Bancroft, the *New Yorker* cartoonist Charles Addams, Irving Stone, Maurice Evans, Henry Tiarks, the lawyer Melvin Belli, and Graham Greene, who based his hotel in *The Comedians* on the Oloffson. Whenever Greene is at the Oloffson he stays in the John Gielgud Suite. Before leaving, he invariably sends Gielgud a note which says: "Last night, I, Graham Greene, slept in your bed."

Seitz's days are much the same. "The old *maison* sort of ticks over by itself. I'm only here to incite polite conversation. It's beaut-ee-ful." At the end of the day, the diplomats return from their embassies, new guests arrive, old guests depart, the rara band, "my string ensemble," squats on the balcony creating orgiastic noises during dinner, and Monsieur Issa, owner of Haiti's finest art gallery, arrives, as he usually does, in the company of two beautiful ladies. When Seitz is on holiday, Issa runs the hotel, and the Oloffson, as a result, is cluttered with primitive paintings. Seitz has run the Oloffson for nine years and has lived in Haiti for twenty. Now at the end of the day he finds his thoughts turning more frequently to America. "I'm tired," he muses, "I'm slightly vexed and recently married. I've been away too long." But it's difficult to imagine the Oloffson without him. His periodic dreams of departure, one suspects, are more of a ruse than a remedy. The deplaned nurse, who had decided to remain another few days after all, came into the bar and asked if any of the paintings were for sale. "Everything's for sale, including the hotel." He smiled with his eyes again, drawing all the while on his cigar.

Seitz never did get around to selling. He married a woman twenty-five years his junior; they had three boys, and ran the hotel together until Seitz died of cancer in 1982 at the age of sixty-four. Celebrities continued to adore the place and rooms were named after many of them, including playwright Harold Pinter and actress Anne Bancroft. Mick Jagger and his then wife Jerry Hall visited as Seitz was dying. Seitz's wife remembers the rock star "climbed into bed with Al and held him in his arms like a child to comfort him. Pretty soon Jerry got in too, and so did I. And we all just lay there to make him feel better."

Blackwell's Island

Rolling Stone, May 27, 1982

"I like to think of Island as a very classy delicatessen. The bigger labels are supermarkets. They'll sell almost anything. And most of them do."

It was twenty miles from the nearest town when the car ran out of gas. Two men stood by the side of the road. A woman was in the bushes taking a pee.

"Brazen," said one of the men.

"Shameless," said the other.

"Get off my back," the woman shouted. "I don't care if anybody finds me. When you gotta pee, you gotta pee." She was a French actress named Nathalie Delon. She had a superb command of American slang, but she spoke English unevenly and with a low French lilt so that it sounded like a siren song.

One of the men was Chris Blackwell. He and Mlle. Delon had been lovers for nearly four years. Tall, with long reddish-blond hair, Blackwell wore sandals, faded jeans, and a Black Uhuru T-shirt, pinned to which was a button that said everything's great. He had the easy air of a man who probably believed it was true.

It is difficult to describe the other man; suffice it to say that his profession was that of traveler and scribe. He didn't know whether the car was actually out of gas or whether it was another of Blackwell's practical jokes.

They were marooned in the desert some eighty miles north of Flagstaff, Arizona. They had just spent two days on the Havasupai Indian Reservation at the bottom of the Grand Canyon. The year before, Blackwell had learned that the Havasupai Indians were passionate about the music of Bob Marley, that they had adopted "Rebel Music" as one of their tribal anthems, and that, because of Marley, they had come to look upon white men as Babylonians and oppressors. Amazed, Blackwell arranged to fly Marley's mother, Cedella Booker; his keyboard man, Tyrone Downie; and a film crew into the Grand Canyon to shoot the beginnings of a documentary on Marley's life.

The night before, as Mrs. Booker, accompanied by Tyrone on piano and guitar, sang her dead son's songs, the large crowd of young braves, many of whom wore Bob Marley T-shirts, roared their approval, occasionally rising to their feet with clenched fists and fierce shouts of "Jah, Jah, Rastafari." Afterward, their favorite film, *The Harder They Come*, was screened. It was all too bizarre, and the two men and one woman helicoptered out the next morning, leaving the film crew behind. In the little town of Grand Canyon, they picked up a car, and now, an hour later, they were out of gas. It would soon be dark.

"I can't think why I agreed to this interview," said Blackwell. "No one knows much about me, you know."

"Your intimates will vouch for that," said the scribe.

"I'm serious. No one's ever heard of me."

"Well, I've always thought of you as a shining example of a rapid rise to obscurity."

"Obscurity? That's what?" asked Mlle. Delon.

"Let's begin at the beginning," said the scribe.

"Well, make it quick," said Blackwell. "I don't have a long attention span."

"Are you going to tell him everything?" asked Mlle. Delon.

"No, I'll tell him the truth, and he'll figure out the appropriate lie."

"I don't understand," she said.

* * * * *

Blackwell was born at home in London on June 22, 1937. His father was Irish—related, though distantly, to the Blackwells of the tinned-goods firm of Crosse & Blackwell. His mother, Blanche Lindo, was of an old Jamaican family—Sephardic Jews who had come from Portugal to Jamaica in 1743 in order to escape the Inquisition. During the late eighteenth century, the Lindos made a fortune in Jamaica trading in rum, sugar, coconuts, and cattle. By the time Blackwell was born, the Lindos were an important family of successful traders, hagglers, and barterers.

At the age of six months, Blackwell was taken to Jamaica, where he would spend the next ten years. He grew up in a spacious house called Terra Nova in an affluent suburb of Kingston. Despite the fact he was living in the tropics, Blackwell spent his childhood in enclosed rooms, suffering from acute bronchial asthma. He had no siblings and no friends, and grew up alone.

From the start, he was a pragmatic boy. His mother remembers reading him the stories of Hans Christian Andersen. One night, when she had finished reading, the five-year-old Blackwell asked if they were true. When told they were fiction, he turned his head to the wall and said that the stories no longer interested him.

There is a poignant photograph of the period. It shows the young Blackwell and his parents' staff on the lawn outside Terra Nova. Blackwell is standing in front, and banked in rows behind him are a butler, chauffeur, and chef, gardeners and grooms and maids and nannies. They look like a football team, and Blackwell, the only white person in the picture, looks like the confident quarterback.

At ten, Blackwell was dispatched to England to a Catholic preparatory school. He had been raised a Catholic and would remain so until his parents divorced in 1949. He was a strange, shy little boy; there was a kind of unspeakable sanity about him. Already, he had developed a keen circumspection in his dealings with the world. He was secretive, *en garde*. He knew something, it seemed, but remained impassive, as though he were concealing three aces in his hand. He was like that at ten, and he would never change.

From prep school, he went to Harrow, one of the more prestigious but backward British public schools. He remained there until 1955, when, at seventeen, he left mysteriously before his final term. He returned to Jamaica, his formal education over.

But what was he to do? And, indeed, why do anything at all? After all, he could afford not to. Nonetheless, he returned to London, where he studied accountancy at the respected firm of Price Waterhouse. But accountancy then, as now, was a monotonous trade, and he soon gave it up. For the next two years, he took up a more romantic form of accountancy—gambling. He learned bridge, poker, and twenty-one. He played the horses at Newbury, Ascot, and Kempton Park. On Monday and Friday nights, he gambled on the greyhounds at Wembley, and on Thursday and Saturday nights, at White City. It was, he now believes, an excellent education; a knowledge of gambling at a tender age gives one a wonderful sense of value for money, imparting essential secrets for one who would one day enter the slippery world of commerce. But commerce had not yet occurred to him.

In 1958 Blackwell again journeyed to Jamaica, convinced he was not cut out to make his way in the world on the capricious proceeds of dogs and horses and cards.

He worked as the aide-de-camp for the governor of Jamaica, Sir Hugh Foot. He sold real estate and hired out motor scooters. He worked as a water-skiing instructor at the Half Moon Hotel in Montego Bay. He worked when he felt like it, and, more often than not, he didn't feel like it.

In 1959 he spent six months in America, hanging out on the New York jazz circuit, where he became friendly with Miles Davis. Jazz became his favorite music. Back in Jamaica, he heard a jazz ensemble at the Half Moon Hotel. The band was led by a blind Bermudan pianist named Lance Haywood, and Blackwell decided to record them and form his own label. Because of the success of Alec Waugh's 1957 novel, *Island in the Sun*, and the subsequent film,

"There are two things you can always count on with Blackwell," said his friend Artie Mogull. "That he'll be late for his own funeral, and that he's so mean, he wouldn't pay five dollars to watch monkeys fuck."

Blackwell called his label Island Records, incorporating it for just under $1,000. One did not require extravagant sums to start a record label in those days—no more, he believes, than one does today.

He recorded the band at a Kingston radio station (there were no local studios) and some weeks later released an album, *Lance Haywood at the Half Moon*. It was a flop, and Blackwell decided to do then what he does today when he has a flop: record another LP immediately. He did, and that too was an unqualified disaster.

In 1960, because of failing family fortunes, his mother sold Terra Nova. Blackwell loved that house, and he promised himself nothing like that would happen to him again. Here he'd been looning through life. The sale of Terra Nova suddenly galvanized him into thinking somewhat more seriously about his future.

He began recording again. There was no popular music being recorded in Jamaica then, and Blackwell was one of the first people on the island to make any noncalypso records. In 1960 he had his first success—a 45 called "Little Sheila," by Laurel Aitken. It went to number one in Jamaica, as did the flip side, "Boogie in My Bones." His next 45 also went to number one. He was never to have that much success again. Flushed with triumph and $1,500 in cash, he opened an office in Kingston with a beautiful Chinese woman who was both his girlfriend and his secretary.

Blackwell next made a deal to manage sixty-three jukeboxes in the little bush towns and villages of Jamaica. When he wasn't in his Kingston offices, he'd travel throughout the bush for days at a time, hawking new records from Kingston and learning slowly but precisely what his Jamaican audiences did and didn't like. He was working hard now, sometimes fifteen and sixteen hours a day. Much later, Blackwell was fond of saying that the working world was divided between those who looked forward to Fridays and those who looked forward to Mondays—he, of course, belonging to the latter school. In any event, he never thought of music as work; he had merely commercialized a hobby.

In 1961 Blackwell worked as producer Harry Saltzman's man in Jamaica during the filming of *Dr. No*, a job he had been recommended for by Ian Fleming. When the filming was completed, Saltzman offered Blackwell a more permanent position in his production company. But Blackwell was undecided. He felt he understood the record business now, although he'd had no real success in it. On the other hand, this was a firm offer, a break, an opportunity. Blackwell sought out a reputable fortune teller in Kingston, asking her to dispel the clouds. The old lady advised Blackwell to continue working for himself, in effect telling him what he already knew—that he was unemployable. He turned down Saltzman.

By the spring of 1962, Blackwell was a full-fledged record producer. Island, of course, wasn't a *proper* company. It was an upstart, maverick record label that had released two LPs and twenty-six 45s. It was successful, after a fashion—a lark, an amusing caper. But what the hell. He was only twenty-five years old.

* * * * *

Blackwell was late. He was always late—so consistently late that there were those who occasionally believed he was ahead of his time. There is a Jamaican expression that goes "soon come." Loosely translated, it means that you'll get there when you get there. In Jamaica, punctuality is considered pushy or a waste of time. Therefore, when Blackwell says, "I'll meet you in Kingston on the fourth *for sure* . . . or the fifth," no one in Jamaica bats an eye.

"There are two things you can always count on with Blackwell," said his friend Artie Mogull. "That he'll be late for his own funeral, and that he's so mean, he wouldn't pay five dollars to watch monkeys fuck."

The scribe, Nathalie Delon, and her Belgian shepherd, Masai, were in Blackwell's hotel suite in the upper reaches of Central Park South. Blackwell had been expected the day before. The suite is one of five homes Blackwell maintains, the others being in England, Nassau, and Jamaica. Depending on whom he's recording and where, Blackwell drifts like a vagrant among these fixed abodes.

He has maintained this suite for five years, decorating it to suit his eccentric tastes. Overlooking the Manhattan skyline, it feels like an airborne discotheque. The floors are carpeted in black Pirelli rubber, many of the walls are mirrored or cluttered with bright sci-fi paintings, the television is built into a wall at the foot of the bed, and an elaborate stereo system occupies yet another wall. From the stereo emanate the loud, primitive sounds of Black Uhuru. At night, the illuminated skyline is so close, it seems like part of the room.

Toward midnight, Blackwell finally arrived in his customary uniform of sandals, T-shirt, and jeans. He is not much concerned with haute couture and, as a friend once pointed out, has been prominently placed on the men's worst-dressed list for more than twenty years.

He made no mention of where he'd been, how long he was staying, or where he intended to go. And Mlle. Delon didn't ask him. She accustomed herself long ago to traveling fast and light at a moment's notice. Mlle. Delon is a startlingly attractive blonde. She was wearing a casquette, an Irish cap, her hair pulled up beneath it so that she looked like an eighteen-year-old boy. She is not eighteen, but she continues to lead her life as though she were. There is an air of recklessness about her, the spunky charm of a woman game for anything. Blackwell calls her Madame Skill.

Curiously, Blackwell is surrounded by strong, independent women: Mlle. Delon; his sixty-nine-year-old mother, Blanche; his Jamaican housekeeper, Pearl; Denise Mills, who runs the Island offices in London; Ivy Chee, who runs Island's property ventures; Lorraine Fraser, who manages the Compass Point studios in Nassau; and his cousin Barbara Cuddy, who runs his offices in New York. Blackwell is hen-*ridden* rather than henpecked.

Blackwell wanted to know how the interview was going. He gave an impression, as he always does, of being both inquisitive and uninterested at the same time.

"It slows down considerably in your absence," said the scribe.

"I've been thinking," said Blackwell. "There should definitely be some bad things in the piece."

The scribe, of course, was well aware that rock 'n' roll was a ruthless business—a treacherous sea on which Blackwell had sailed without serious mishap for twenty years. Long ago, Ahmet Ertegun, the wily head of Atlantic Records, had dubbed Blackwell "the baby-faced killer" —a moniker no one, in rock 'n' roll at least, saw fit to refute.

"Some people think I'm a complete bastard."

"Rumors, probably," said the scribe.

Blackwell smiled. "Probably," he said.

*****

By the spring of 1962, Blackwell's little business was booming, but he was confronted with two problems: he was now selling more records in England than in Jamaica, and he was encountering fierce local competition from such record producers as Sir Coxsone Dodd, Duke Reid, King Edwards, and Leslie Kong. Blackwell decided that rather than compete directly with his competition, he would go to England and represent them there. He left for England in May 1962.

In London, Blackwell rented a house near Harrods in Knightsbridge and formed a company called Island Records. The initial investment from five investors, most of them Chinese Jamaicans, was to have been $8,000, but one of them—probably Blackwell, he later recalled—failed to come up with his share. So Island Records was founded in May 1962 from a capital outlay of $5,300.

For the next two years, Island Records was just a tiny business, lazily, imperceptibly ticking over. Blackwell's house became his office, where he maintained a secretary who was not Chinese. He kept his stock in the back seat of his blue Mini Cooper, and during the day, he flogged around the black ghettos of the city, visiting record shops in Brixton, Lewisham, Stoke Newington, and occasionally up in Birmingham, replenishing the records as they were sold. That first year, Island Records made a net profit of $8,000; in 1963 it made a profit of $6,000.

Even so, Blackwell considered his company a success. Island's first release, during the summer of 1962, was a 45 by Jamaican singer Owen Gray called "Twist Baby." Blackwell pressed five hundred records and sold them all. Success, he believed, was relative; there was not a line beyond which lay success and behind which was failure. In any event, success was largely imaginary, an Anglo-Saxon myth foisted on the unsuspecting by their superiors. He had pressed five hundred records and sold them all. He was having a wonderful time, and so, if one chose to see life in limited terms, he was successful. More important, his little business was growing.

In effect, what Blackwell had done was to create a specialist's market in which he had little or no competition. Out there, in the rest of England, was a flourishing, predominantly white pop-music business, but he wasn't competing with it. It didn't interest him, and so it was as if it didn't exist at all.

One of the very first 45s Island released was "We'll Meet," sung by two young Jamaican singers called Roy and Millie. The record sold well in England, primarily, Blackwell believed, because of Millie's unusual voice. He decided to bring the fifteen-year-old singer to England. He wrote her mother in Jamaica, enclosing an airline ticket, and one day in early 1963, Millie simply materialized at Heathrow.

Five years before, Blackwell had bought a 78 in New York called "My Boy, Lollipop." He now decided to cut it with Millie. When the record was completed, Blackwell reckoned he had a big hit on his hands—too big, he felt, for Island Records to handle alone, so he licensed it to Philips (now PolyGrám).

Released in 1964, "My Boy, Lollipop" was an enormous hit in England and the rest of the world, selling some six million copies in one year alone and netting Island about $150,000. Blackwell was not surprised. Millie was the white person's dream: she was black and cute and fresh from the bush.

Millie's success catapulted Blackwell into the pop business as Millie's manager. Leaving the distribution of records to others at Island—the company now had six employees—Blackwell went on a world tour with Millie. She was a great success, and so was her twenty-seven-year-old manager.

In 1964, during a tour of Birmingham clubs in the Midlands, Blackwell heard a band called the Spencer Davis Group. The lead singer was a fifteen-year-old kid named Stevie Winwood. He had been greatly influenced by American R&B of the '50s, and Blackwell thought he sounded just like a young Ray Charles. He fell in love with the band and signed them to Island. The Spencer Davis Group was the first white band with which he became involved. Again, because

Bradshaw, Chris Blackwell and Nathalie Delon celebrating at Blackwell's home in Nassau

he felt that Island was not yet ready to handle mainstream pop music, Blackwell licensed them to Philips.

In December 1965, the Spencer Davis Group had its first English number one hit song, "Keep on Runnin'." In 1967 they had two international hits in "Gimme Some Lovin'" and "I'm a Man." When the group broke up the next year, Stevie Winwood formed a new band called Traffic; it became Island's first rock group.

"The film and the record businesses, as we know them today, are finished. Dinosaurs. In the record business, the top executives, most of whom are lawyers and accountants, operate entirely on computer runs."

Island's first really successful year was 1967—the year, Blackwell believes, that the music business changed from pop to rock. Musicianship was now becoming of paramount importance, and the musicians themselves were becoming stars—such as guitarists Eric Clapton and Jimi Hendrix. That year, Island ceased to be a predominantly ethnic record company and went into the rock business. During the late '60s, Blackwell signed such quintessential English rock and folk acts as Free, Spooky Tooth, Robert Palmer, John Martyn, Fairport Convention, Jethro Tull, King Crimson, Emerson, Lake & Palmer, and, most successful of them all, Cat Stevens.

Blackwell now believed that he had the best and the most interesting record company around. Island was doing something fresh and innovative; it was not only making heaps of money but was helping to create a completely new sound. For the next four years, Blackwell would virtually ignore Jamaican music, concentrating instead on his English rock groups.

* * * * *

In June 1970, Blackwell flew from London to Los Angeles to negotiate a deal whereby Capitol Records would become Island's first distributor in America. The negotiations were extremely important to Blackwell. The executives at Capitol believed that Island was a hot label; only Blackwell knew that Island was overextended, nearly broke in fact. He intended to obtain from Capitol as much as possible.

The two negotiating teams met at the Capitol Tower near Hollywood and Vine, and negotiations stretched over the next five days. The Capitol Records team consisted of its president, the head of business affairs, the head of A&R, plus three or four in-house experts who drifted in and out of the room with bits and pieces of significant information. They all wore suits and ties. Island's negotiating team consisted of Blackwell and his lawyer. Blackwell wore crumpled jeans, a Spooky Tooth T-shirt, and dilapidated Jamaican sandals.

By the fifth day, they had agreed on almost everything except a basic royalty rate on the projected sales of singles. The dispute was over a 4 percent differential on what Capitol preferred to pay and what Blackwell wanted. The disputed figure amounted to $250,000 a year for the five-year contract—or a total of $1,250,000. Capitol thought it was exceedingly high. Blackwell felt it wasn't nearly enough.

Negotiations continued throughout the day. Toward seven o'clock, Blackwell became impatient and more than a little bored; he had never been partial to extended conversations. He suggested that they toss a coin for the 4 percent. He would take heads or tails; it didn't matter. At first, the Capitol executives were appalled, but not being able to reach an amicable solution, they finally agreed. Artie Mogull, Capitol's canny head of A&R, elected to toss the coin. Blackwell called tails. The coin came up heads. The Capitol executives were much relieved and congratulated one another on their astute negotiating skills.

For the rest of the evening, the two sides negotiated the final points of the contract, and at about four in the morning, everything finally seemed concluded. Throughout the night, lawyers scuttled in and out of the office. In an adjacent room, two secretaries tirelessly typed out the contracts. And, at some point, a check for $1,500,000, representing Capitol's advance to Island, was conspicuously placed on the table—in order, Blackwell presumed, that he might betray some significant emotion.

When the contracts were ready, Capitol asked Blackwell to sign. But, no, Blackwell was exhausted. It was late, and he had a plane to catch back to England. He would take the contracts with him, look them over, sign them, and send them back in a few days. And, most important, Blackwell had neglected to bring his lucky pink pen; he never signed anything without his lucky pink pen (in those days, Island had a pink logo). But Capitol was adamant. They had negotiated for five days. They were tired. It was not only fair but imperative that Blackwell sign the contracts *now*.

Artie Mogull looked around the table at his tired and disconsolate colleagues. Mogull knew, as they did not, that Blackwell believed a signed contract was merely a piece of paper that gave him the right to begin negotiations again. Mogull decided not to mention this until the following day.

The disagreement continued for some time, and finally Blackwell shrugged and suggested to Capitol that they make a deal. A corporate groan rose from across the table. Unperturbed, Blackwell said that he would sign immediately if Capitol returned the 4 percent to him. For a moment, there was a terrible silence in the room, and then the exhausted Capitol executives gave in. Blackwell signed the contracts. He picked up his check, slipped into his sandals—which, presumably for negotiating purposes, he had taken off—and, smiling, left the room.

"Things must be allowed to have time to grow. The best advertising in any business is still word of mouth. So start small and let it go. If it's no good, it's never going to build. But if it is good, nothing will ever keep it down."

* * * * *

In 1971 Blackwell became involved with his first film—the Jamaican ghetto classic *The Harder They Come.* The film cost $200,000. Blackwell invested only $3,000 himself, but he secured the leading role for Jimmy Cliff, whom he still managed. The film went on to become a worldwide cult hit.

That same year, Blackwell met Bob Marley, with whom he would have a close personal and professional relationship until Marley's death from cancer ten years later. Marley just walked into Blackwell's London office one day after having been stranded in Sweden without cash while touring with Johnny Nash. Blackwell had long admired Marley's work and signed him to Island within days. (Marley had originally been signed to CBS, but Blackwell bought his contract for $9,000 and a 2 percent override on his first six albums. Obviously, CBS had no idea of Marley's potential.)

At that time, Marley was something of a star in Jamaica, but few people had heard of him off the island. To launch his international career, Blackwell gave Bob Marley and the Wailers $8,000 to make their first album, 1973's *Catch a Fire*. Music executives ridiculed Blackwell, telling him he was mad, that Marley would spend the cash and never make an album. And, even if he did make it, what difference would it make? Jamaican music had no credibility; it was joke music for Caribbean discotheques.

But Marley made the album. *Catch a Fire* was the first Jamaican album ever conceived as an album and not just a collection of 45s. (Reggae, in fact, is the only Jamaican music born completely in the studio—possibly, Blackwell believes, because the musicians could not afford their own instruments.) When the album was completed, Blackwell released it in America through Capitol. Capitol gave the album almost no promotion or advertising, a point that rankled Blackwell for a long time. Even so, *Catch a Fire* sold fourteen thousand copies that first year and has since sold more than a million copies throughout the world.

During the next few years, Blackwell toured with Traffic in America, until their breakup in 1974, and spent more and more of his time in Nassau and Jamaica directing Bob Marley's burgeoning career—a career that, with the release of *Rastaman Vibration* in 1976, catapulted Marley to stardom.

Blackwell personally produced the majority of Marley's albums. Oddly, he had not intended to, but felt compelled when he was unable to find anyone else. Marley would cut the tracks and then send them to Blackwell to mix. He trusted Blackwell implicitly, and Blackwell came to think of himself not as a producer but a translator of Marley's work.

Unlike many other producers in the music business, Blackwell pays close attention to his artists, listens to their criticisms and complaints, talks to them about how their records sound and what they prefer in the way of cover artwork. Most of his concern with them is reflected in the unusual fact that Steve Winwood has been with Island for eighteen years, Toots and the Maytals for twenty, Robert Palmer for twelve. And, at the time of his death, Bob Marley had been with Island for ten years.

During the mid-'70s, Blackwell did sign some new acts—notably Bryan Ferry and Roxy Music—but he paid almost no attention to them, concentrating instead on trying to break Jamaican music on the international market. To that end, he promoted Marley and Toots and the Maytals, signed Third World and Burning Spear, and created an elaborate studio complex in Nassau called Compass Point.

In the late '70s, Island once again broadened its musical horizons when Blackwell signed Grace Jones, Marianne Faithfull, U2, the B-52's, and, most recently, Joe Cocker and James Brown. Today, Island is a large company—larger, at least, than Blackwell had ever meant it to be—with offices in London, Paris, New York, Los Angeles, Nassau, and Kingston. The main headquarters are in Nassau, where Blackwell prefers to live. He spends more of his time there, moving between his seaside home and Compass Point studios. Though Compass Point is mainly a production center for Island Records, it also attracts musicians from around the world, including AC/DC, Talking Heads, the Police, and the Rolling Stones.

Blackwell claims not to know how much Island Records is worth today, but he will admit that it is one of the oldest and most successful privately owned companies in the record business. In late May, the company will celebrate its twentieth anniversary. Recently, Blackwell decided to widen Island's scope by moving into movie production.

"The record business is in a serious state of stagnation today," he said. "I mean, things have come to a pretty pass when I'm the only chief executive of a record company who actually *makes* records. It seems to me that if you're in the record business, it's important to know how to make records. A similar madness prevails in Hollywood. The people who run studios don't know how to make films, you know? It's beyond them, mysterious snippets of celluloid. But they control the films, and that is inefficient.

"The film and the record businesses, as we know them today, are finished. Dinosaurs. In the record business, the top executives, most of whom are lawyers and accountants, operate entirely on computer runs. That is to say, they only record the past. But these people don't know that. They continue to base their decisions on what's happened before. Anything that is happening or might happen doesn't compute. And they won't support it.

"They can't sign and develop new talent. They don't have the time, and they may not even have the interest. The companies they run are structured to deal with names and trademarks. Who's a star? Who can draw? Package this, package that. Presell this or that. Don't take a chance, play it safe, look before you leap. In fact, don't leap at all; you might lose your job."

* * * * *

Blackwell and the scribe lay in a boat, riding smoothly at anchor in the southern sea. Some sixty yards away was Blackwell's Nassau home, a red-tile-and-stucco hacienda sitting on a cliff above the sea. In the distance curved the bare, unpopulated beach—brown and inviting. From the jetty below the house, Nathalie Delon and her dog, Masai, leaped into the sea and swam leisurely toward the boat. The day was cloudless, hot and blue.

"You see," said Blackwell, "the films I've made are rather like the records I cut back in 1962—small and inexpensive and made with a specific audience in mind. Since none of them had stars, I could not have gone to a big company and presold them, so I released them myself, hoping they would build and find their own market. Only then would I approach a major distributor.

"The main thing is to control your own destiny. And that's why it's terribly important that both Island Records and Island Pictures be independent. You've created something, you've nurtured it. Why, then, at the outset put it into the hands of someone who doesn't care about it as much as you do? It would be rather like designing a great car and then asking General Motors to help build it.

"Things must be allowed to have time to grow. The best advertising in any business is still word of mouth. So start small and let it go. If it's no good, it's never going to build. But if it is good, nothing will ever keep it down."

Moments later, Mlle Delon and Masai clambered aboard the boat. She was wearing a black bikini bottom and a Grace Jones T-shirt.

"You shouldn't wear that shirt in the sea," said Blackwell. "The salt water might shrink it. And, besides that, it's expensive."

"Give me a break," she said.

Although it is true that before going to bed at night, Blackwell walks round his house and turns off all the lights, his reputation for parsimony is largely undeserved. He is, as his cousin John Pringle said, terribly generous with people—provided they don't tell anyone about it.

"Well, the piece is finished," said the scribe.

"That's great," said Blackwell.

Two of Blackwell's favorite expressions are "that's great" and "that's a drag," both of which are said in exactly the same tone of voice.

It was nearly three o'clock, and gray clouds began to bunch above the far horizon.

"It's getting cloudy," said Mlle. Delon, who was attempting to perfect her tan before returning to Paris the following day. "I knew it would rain."

"No problem," said Blackwell.

"*Merde*," said Mlle. Delon.

Blackwell smiled. "I guess it's just another shitty day in paradise," he said.

Bradshaw was great pals with Blackwell, who eventually sold his stake in Island Records for a lot of money and went on to own a string of fabulous luxury boutique hotels in Miami and Jamaica. Blackwell is godfather to Bradshaw's daughter, Shannon. He also gave Carolyn away at Bradshaw's second wedding.

The Man Who Would Be King
Esquire, March 27, 1979

He had always had his baraka*—an Arabic word denoting luck.* Baraka, *in fact, was more than luck; it was a kind of invincibility.*

There was little hope for him this time. He had come to the end. His luck had gone. And worse, he would soon be fifty. Robert Denard sat in the cluttered office of his Citroën sales and service station. Outside, the heavy traffic beat down the main road to Bordeaux. He stroked his mustache and dreamed, waiting for his manager to present the monthly billings.

Over the years, Denard had fought in seven separate wars as a professional soldier, or, as the papers put it, a mercenary, one of *les affreux*—the terrible ones. He was known throughout black Africa as Le Colonel. He had taken five wounds. He walked with a limp. He suffered from recurrent bouts of malaria. He had a wife, a light-skinned Congolese. He had a child. He maintained secret bank accounts in Gabon, Geneva, and Luxembourg. He owned a successful Citroën station. But what was that? It wasn't much. And he had not expected to end his days in trade.

Denard fiddled with the bracelet of elephant hair he always wore round his right wrist. He was a handsome man—a Gascon with a hooked nose, cropped brown hair graying at the sides, blue eyes that seemed always still and cold. Denard was what the French call a *baroudeur*, an adventurer. He believed that men are made by circumstances; he himself had come of age during the German occupation of Paris. After that, there had always been war for him. He had been a marine gunner in Vietnam, a policeman in Morocco, a legionnaire in

Now, sitting in the cluttered office of his Citroën station, he recounted the grim litany of his defeats and waited for his manager to present the monthly billings. Once there had been heroics; now there were only Citroëns.

"Denard was what the French call a *baroudeur*, an adventurer. He believed that men are made by circumstances; he himself had come of age during the German occupation of Paris."

Algeria, a mercenary in Yemen and the Congo. "*La guerre c'est mon metier*," he had long been fond of saying. It seemed mere bluster to him now.

But he remembered it all so well. Even here in Bordeaux, the Congo was always with him. It was in the Congo that he had assumed his first command and acquired a reputation for cold-blooded bravery. During the battle at Kolwezi against a superior United Nations force, he and his little band of mercenaries resisted for days, inflicting heavy casualties, before slipping across the border into Angola. Later, in 1966, they held Stanleyville against the mutinous Katangese, then drove the rebels from the city and destroyed them in Maniema.

Each skirmish, each ambush and attack, was clear to him—how they drove through the damp weight of the jungle in their Jeeps, the heavy machine gun mounted on the back; how they swooped into enemy villages, their morale so high that they attacked while standing up in their Jeeps. He could still hear the crash of the mortars, the machine-gun and automatic-rifle fire. He could still see the oncoming waves of screaming Katangese, drugged on *chanvre*, which gave them, they believed, the *dawa*, or magic, that enabled bullets to pass through them harmlessly; and afterward, when the battle was done, the piles of dead black bodies along the jungle road, so thick at times that the Jeeps were unable to pass until the bodies were heaved into the bush. He had killed . . . he could no longer remember how many men he had killed.

In those days he had always had his *baraka*—an Arabic word denoting luck. *Baraka*, in fact, was more than luck; it was a kind of invincibility. He believed in it with the odd and obstinate faith of the superstitious. And so did his men, the little group of thirty or forty mercenaries whom he had trained in the Congo, taken to the war in Yemen, and brought back to the Congo again. They believed he had a great vein of it, that it was powerful not only for him but for them, and that it would never run dry. But in July of 1967, while inspecting his troops entrenched along the Congo River, he was hit in the head by a bullet. He was flown in a stolen DC-3 to Rhodesia for an operation. The bullet was removed, but he was partially paralyzed in the right leg, and for months thereafter, he walked with a cane.

By then, the war in the Congo was nearly over. In November of 1967, only partially recovered and still using a cane, he and sixteen of his men crossed into the Congo from Angola in order to support the Belgian mercenary Jean "Black Jack" Schramme's mutiny against the Congolese government. Having no transport, they came into the Congo on bicycles. In a series of sudden ambushes, they lost four men and were forced once more to retreat into Angola. He was finished, his Congo days ending in defeat and ignominy. This was made quite clear to him that fall. Hearing that there would be clandestine but official French support for a mercenary venture in the recent outbreak of war in Biafra, he offered his services; but his reputation was tarnished, and, despite his intrigues, he was rejected as its potential leader. It was the final blow, he believed at the time, and he withdrew to Bordeaux.

Since late 1967, Denard had been one of the trusted agents of Jacques Foccart, then the French Republican presidency's secretary-general in charge of African and Madagascan affairs. Appointed to this position by President de Gaulle in 1961, Foccart quickly became the éminence grise of French covert operations in Africa. Called Le Phoque (the seal), Foccart had been one of the leaders of the Gaullist Service d'Action Civique (SAC), whose specialty was dirty tricks against left-wing parties in France. Now, independent of the official services, Foccart took Africa as his fief.

In the early '60s, at a time when African nations were becoming independent, the Gaullist regime backed those African politicians who were favorable to or dependent on France—particularly in its former colonies. Independence was necessary, acceptable even, but de Gaulle, Foccart, and Denard himself were men who continued to believe in the efficacy of the French Empire. To that end, France used its secret services to combat threats to its interests by radical African political organizations in its former colonies. Thus, whenever there were secessionist movements or important mineral or

Denard took the body of Ali Soilih, the Comoran head of state, to the village of Chaoueni and placed it before Ali's eighty-one-year-old mother.

MARCH 27, 1979/ESQUIRE 69

The Man Who Would Be King by Julian Allen

petroleum resources in question, Foccart and, hence, Denard were actively engaged. Denard was Foccart's pawn, and he was moved about Africa accordingly.

In July of 1975, Denard received new marching orders, this time to the Comoro Islands. The Comoros, lying in the Indian Ocean between Madagascar and Mozambique, were the poorest of France's dependencies. The four small islands have a population of some 370,000 Muslims of mixed African and Arab descent. They survive for the most part on the exportation of vanilla beans, cloves, a little copra, and a curious plant called the ylang-ylang, essential to the making of many French perfumes. A poor and inauspicious place, the Comoros have a per capita income of under $153 a year. The islands, however, were of strategic importance to France, since they lay at the northern end of the Mozambique Channel, through which all the supertankers came from the Persian Gulf bearing oil round the Cape of Good Hope to Western capitals.

On July 6, 1975, the Comoran parliament declared unilateral independence and appointed Ahmed Abdallah as president, thereby ending 132 years of French rule. Nearly a month later, Denard and seven mercenaries arrived by night in the Comoros, captured Ahmed Abdallah, and installed Ali Soilih, the leader of the opposition, as the new Comoran president. Ahmed Abdallah was exiled to France. Denard remained to train the 1,600-man Comoran army. He spent some two months in the Comoros, and gradually he came to look on the islands as his own kingdom. He was not king, of course, but it was he, Denard, who had made the king. Those were rapturous days for him. Ali Soilih followed orders. Denard soldiered; he swam and lay in the sun and consorted with several of the local girls. At last, everything worked. The Comoran coup had restored his confidence and he believed that nothing would ever deter him again. That autumn he received a new assignment, and when he left for Gabon, he promised himself that one day he would return.

During the next few months, he remained in Africa running invidious errands for Jacques

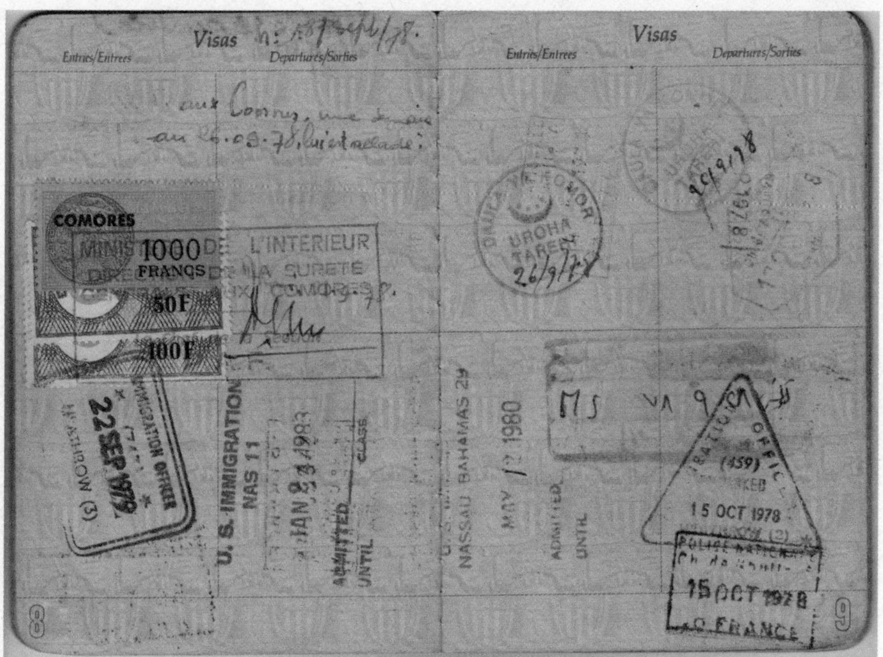

Bradshaw's visa to the Comoro Islands

Foccart and the CIA. In the fall of 1975, he recruited thirty mercenaries to support President Mobutu of Zaire's invasion of oil-rich Cabinda. The invasion failed. In early 1976, he was paid $500,000 by the CIA to recruit twenty mercenaries to support the right-wing UNITA forces during the Angolan war. The mercenaries failed to complete their six-month contract. Denard was vexed, but these were minor setbacks and he continued to believe that his *baraka* was as strong as ever.

On Sunday morning, January 16, 1977, Denard and ninety-one mercenaries were aboard an unmarked four-engine DC-7 en route from Libreville, in Gabon, to Cotonou, in Benin, a small "Marxist-Leninist" republic on the western coast of Africa. The mercenaries were called Force OMEGA, and Denard, their leader, was traveling under his usual pseudonym of Colonel Gilbert Bourgeaud. The group, trained at Benguerir, a military base near Marrakech, in Morocco, had flown the day before from Morocco to Gabon.

Force OMEGA's objective in Benin was "to eliminate the present regime, to install the new team from the Front for the Liberation and Rehabilitation of Dahomey [Benin] and to seize and neutralize the President." Denard reckoned the coup d'état would take a maximum of three hours. With Denard was Gratien Pognon, Benin's former ambassador to Brussels and a longtime agent of SDECE [Service de Documentation Extérieure et de Contre-Espionnage]. Pognon was to be Benin's new president. He carried a copy of his victory speech inside his safari jacket. The speech began: "Children of Dahomey, arise. The tyrant is no more." At seven o'clock that morning—because of a breakdown in Gabon, they were already an hour late—the old DC-7 flew in low over the Bight of Benin and landed at the small airport in Cotonou.

As the plane taxied round, Denard saw a tank move slowly up the airstrip toward them. The plane wheeled and stopped. Chutes were extended from the doors through which the mercenaries slid to the ground. An 81-mm mortar was set up near the starboard wing, and they knocked out the tank on the second shot. Fifteen minutes later, the airport was theirs. There were only five soldiers on duty, three of whom were shot. The other two and seven airport technicians were taken hostage. Denard set up his staff headquarters in the main terminal and dispatched his men in three separate units to the presidential palace, 2.5 kilometers away.

From the roofs of the Ministry of the Interior and a five-story apartment building, the mercenaries began to shell the palace with 81-mm mortars. One of the shells hit the palace roof just above the president's bed, but he had spent the night in his private residence five kilometers away. The mercenaries' fire was returned by the palace guard, who swiftly grouped on the palace roof. The firing from the palace was fierce and accurate, and the mercenaries were unable to advance. Three hours later, supported by two hundred troops from the nearby army camp, the palace guard counterattacked, and slowly the surprised mercenaries were forced to retreat.

Only minutes later, it became a rout. Dozens of civilians wielding machetes joined the advancing soldiers. The mercenaries broke and ran for the airport, shooting haphazardly over their shoulders as they went. At the airport, Denard was stunned. Leaving the terminal building, he saw his men in full flight and, beyond them, the oncoming Beninese. Without thinking, and clutching his bad leg, he joined them in their dash for the plane. The DC-7 taxied round and moved slowly up the airstrip, the mercenaries running alongside until one by one they were dragged aboard. Two mercenaries were killed and a young Belgian mercenary was shot in the arm; it was later amputated.

Somehow, the DC-7 managed to take off without receiving a direct hit. Sitting in the back of the plane, Denard could see the Beninese soldiers below jumping up and down and brandishing their rifles in the air. It was only later he discovered that in their panic, they had left behind their mortars and machine guns and a 300-watt radio transmitter and that he had forgotten his briefcase containing photographs of the mercenaries, their real names, addresses, and bank accounts, and detailed plans for the coup d'état. He was sick. He had never felt so sick.

It had been a terrible fiasco. His *baraka* had finally gone. In the next few months, many of his men who had been loyal for years deserted him for other campaigns and other commanders. In 1977 there were wars enough to keep them occupied. Some went to Rhodesia, others to Somalia and Saudi Arabia, and others still to Thailand and Chad. Denard returned to Bordeaux.

Now, sitting in the cluttered office of his Citroën station, he recounted the grim litany of his defeats and waited for his manager to present the monthly billings. Once there had been heroics; now there were only Citroëns. When he finished work at five o'clock, he drove the sixty kilometers to his home in the little village of Lesparre. Over dinner, his wife said he had had an urgent call from Paris that afternoon. Denard said he did not believe in urgency anymore.

"Denard refused to see me the first ten days I was [in the Comoro Islands]," Bradshaw said in an editor's note for Esquire. *"So, I hung out with his subordinate officers, mostly in bars and brothels—the usual droll life one lives in such places—particularly in a bar called La Rose Noire (to be avoided, should you go there). Three days before I left, Denard summoned me to his office, where we had a long talk, and he informed me he had to leave the islands. Denard is a very cold Gascon with calculative charm. But he was a defeated man—the dream that he had, that is, to be king, had come to naught." Denard died in 2007 at the age of seventy-eight.*

Bradshaw was indeed a scoundrel. But softly so. His caught-in-the-act smile always returned quickly, it's who he was. Infuriating and lovable simultaneously, no real malicious intent—though fascinated by it in others. Bradshaw himself was never counterfeit. Each moment was an accurate snapshot of his entire being. He played the role he wanted—himself—and it was a wonderful performance. A seasoned listener and storyteller. A humorous and charming man of the people—preferably people with resources. There's a reason no one called him Jon.

Alan Rudolph

July 18, 1978 $1.50

ESQUIRE

FORTNIGHTLY

A Dream of Terror

The Life and Death Of the Man Who Set Out to Destroy A Country By Jon Bradshaw

Will There Be a 1979 Recession? By Dan Dorfman

The Elusive Editor Behind America's Greatest Authors

Baader-Meinhof Gang Leader Andreas Baader

A Dream of Terror Illustration by Julian Allen

A Dream of Terror

Esquire, July 18, 1978

The product of terror is terror. —Nikolai Lenin

The German Institute for Social Questions is in the bleak suburb of Dahlem in West Berlin at Miquelstrasse 83. It is comprised of two separate buildings, their small gardens backing onto each other. One building faces the Miquelstrasse; the other, the busy Bernadottestrasse. Like many of this city's buildings, they have been constructed since the war and have that gray and featureless façade that is now the new Berlin. The northernmost building contains the institute's library, and it was here, on May 14, 1970, that Andreas Baader had arranged to begin research on a book concerning the organization of youth on the fringes of society.

At the time, Baader was residing in West Berlin's Tegel Prison, where he had been for some six weeks. He was serving three years for his part in setting fires in two Frankfurt department stores in 1968. Baader's lover and co-arsonist, Gudrun Ensslin, had been given a similar sentence; but she had eluded the police and gone underground. Even so, in late April she contrived to visit Baader in Tegel Prison, using the pseudonym of Dr. Gretel Weitermeier. On five other occasions in early May, Baader was visited by his new friend Ulrike Meinhof, West Germany's most famous left-wing journalist.

In April, the thirty-five-year-old Meinhof drafted a letter from a bogus publisher stating that Baader had been commissioned to write a book for them; she requested official permission that he be allowed to research it at the Dahlem Institute. Oddly, there were no complications, and it was arranged that Baader would begin his researches there that

Thursday morning in May. In Tegel Prison, Andreas Baader had thought about little else for days.

Just after eight o'clock that morning, Ulrike Meinhof rang the institute's front bell. Frau Gertrud Lorenz, the head librarian, let her in, and Ulrike explained that she had come to assist Andreas Baader. Taking the well-known journalist at her word, Frau Lorenz escorted Ulrike into the main reading room. Ulrike placed an empty chair next to her own and sat down at the table to work. She put her handbag on the floor between the two chairs; the handbag contained cosmetics, keys, her identity papers, two paperback books, and a small handgun.

Frau Lorenz and her assistants went about their work, and at nine-thirty, when the doorbell rang, everyone knew who it was. Looking out the window into the Miquelstrasse, Georg Linke, an elderly librarian, saw a prison car parked at the curb. He opened the front door. Andreas Baader, dressed in jeans and a black pullover, stood there handcuffed between two armed guards. A dark, attractive man of twenty-seven, Baader seemed nervous, irresolute. The three men were taken into the main reading room. Ulrike Meinhof looked up, gesturing to the empty chair beside her. Baader's handcuffs were removed, and the two guards walked round the room checking the exits and the window locks. They did not, of course, notice Ulrike's gun, nor did they see the young man in the window of a flat across the street. He had been directed to hang a white towel from the window if there were police cars in the neighborhood. At the main table, the two researchers riffled books and papers and whispered to each other. It was not until later that one of the assistant librarians remembered Baader saying to Ulrike, "Well, if things don't work out today, we can try again on Monday." It had not seemed important at the time.

Shortly before eleven, the front bell rang again. Georg Linke admitted two women who needed, they explained, to research some facts for an essay on juvenile delinquents. Linke told them they were not permitted in the main reading room, but that they could work at a table in the front hall. The two girls, students, Linke remembered thinking, sat down, putting their briefcases on the floor. The younger girl was Irene Goergens, the illegitimate daughter of an American soldier who had run away from a state home two years before. She was Ulrike Meinhof's friend and protégée. Her companion was Ingrid Schubert, a pretty twenty-five-year-old brunette who had been trained to be a doctor. Both girls wore wigs.

Minutes later, the doorbell rang yet again. Ingrid Schubert crossed the hall and let in a tall man wearing a green hooded mask, a balaclava, over his head. His name was Hans-Jürgen Bäcker. An electrician by trade, he had long sought a more romantic role. He hurried into the front hall brandishing a Beretta with a silencer.

Georg Linke had also heard the doorbell. The sixty-two-year-old librarian opened his office door and looked into the front hall. The masked man promptly shot him in the stomach. Linke lurched back into his office, slamming the door behind him. The masked man moved into Frau Lorenz's office, pointed the Beretta, and shouted, "Stay where you are or you'll be shot." Frau Lorenz closed her eyes and slumped in her chair.

Ingrid Schubert and Irene Goergens walked into the main reading room and swung their guns slowly round the room. Their guns contained gas pellets. The two startled guards rose to their feet. They did not reach for their guns. Ulrike Meinhof ran across to the window, opened it, and jumped out into the garden. Baader was right behind her. The masked man and the two girls fired several rounds of bullets and gas pellets low along the floor. As Ingrid attempted to get out the window, one of the guards grabbed her, pulling off her wig, but the masked man shot him in the face with pellets. The two girls and the masked man then jumped from the window and ran across the garden into the Bernadottestrasse. A silver-gray Alfa Romeo Giulia Sprint, its engine running, waited at the curb. Another of their accomplices, Astrid Proll, sat behind the wheel. Ulrike and Baader huddled in the back seat. Within seconds, the car was gone.

Some hours later, the Alfa Romeo was found abandoned in the street by the Kripo—the criminal police. Under the front seat they found a tear gas pistol, a long flashlight, and a book entitled *Introduction to "Das Kapital."* But they were not to find Andreas Baader or his comrades for more than two years.

Three days later, the German Press Agency received a letter, portions of which were also published in the Berlin anarchist paper *Agit 833*. Written by Ulrike Meinhof, it said in part, "Did the pigs really believe that we would let Comrade Baader languish in prison for two or three years? Did they really believe we would talk about the development of the class struggle and the reorganization of the proletariat without arming ourselves at the same time? Did the pigs, who shot first, believe that we would allow ourselves to be knocked off like cattle? Those who don't defend themselves die. Those who don't die are buried alive in prisons, in reform schools, in the slums of the working districts, in the stone coffins of the new housing developments, in the crowded kindergartens and schools, in the brand-new kitchens and bedrooms filled with fancy furniture bought on credit. Start the armed resistance now. Build up the Red Army!"

And there it began—the Rote Armee Fraktion, the Red Army Faction, the RAF. But it was not as the RAF that the group achieved its notoriety; rather, it did so as the Baader-Meinhof gang. Ulrike Meinhof, already prominent in left-wing circles, became the gang's pamphleteer and its most potent martyr. But it was Baader, the boy bandit, who became the hobgoblin of the German press and hence the German public. Before the year was out, Andreas Baader would become the most notorious terrorist in Europe.

* * * * *

Berndt Andreas Baader was born in Munich on May 6, 1943. His father, Dr. Berndt Philipp Baader, a historian, was employed as an archivist by the state of Bavaria; he was drafted into the German army in World War II and was killed on the Russian front in

"Baader desired destruction as some men desire country homes. He wanted to kill complacency."

1945. His widow, Anneliese, never remarried. Andreas, or Andy, as his mother liked to call him, was an only child. He was raised in a small flat in the Schwabing district of Munich by his mother, an aunt, and a grandmother. In order to support him, Frau Baader worked as a typist and occasionally as a secretary. Andy was her whole world, and she doted on the boy.

By all accounts, Baader was a beautiful child. But he was spoiled and obstinate. Once, when he was about eight, his mother took him boating on the Starnberger See, a large lake just southwest of Munich. The boy scrambled all over the boat, and his mother warned him not to fall into the water. Although fully dressed, Andy jumped in and, smiling, swam easily behind the boat. On another occasion, Andy was suffering from a toothache. "I tried to take him to the dentist," his mother said, "but he refused. He told me he wanted to see just how much pain he could bear." Frau Baader always found it difficult to scold the boy, and she was never able to control him.

Baader was sent to a series of private schools in and around Munich; he did not do well. At sixteen, he was dispatched to Dr. Florian Unerreiter's school. Peter Müller, now a Hamburg architect, spent two years with Baader at Dr. Unerreiter's and remembered him as being "very middle class; his family didn't have much money. I think he must have been ashamed of them since he never took anyone home with him.

"The German educational system is very strict, very orderly," Müller said. "It caters to the averagely intelligent. Andreas was brighter than that, of course, but he was cocky and freewheeling and he couldn't cope with the rules. He hated taking orders from anyone. He was dark—he might have been Irish or French—and he tended to be romantic. He once pretended to have lung cancer, or perhaps it was tuberculosis. He walked around Munich with the face of a man who knows he is dying but who is determined to make the best of it. He always tried to cough up blood into handkerchiefs, and invariably the handkerchiefs stayed white.

"He was not the fool the newspapers made him out to be. At sixteen, Andreas was reading Sartre, Nietzsche, and Balzac. He loved Balzac, especially

The Droll Tales. He always liked the shadowy part of society. He was opportunistic, and he had no fear of anything. During his last year at school, he stole one of those old-fashioned East German motorcycles. He didn't have a license, but he liked driving through the English Garden at 120 kilometers an hour. I don't think he was ever caught." Baader was, however, caught for driving another motorcycle without a license and was sentenced to three weeks in reform school.

"There was another side to Andreas," said Müller. "He was obsessed with the high life. He was often taken in by people who thought he was fascinating. I remember a queer man once kept Andreas in the way some people keep exotic animals. And Andreas loved it. But he never submitted to these people. They did what he told them to do or he walked out."

In one of his school reports, Dr. Unerreiter described Baader as "sympathetic" and added, "There is hope of good results. The pupil should be capable of the high school diploma." Dr. Unerreiter was certain of one thing. "He was an extremely gifted young man," he said. "At the time, I supposed Andreas would go on to become a journalist or a writer of some sort. He wrote marvelous essays."

During his last year in school, however, Baader developed a tendency to fight with his fellow students, and somewhat later, he was expelled without having obtained his Abitur—the examination that dictates the future of every German student. Baader was eighteen. It was the end of his formal education. With friends, he maintained a cheerful insouciance, but he had, he felt, been unfairly chastised, violated.

* * * * *

The twentieth century, as Lenin predicted, has become a century of wars and revolutions. But Lenin had not envisaged terrorism, possibly because both he and Marx dismissed it as counterproductive, ineffectual. Terrorism, in fact, does little more than alienate the very people it hopes to set free. Even so, the use of violence to obtain political demands continues to have its advocates—including Andreas Baader's favorite author, Jean-Paul Sartre. "Violence," Sartre wrote, "like Achilles' lance, can heal the wounds it has inflicted." Baader believed that slippery axiom. He dreamed of violence, and his dream became one of the many nightmares of our time.

Following his escape from prison, Baader felt a great impatience; it was imperative that the mission begin. Using false passports, the little group traveled to Jordan, where they had been invited to a Popular Front for the Liberation of Palestine training camp. The group included Baader, Gudrun, Ulrike, and Horst Mahler, a prominent left-wing lawyer who had given up a lucrative law practice to devote himself to the Berlin protest movement and to defending radical students.

They were to spend two months in Jordan undergoing training in the use of explosives, weapons, and guerrilla tactics. Baader did not get on with his Arab brethren; he flatly refused to crawl under barbed wire in the mud, for example, which antagonized the Arabs. Baader felt the exercise would not be particularly useful in Frankfurt or West Berlin.

At the end of August 1970, this self-styled "People's Army" returned to Germany to prepare for the coming conflict. They devised code names (Baader was Hans, Gudrun was Grete); they acquired weapons, electronic devices, false identity cards, and large, fast cars. But their most pressing need was for funds, and so, according to the precepts of Carlos Marighella, the Brazilian revolutionary, they decided to rob banks. Was that not the legitimate course? Given the fact that the state was immoral, how could there be a crime against the state? And besides, Baader had come to believe that a violation of social laws was, in itself, a revolutionary act.

Accordingly, on September 29, 1970, just before ten in the morning, the gang hit three West Berlin banks simultaneously. The thirteen gang members, seven of whom were women, came away with nearly 220,000 deutsche marks (about $60,500). Their first conflict had been extraordinarily successful, and Baader was jubilant. Concerning the robbery of banks, Ulrike Meinhof was to write, "No one claims that bank robbery of itself changes anything . . . but for the revolutionary organization, it means a solution to

"Baader saw himself as a Marxist, not an anarchist. The system must be torn limb from limb."

its financial problems. It is logistically correct, since otherwise the financial problem could not be solved at all. It is politically correct because it is an act of dispossession. It is tactically correct because it is a proletarian action."

But their triumph was short-lived. On October 8, the West Berlin police raided their Knesebeckstrasse hideout and arrested four girl gang members and the luckless Horst Mahler. He had been an active urban guerrilla for just nine days. Two days later the rest of the group met and spoke bitterly of Mahler's capture. "Don't shit in your trousers," retorted Baader. "So the cops have caught a few of us, that's no reason to lose our nerve. We have to learn from it." But Baader was convinced that Mahler had been betrayed. He attacked the others for whining and assured them that they would go on as successfully as before. Most of them believed him. "Baader exerted a very strong *personal* influence on the others," said Mahler. "That influence more than made up for his political shortcomings."

But Baader was learning. In a letter to a Frankfurt newspaper, Baader neatly restated one of Marighella's precepts: "The pigs will stumble around in the dark," he wrote, "until they are forced to transform the political situation into a military one." Although commonly described as an anarchist, Baader saw himself as a Marxist striving for radical social change. The system, he insisted, must be broken, torn limb from limb.

That kind of savage rhetoric created much consternation in Germany. The government and leading social commentators simply did not understand. What in the world did they mean? With one or two exceptions, the Baader-Meinhof gang were from the haute bourgeoisie; they were, for the most part, students or university graduates, trained to be sociologists, teachers, journalists, and lawyers. They had been reared in one of the most successful liberal democracies in the world, a country that had risen from the ashes of World War II in less than twenty years to produce its *Wirtschaftswunder*—its economic miracle. On average, German workers bring home as much as 2,300 deutsche marks a month (they are the highest-paid workers in the world), and these middle-class malcontents from good, clean German homes were calling them "wage slaves." It was outrageous; in Germany it was almost sacrilegious.

"It is not pure coincidence," Horst Mahler said, "that the countries with the most violent terrorist movements today are Italy, Japan, and Germany." As in Italy and Japan, the Germans rejected so much of their immediate past that a kind of national amnesia set in. Their past stank of pain and guilt and a still unconquerable shame. And so, when the war was done, they attempted to construct a rational, materialistic Germany, a clean and ordered place where their past could not only never be repeated but where the memory of it would be obliterated forever. And, had they not had children, they might have succeeded.

*****

It is difficult to say just why terrorism began in Germany at precisely this time. The theories are numerous and, more often than not, contradictory. But according to Dr. Richard Clutterbuck, a senior lecturer at England's Exeter University and the author of *Living with Terrorism*, the terrorism was born out of imitation, disenchantment, and a profound frustration with the German political process.

In the late '60s, German students, in much the way Baader had imitated the mannerisms of [Humphrey] Bogart, began to imitate the American violent dissent against the war in Vietnam, culminating in the protest demonstrations in West Berlin in 1968. Secondly, German youth were deeply disenchanted—"disgusted" is Clutterbuck's word—by their parents' generation. They despised their parents' sanctimonious talk and that a majority of them had supported Nazism; even more, they hated the fact that many of that generation, including active Nazis, still held influential positions of power in German society.

In Germany's institutions of higher learning, the number of students has more than doubled in the past decade to about eight hundred thousand. German universities are free to any student who achieves a certain mark in the Abitur, the high school final examination. (Curiously, in German high schools, there is little teaching of German history between 1914 and 1945; the Germans would seem to be the one nation on earth not to know what Nazism was.) Once admitted to a university, many students are given allowances and grants; there are few academic requirements and equally few time limits on when to complete their studies. It is not uncommon to find German students in their thirties.

The early '60s were heady times in the overcrowded German universities. The students were restless and hungry for change. Given the ban-the-bomb movement, the Berlin Wall, Cuba, and Vietnam, many students, as they did in America, turned to the teachings of Marx and Lenin, of Trotsky, Mao, Marcuse, and Guevara. Today, it is believed that there are some 170,000 students who are radical sympathizers. They believe, as Stephen Spender put it, that the future is like a time bomb, but ticking away in the present. Thus, many of that generation of radical German students became communists, others Maoists, and still others turned to terrorism, to what Irish patriots call the politics of despair.

The effects of violence are always indiscriminate, and what began as an academic crisis rapidly became a governmental one. In the beginning, the federal government seemed powerless against this small but determined band of terrorists. That such a thing could happen in Germany was incredible to them. But they reacted with violence and hysteria. In the early '70s, helmeted policemen with truncheons and automatic weapons began twisting arms and pulling hair and interrogating anyone who looked unpleasantly nonconformist. New search, arrest, and gun laws were passed; daily roadblocks on autobahn off-ramps and at border posts were mounted by paramilitary units using armored cars, machine guns, dogs, and helicopters. The police maintained surveillance on the homes, telephones, and mail of thousands of friends, relatives, and acquaintances of group members. They refused to reveal just how many homes had been searched, how many people had been interrogated, or how many had been arrested and held in detention. And these draconian measures were put into effect with the public's blessing. When given a choice between civil liberty and order, the German has rarely hesitated to choose the latter.

In the winter of 1970–71, the Baader-Meinhof gang consisted of twenty-two persons who were wanted for robbing three banks. Five thousand heavily armed police were now in search of them. One of the chief reasons for the gang's unwarranted notoriety was the presence of Ulrike Meinhof among them. She was well-known, she was the group's most articulate spokesman, its intellectual leader, and most significantly, she had been a respected and successful member of the bourgeoisie. That winter, the gang, hell-bent on its *Klassenkampf*, its class war, had many sympathizers in the radical Left, and Ulrike's photograph, it was said, was secretly carried in the pockets of thousands of young German students. They understood Ulrike's action, but no one else did, least of all the "shit liberals," as Baader dubbed them—consumed with radical chic, or *Schickeria*, as it is known in Germany.

* * * * *

On June 1, 1972, just before six in the morning, three young men drove slowly into Hofeckweg 2-4 in a purple Porsche Targa. It was not quite light. The three men were Andreas Baader, Holger Meins, and Jan-Carl Raspe. They got out of the car, and Baader and Meins walked toward the garage while Raspe lingered behind. They did not see the sharpshooters on the opposite rooftops, the highway patrol and their *Panzerwagens* in the next street, nor did they hear the helicopters hovering three hundred feet in the air a mile away.

Wearing bulletproof vests, the police closed in. Baader turned and saw them, and he and Meins sprinted into the garage, slamming the double doors behind them. But Jan-Carl Raspe ("Herr Allerman") had been too slow. He turned and ran, firing several shots, but two policemen tackled him and brought him down. Inspecting the Porsche, the police found several homemade hand grenades and a large box of gunpowder.

"Baader lay on the cement floor, unshaven and in dark glasses. His thigh was bleeding badly."

Despite the early hour, a large crowd of spectators gathered nearby. In an apartment across the street from the garage, a television camera team had taken their positions. They filmed the entire proceedings and their film was shown eight times that day on German television. It was now light. A police captain, holding a megaphone, shouted, "Come out one by one and nothing will happen to you. You are surrounded. Your chances of escape are zero. Think about your lives. You are young. It's only a matter of time." But there was only silence.

At about six-thirty, the police drove an Audi up to the garage doors and left it there. But an hour later, they dragged it away, and immediately the double doors flew open. The police hurled tear gas into the open garage, but the two fugitives batted the canisters away with wooden planks. Baader, in an open shirt and dark glasses, could now be seen in the dim garage. A Gauloise hung from his mouth as he changed the magazine in his pistol. Across the street, a sharpshooter took aim, fired, and missed, but the bullet ricocheted, striking Baader in the thigh. He cursed and retreated into the garage.

Some two hours later, Holger Meins decided to surrender; he had been grazed by a bullet on the left thigh. He threw his pistol into the courtyard and the police ordered him to take off his clothes. Moments later, Meins walked out in his underwear, his hands above his head. Two police officers grabbed him and twisted his arms behind his back. Meins screamed in pain, and the officers led him away. "Who's still in there?" Meins was asked, and whispering almost inaudibly, Meins said, "Andreas."

Ten minutes later, an armored car drove up to the double doors; in its wake came nine or ten police officers wearing bulletproof vests and gas masks. Inside, Baader lay on the cement floor. He was unshaven and wore dark glasses. His thigh was bleeding badly. They grabbed him and dragged him outside. As they put him on a stretcher, Baader shouted, "Pigs, you're all pigs." He was taken, under guard, to the Frankfurt University Clinic, where it was discovered he had lost nearly 40 percent of his blood; only a blood transfusion saved him. The next day, the influential *Frankfurter Allgemeine* said in a banner headline: FINALLY, A SUCCESS.

And now, the end came very quickly. A week after Baader's arrest, Gudrun Ensslin was arrested while buying clothes in a Hamburg boutique. She struggled when the police arrived, but it was over; with Baader's capture she had lost her taste for revolution. In her handbag, the police found a gun, a forged identity card, and newspaper clippings of Baader's arrest.

Another week went by, and the police received another of their fortuitous tips, this one from a young left-wing teacher. He had decided that the Baader-Meinhof gang was helping to sabotage the new left movement. To that end, he informed the police that Ulrike Meinhof had taken refuge a few days before in his flat in Hannover. Ironically, the young teacher was just the sort of radical who only a year before would have been an ardent Baader-Meinhof sympathizer.

The police went to the flat. When Ulrike opened the door they took her. She struggled, furiously at first, calling them "pigs," but she was easily subdued. In her luggage, the police found three 9-mm pistols, a submachine gun, two hand grenades, a gift-wrapped homemade ten-pound bomb, boxes of cartridges, and forged identity papers. There was also a letter from Gudrun, written after her capture, which said, "Shut your trap and stay in the hole." But it was already too late, Ulrike Meinhof's two-year mutiny had ended.

After the capture of Andreas Baader, the federal government believed that there would be an end to the violence, an end to the hysteria and turmoil the gang had done its utmost to create. The feeling in Germany during that early summer of 1972 was that the Baader-Meinhof gang had been routed, that but for the trial, it was all over. The revolt, which novelist Heinrich Böll called "the war of the six against the sixty million," had run its course. Germany would return to its senses again.

* * * * *

A Dream of Terror Illustration by James McMullan

"As long as Andreas Baader lives," one of the gang defectors said, "the terror will never end."

But the war had just begun. And it would not soon be over. Baader was now incarcerated in Schwalmstadt Prison in Düsseldorf. He continued to nurse his smashed thigh. He read *Uncle Tom's Cabin* in German. He harangued his captors. He hatched extravagant intrigues. It is not known to what extent Baader involved himself in the bombings, the hijackings, the kidnappings, and the assassinations that were to come. He may have helped to plan them; the federal government believed he had. He certainly gave them his encouragement and support. But one thing, apparently, was certain. "As long as Andreas Baader lives," one of the gang defectors said, "the terror will never end."

Baader, Gudrun, and Ulrike were kept in separate prisons. Gudrun was shunted from prison to prison and ended up in Essen. There, in protest against an investigation into whether her lawyer had smuggled letters from her to Ulrike, Gudrun began a hunger strike. Baader disapproved of Gudrun's tactic, since it impaired her ability to think clearly. "And we must," he said, "think clearly now."

Because the authorities feared there would be attempts to free them, Baader and Gudrun were kept in strict isolation. Ulrike was locked away in the women's psychiatric examination wing of Ossendorf Prison in Cologne. She was kept in a section called "the silent wing." She was its only inmate. Following her capture, Ulrike would spend 231 days in solitary confinement; she was kept in a small cell in which everything was painted a luminous white, where the neon white lighting was never extinguished, where the only window was covered so that nothing, not even the sky, could be seen.

* * * * *

Ulrike's cell was virtually soundproof. She could hear no voices, no footsteps, none of the normal sounds of prison life. The silence was called "the white noise." She never saw another prisoner; but she was permitted a radio—permanently tuned to one station. "It sounds in the silence," Ulrike wrote, "but it does not relieve it." The eight-month confinement did much to derange her. In a letter Ulrike had smuggled from prison she wrote, "The feeling that one's head is exploding, that the spinal marrow is being pressed into the brain. The feeling that the brain is slowly shriveling up like a baked fruit. The feeling that one's spine is drilling into the brain. The feeling that one is pissing one's soul away. Pains in the head, flashes. The feeling that one is in a mirrored room that distorts one's image, weaving back and forth. Frantic aggressiveness for which there is no outlet. The feeling that a whole layer of one's skin is being stripped away." Ulrike likened the silent wing to "uninterrupted rollercoaster riding," to "Kafka's penal colony."

Shortly thereafter, Ulrike was moved to another part of the prison and was allowed meetings with Gudrun Ensslin. By June of 1974, Ulrike, Gudrun, and Baader had been in what West German law calls "investigative detention" for two years. As a protest against solitary confinement and to demand the normal rights of prisoners, Ulrike called on the imprisoned members of the gang to begin a hunger strike. "We will fight them now with our lives," she said. "Better be dead than be reduced to vegetables."

This hunger strike, the gang's third, began on September 13 and was to last until February 5, 1975. Thirty-nine prisoners joined the strike, the motto of which was "Strength from Weakness." "I don't think we'll break off the hunger strike this time," said Baader. "That means that this time someone will be destroyed." It did not take long. On November 9, 1974, the thirty-three-year-old Holger Meins died in the prison hospital. The official cause of death was "cardiac arrest." Meins, who was more than six feet tall, had been forcibly fed for about five weeks. At the end he weighed about sixty-eight pounds.

The day after his death, four youths, carrying bouquets of flowers, called at the home of Judge Günter von Drenkmann. As president of West Berlin's appeals court, Drenkmann was one of the most important judges in the country. When he opened his front door, he was shot and killed. Responsibility for his "execution" was claimed by a revolutionary group called the Movement Second of June (the date Benno Ohnesorg was killed), and their public statement was signed "Kommando Holger Meins."

Besides the Baader-Meinhof gang, there were several terrorist groups operating in Germany at the time, the most violent of which was the Movement Second of June. Derisively, they called the Baader-Meinhof gang "Leninists with guns." They were younger, more efficient, and had never been involved in the student political movement. "They decided to make careers as terrorists," one of their defectors said, "because they felt impotent to change politics immediately. They saw how the courts and the lawyers worked, that they simply didn't care about the law; and they saw how Germany reacted to bombs and kidnappings, and it excited them. The society's hysterical reaction had actually produced a raison d'être for becoming a terrorist."

The Baader-Meinhof hunger strike was now entering its fourth month, and several of the younger members began to rebel, calling the strike pointless. But Baader remained firm. "If one of you eat or has eaten," Baader ordered, "he is out. There will be no extra money, no intercell memos, and your lawyers will be withdrawn." No one complained again. Finally, on February 5, 1975, Baader and Ulrike called off the strike. "Our lives are now our only weapon," said Ulrike. "It fell to me to try and persuade you to eat again, to live. I act not at the state's orders, certainly not to help solve a problem for the authorities, but to save lives. Not for a moment will I accept that the life of a terrorist is more expendable than the life of a politician."

But the hunger strikes and the long spells of solitary confinement had already taken their toll. Three months before, Baader, Gudrun, and Jan-Carl Raspe had been transferred to Stammheim Prison in Stuttgart. In December of 1974, Baader's lawyer, Klaus Croissant, arranged for Jean-Paul Sartre to visit Baader there. During his two-hour visit, Sartre recalled, Baader was very weak and held his head in his hands in order to prop it up.

Later, at a press conference, with Daniel Cohn-Bendit acting as interpreter, Sartre said there "were many lines in Baader's face. He has the face of a tortured human being." Concerning the prison conditions, Sartre said, "This is not a torture like the Nazis. It is a torture which is meant to bring on psychic disturbances." He said an attempt was being made to destroy "the psychic and intellectual capabilities of a human being . . . in order that Baader would become insane . . . or in order that he would die, as has already been witnessed here.

"Baader and the others live in a white cell," said Sartre. "In this cell they hear nothing except the steps of the guard who brings the food. For twenty-four hours round the clock, the light is left on, except for Baader's, which is turned off at eleven o'clock." Sartre said that Baader had lost between thirty-five and forty pounds. "We can say this about the politics of Baader," concluded Sartre, "the proletarians cannot follow him, but it is not the principles of Baader which are wrong, but his deeds." The German government denied all of Sartre's allegations.

On February 27, three weeks after the hunger strike ended, Peter Lorenz, the Christian Democratic candidate for mayor of West Berlin, was kidnapped in West Berlin by the Movement Second of June. The inevitable letter, listing their demands, duly arrived. The sentences passed on demonstrators who protested the death of Holger Meins should be annulled. Six imprisoned comrades, including Horst Mahler, should be released. There was to be an immediate cease-fire on the part of the police—no house searches, no arrests, no wanted posters. "If all the demands are precisely met," the letter said, "the safety of the prisoner Lorenz is guaranteed. Otherwise, a consequence as in the case of Chief Justice G. von Drenkmann is unavoidable."

The government capitulated. Five terrorists, each of whom was given a ransom of 20,000 deutsche marks, were flown to Aden. Horst Mahler refused to go. The next day, at midnight on March 4, Peter Lorenz was released unharmed in the Volkspark.

Early on April 25, nine of the Baader-Meinhof prisoners burned their papers and gathered their belongings together. "I'm going out today," one of them joked to her guard. It was a cold, rainy Thursday. At eleven-thirty that morning, six heavily armed youths forced their way into the West German embassy in Stockholm; they were members of the

Socialist Patients' Collective, those who had sworn to "strike a death blow against the sick system." They took twelve hostages and demanded the release of twenty-six political prisoners.

This time Chancellor Helmut Schmidt rejected their demands. In retaliation, the terrorists shot the German military and economic attachés. The Swedish police decided to attack with gas, but just before they rushed the embassy, a terrible explosion occurred on the third floor. Parts of the roof were blown off, and all the windows were blown out. The terrorists' arsenal had accidentally exploded, and one of them and one hostage died in the blaze. The remaining hostages were wounded but survived.

The next day, Chancellor Schmidt went before the Bundestag and said, "We didn't make it easier on ourselves yesterday, but today I am convinced that we fulfilled our duty correctly. A release of these criminals, some of whom are still awaiting their trial, would have meant an inconceivable shattering of security for all of us and for our state."

* * * * *

The Baader-Meinhof trial was scheduled to begin on May 21, 1975, in Stuttgart. It would become the most widely followed judicial proceeding in Germany since the Nuremberg trials. The trial was deemed important, and, eventually, it was decided to build a completely new courthouse, which cost, in the end, some $10 million.

The courthouse was built in a sugar-beet field near Stammheim Prison. The steel-and-concrete fortress had an antiaircraft defense built in to eliminate the possibility of attacks by helicopter. Around the building, listening devices were planted in the ground, and the interior was glutted with scores of closed-circuit television cameras. Photographing the new courthouse was strictly forbidden. The streets around Stammheim were guarded by five hundred policemen in tanks, patrol cars, and motorcycles. The five judges (there are no trials by jury in Germany), the accused, and all the witnesses would sit behind bulletproof glass security screens. There were walls and steel nets, searchlights and sharpshooters. The workers who built the courthouse were sworn to secrecy.

The trial was expected to last for two years. The 354-page indictment covered a catalog of common crimes—murder, attempted murder, robbery, theft, and arson. Because the death penalty had been abolished in Germany in 1948, most observers expected a minimum sentence of life imprisonment. Judging by the letters received at Stammheim and at newspaper offices, however, many Germans preferred that the terrorists be put up against the wall and shot. Others, however, pointed out that prominent ex-Nazis had been tried in far less oppressive surroundings. Some Nazi war-crime trials were still being held; for example, the prosecution of former SS guards at the notorious Majdanek concentration camp in Poland, where at least a million people had died in gas chambers. But none of these trials held the German imagination as Stammheim did.

Incited by the right-wing popular press, Germany was consumed by terrorism. A kind of lex Baader-Meinhof was introduced. "In the last two years, we've changed so many laws you can't imagine," said Heinrich Albertz, the ex-mayor of West Berlin. "There are laws changed every day, and you can blame it all on the government's reaction to the Baader-Meinhof gang."

The new decrees of the Bundestag stated, among other things, that defendants could not have more than three defense attorneys of their own choice; defense attorneys could be excluded from trials on *suspicion* of participating in the criminal acts of their clients; and defendants could also be excluded for "behavior contrary to the rules."

By the time the Stammheim trial began, lawyers Klaus Croissant, Hans-Christian Ströbele, and Kurt Groenewold had been excluded because they were suspected of complicity in the criminal activities of their clients. And, because of legal actions instituted against them by the state, lawyers Jörg Lang, Eberhard Becker, and Siegfried Haag had vanished into the underground. Less than a month before the trial began, the court appointed new defense attorneys for all the accused—attorneys who had not exchanged a single word with the defendants and who had not seen the fifty thousand pages of trial documents collected by the prosecution. The stage was now set for what one lawyer called "this sad and embarrassing legal circus."

Inside the windowless courtroom, the prisoners sat in a row in blue jeans and loose black sweaters. The hunger strikes and the three years of "investigative detention" had taken their toll. Baader's skin had turned yellow, and now and again he screamed abuse at the judges. Gudrun, her hair unevenly shorn, was grim and haggard, and for no apparent reason she occasionally emitted little shrieks. Ulrike wore her hair in a braid over one shoulder. She wore round spectacles and looked round the room with vague, uninterested eyes. The trial took place only three hours every day, but Ulrike complained she could not concentrate for that amount of time. It was clear that she was now completely disoriented. Occasionally, the defendants, claiming weakness, absented themselves from the court. But because of a new law, it was ruled that they could be tried in absentia, as their weakness was self-induced.

During the late summer of 1975, the long contretemps over prison conditions and the fitness of the defendants to stand trial seemed settled when four professors of medicine unanimously agreed that they were able to stand trial "only on a limited basis" and were "in need of treatment." Since the court had appointed the four medical experts, it could not dismiss them as sympathizers. And their judgment had come none too soon. Baader's ears were buzzing, and he had lost forty-six pounds. Ulrike had difficulties with articulation and concentration and no longer recognized her surroundings. She had lost twenty-eight pounds. Gudrun's blood pressure had dropped alarmingly, and she too had lost nearly thirty pounds.

But medical opinion now confirmed what the defense lawyers had claimed for years—that the prison conditions were endangering the prisoners' lives. Even so, after postponing the trial for a week, Judge Prinzing declared that the trial would proceed without the defendants. A few days later, in the face of overwhelming criticism, the judge reversed himself. But by this time, the court's impartiality was no longer credible.

* * * * *

On Saturday, May 8, 1976, after nearly forty-four months in prison, Ulrike Meinhof appeared headed for another routine day. In the morning and again in the early afternoon, Ulrike, Gudrun, Jan-Carl Raspe, and Baader met and discussed "identity and consciousness." Ulrike skipped the exercise period because, as Gudrun recalled, it was too hot for her. Ulrike worked at her typewriter during most of the evening; shortly before ten o'clock, Gudrun and Ulrike visited each other and, according to Gudrun, "had a good time."

The next morning at seven-thirty-four, when the duty officer unlocked her cell, Ulrike Meinhof was dead. She was hanging from a crossbar of her window, her body kneeling on a chair, which had toppled over, her head drooping, her eyes open wide and popping. There was no farewell note.

And the interminable trial, now in its twenty-second month, went on. In March of 1977, defense lawyers discovered that government security services had been bugging private conversations between them and their clients. The state government of Baden-Württemberg admitted to the bugging operations but insisted they had been conducted for reasons of security. The judge and the public prosecutor claimed that they had not been privy to the contents of the tapes and that, therefore, the bugging had nothing to do with the trial. And the court claimed that because it had not sanctioned the buggings, the trial should not be abandoned. This decision was upheld. Earlier, for reasons of bias, Judge Prinzing had been forced to step down. He was promptly replaced by another and presumably less prejudiced colleague. In retaliation for this and the buggings, Baader initiated another hunger strike and his lawyers decided to boycott the trial. By now, even the insatiable German public had become bored with the proceedings.

There was to be one further interruption. On April 7, 1977, Siegfried Buback, West Germany's federal attorney general and the man in charge of the entire Baader-Meinhof prosecution, was murdered. While driving to work, two youths on a Suzuki motorcycle riddled Buback's Mercedes with machine-gun fire, killing Buback, his driver, and a bodyguard. The RAF claimed responsibility for the murders the next day. Their open letter was signed "Kommando Ulrike Meinhof." It now seemed there was a new group of terrorists, a so-called third generation, in operation. The members of this group were, on average, some six years younger than the original Baader-Meinhof members and came from even more affluent backgrounds. And despite their shrill political posturings, they were little more than a death squad with a distaste for the prosperous consumerism in what Gudrun Ensslin called the "Raspberry Reich."

Three weeks later, in Stuttgart, the Stammheim trial finally came to an end. Andreas Baader, Gudrun Ensslin, and Jan-Carl Raspe were sentenced to three times life imprisonment plus fifteen years. They were convicted of murdering four American servicemen, of complicity in thirty-four attempted murders, and of forming a criminal association.

And that was that. During the early summer months even the Springer press found other things to fill its pages. Germany, as *Die Welt* assured its readers in mid-July, had, at last, returned to normal. But on Saturday, July 30, Dr. Jürgen Ponto, the head of the Dresdner Bank, Germany's second largest, was murdered in his Frankfurt home. Among his killers was twenty-six-year-old Susanne Albrecht—one of his daughter's best friends and his own goddaughter. A member of the RAF's third generation, she had performed her mission with a bunch of red roses in her hand. Explaining her actions, she said that she "was tired of gorging herself on champagne and caviar."

At Dr. Ponto's memorial service in Frankfurt, many of West Germany's industrial leaders were in attendance. When the service ended, Dr. Hanns Martin Schleyer, the head of the German Industries Federation, turned to friends and said, "The next victim of terrorism is almost certainly in this room now." Glumly, his friends agreed.

*****

At seven-thirty the next morning, the guards on the seventh floor of Stammheim Prison unlocked Andreas Baader's cell, number 719-720. The group leader was lying on his back on the floor in a pool of blood, his sunglasses hanging from his left ear. A bloody bullet was next to his body, another in the mattress, and a third near his feet. He was dead. He had been shot in the nape of the neck with a Heckler & Koch 7.62-mm pistol; the pistol lay next to him.

Gudrun Ensslin was also dead. She was found hanging from one of the vertical bars in her cell window, a piece of electrical wire from her record player wrapped twice around her neck. Jan-Carl Raspe had been shot just above the right ear; he was still alive but died in the hospital before noon. Another terrorist, Irmgard Möller, had been stabbed several times in the chest; she too was taken to the hospital, where she survived. When Chancellor Schmidt heard of the deaths, he turned to an aide and shouted, "But that's impossible." An immediate investigation was ordered. Hans Nusser, the prison's chief of security, was fired, and Dr. Traugott Bender, the head of the Justice Department in Baden-Württemberg, who had called Stammheim the safest prison in the world, was forced to resign.

It was most odd. For the past six weeks, the four prisoners had been forbidden visitors, including their lawyers; they had been denied access to newspapers, personal mail, radios, and television sets. Their cells had been thoroughly searched almost every day. Security had been very strict. And yet, three terrorists had died.

The same day, a team of pathologists were brought in from Switzerland, Austria, and Belgium to help conduct the autopsies. This unusual step was taken to forestall any suggestion that the three terrorists had been murdered. Concluding their examination, the three doctors agreed that Baader, Gudrun, and Raspe had committed suicide. Meanwhile, prison authorities had ripped the seventh floor of Stammheim apart. According to a government report, two secret holes were found in the walls of the cells of Baader and Raspe. One was large enough to hold a pistol. The second contained elements of a communications system—batteries, wires, sockets—which, when connected to the cell's thermostat, formed an efficient telegraph over which the two terrorists could signal each other in code. Two pistols and 670 grams of dynamite were found in another cell, and 9.5 ounces of ammonium nitrate were found in another.

Following their deaths, Chancellor Helmut Schmidt said, "Words fail me in the face of this vicious circle of violence and death." Schmidt believed that the three terrorists had committed suicide not out of repentance but "as a beacon for their comrades still at large." The West German president Walter Scheel went on national television to plead with the abductors of Hanns Martin Schleyer. "The whole world, East and West, is against you," he said. "I appeal to you to set your hostage free."

But Schleyer was already dead. Later that day, October 19, a terrorist message was received by the left-wing Paris daily *Liberation*. "After 43 days," it said, "we have put an end to the miserable and corrupt existence of Schleyer. His death does not measure up to our grief and anger over the slaughter at Mogadishu and at Stammheim. Schmidt can take delivery in the Rue Charles Peguy in Mulhouse. The battle has just begun."

The police found Schleyer's body in the trunk of a green Audi in the Alsatian town of Mulhouse, some ten miles from the German border. Schleyer was wearing the same clothes in which he had been kidnapped some six weeks before. He had been shot just once in the head.

On October 27, Andreas Baader, Gudrun Ensslin, and Jan-Carl Raspe were buried in a common grave in Stuttgart's tiny Waldfriedhof cemetery. The local citizens complained bitterly that the three terrorists were being buried in a cemetery at all. Some demanded that their bodies be dumped in the town sewage plant. But Manfred Rommel, Stuttgart's mayor, said, "I refuse to accept that there are first- and second-class cemeteries. All enmity should cease after death."

Nearly a thousand policemen with machine pistols ringed the little cemetery. As the three plain pine boxes were carried through the crowd, there was a great shout of defiance. Masked and hooded demonstrators flourished posters: GUDRUN, ANDREAS, AND JAN WERE TORTURED AND MURDERED AT STAMMHEIM. THE FIGHT GOES ON. There were nearly a thousand mourners, many of whom wore Arab kaffiyehs. As the boxes were lowered into the grave, the mourners raised their fists in salute. "It must come as a shock to the government," a professor said, "that all these young people showed up at the grave. That's no small demonstration of faith."

Baader would have been pleased with that. He had not wished to die; death lacked panache. One could not brag about it. But this would have been an acceptable compromise. From the very beginning, when he and Gudrun made their pact—"*auf Leben und Tod*," for life and death—they had talked of sharing "a beautiful death together, a martyrdom." In Stammheim for the remainder of their lives, there could have been no other way. And so, for Baader, suicide (disguised as murder) may have been the brightest martyrdom.

Andreas Baader was a peculiarly German aberration. Because the authorities failed to treat them as common criminals, the Baader-Meinhof gang were allowed to seize a gruesome power over Germany. Goaded by the right-wing press, the gang convinced the government to decree new, illiberal laws to deal with them. By considerably reducing the civil liberties of all German citizens, the German state, as Pastor Paul Oestreicher has said, allowed Baader and his comrades to push it a little nearer to being the repressive system they always believed it to be.

There are two distinct and separate strains in the German character—one, imaginative, romantic, tyrannic even; the other, docile, sober, orderly. They have never been able to reconcile them. Andreas Baader was a symptom of that schizophrenia. He was not the cause. He reflected it. He flaunted it. He was excised. But the schism remains. It produces discord, disorder. As Otto Schily, one of the most distinguished civil rights lawyers in West Germany, said, "You can put your house in order ad infinitum by sweeping terrorism *and* the government's repressive policies under the carpet. It won't help. There is a new fascism growing in Germany—and the old fascism is not yet dead."

When Bradshaw died, Lee Eisenberg, Esquire*'s editor in chief, said this piece "was, and remains, one of the most impressive pieces of the '70s."*

Savage Skulls

Esquire, June 1977

"The last writer came up here . . . wanted to go and live with them for a couple of days—and that was the last we ever saw of him."

The dumb name his old lady laid on him was Renaldo Garcia. Renaldo Garcia? It sounded like the name of a goddamn garbage collector. It had no jive; it was ordinary. He hated that name. When he joined the Savage Skulls, he began calling himself Snoopy. All the dudes in the gang had street names, names like Batman and Bam Boo, Popeye, Nazi, Speed. "Like that, man," said Snoopy. "I don't know what their real names was."

His fourteen-year-old older brother was called Snoopy also. But young Snoopy really liked the name and so the rest of the Skulls called him Snoopy Two. It was a good arrangement and no one confused the brothers. Two years later, in a rumble down on Fox Street, one of the dudes in the Spanish Mafia stuck a shotgun in Snoopy Two's brother's face and pulled the trigger. After that, everyone called him Snoopy. A few days after the funeral, Snoopy bought some needles and India ink and tattooed his brother's tombstone on his arm. It took him three days and it hurt like hell.

It was during my third or fourth day in the ghetto that I encountered Snoopy and we were introduced. Which is to say, the cops pointed him out to me because he was between gangs at the time and likely to be hospitable. As it turned out, Snoopy was almost affable; he was on the straight and narrow, he said, and had nothing much to hide.

A small, husky Puerto Rican, Snoopy was now nearly seventeen. He was a cocky kid, given to boast, and had a tedious habit of insisting he was always telling the truth. He wore jeans, a denim waistcoat covered with dozens of badges, a red-and-black bandanna around his head to keep his pitch-black hair from his eyes, and heavy black jackboots with silver studs in the heels. In his right ear he wore a small gold hoop in the center of which dangled a golden cross. Sometimes he carried a heavy walking stick. I often gave Snoopy a lift to mid-Manhattan, where he had taken a job as a dishwasher. But most of the time we hung around the ghetto, talking at his girlfriend's apartment or playing pinball at the candy store. Snoopy was a pinball wizard and claimed to have broken the world record several times.

Snoopy's view of the world was pleasantly parochial. He often bragged that there was *nothing* he hadn't done, except murder, maybe. He'd done drugs, all kinds of drugs, a little mugging and some burglary. He knew about knives, about guns, the different calibers, where to buy them and where to sell them profitably and quickly. He knew about cars; he'd stolen Cadillacs. He'd gang-banged—"chicken-plucking," he called it—and copped a rape or two. "Hey, I ain't even *seventeen*," he said, "and I ain't never done time, man, not a lousy day. I'm clean as a cat's ass. And that's the truth." On the street, Snoopy was considered one stand-up dude.

Snoopy was born in the old Lincoln Hospital. His parents had drifted to the South Bronx from Puerto Rico in the late '50s, moving into a four-room apartment on 161st Street near Intervale Avenue. He never knew his father, who vanished one night when Snoopy was five. But Snoopy figured the old man had spent a lot of time in bed, since he had four brothers and five sisters.

"That dump was a rathole," he said. "Them four rooms wasn't big enough for *us* and that ain't countin' the goddamn rats. There were a gang of rats around. All I know is my old lady busted her ass in a laundry in Manhattan, pressin' white boys' pants and screamin' for me to stay off the streets at nights. What a stinkin' rathole that was." Snoopy picked up most of his English in the street and perfected it at Intermediate School 52. At thirteen, he left school for good, and a month or two later he ran away from home.

Snoopy was already a member of the Savage Skulls. His older brother, the one who had been killed, had been tight with Popeye, the Supreme Prez of the Skulls. As a favor, Popeye let Snoopy join the Young Skulls. The next day, Snoopy scored a black leather jacket and one of his sisters sewed YOUNG SKULLS in large white letters on the back. Snoopy flew his colors everywhere.

He became a Savage Skull at fourteen. During his initiation ceremony at the old clubhouse on Fox Street, the other Skulls hung him upside down from a pipe and beat him with their fists and baseball bats. But Snoopy never said a word. He didn't even cry. "I had *heart*, man," he said. "They broke my goddamn arm, you know, but I got me some real respect after that."

Throughout the early '70s, the Savage Skulls were the most notorious gang in New York. There were other gangs—the Tomahawks and the Crazy Homicides in Brooklyn, the Eagles and the Ghost Shadows in Chinatown, the Hell's Angels in the East Village, and the Savage Samurai in East Harlem. The main Bronx gangs were the Dirty Dozen, the Bachelors, the Ching-a-Lings, and the Black Spades, but the Savage Skulls were the oldest and most powerful of all. They still maintain three divisions in the Bronx and one in Brooklyn. The Bronx Youth Gang Unit estimates the Skulls have 250 to 300 members in the Bronx today. They are well organized and heavily armed. They operate in the Forty-First and Forty-Fourth Precincts, moving continually from one location to another in order to avoid police.

"The Skulls used to brag a lot," said Snoopy. "They was never anything more than a dirt gang, you know, rapin' and sniffin' glue. But they had them a pretty rep. Man, they was *mean*. They really stuck it to you."

As a Young Skull, Snoopy used to hear the stories. He was too young to be involved himself, but he knew all the stories by heart. Everybody in the street knew the stories and sometimes they were even in the newspapers. Like the junkie massacre in 1971. "A few of the dudes," said Snoopy, "they moved into one of them abandoned buildings the junkies used as shooting galleries, you know, and they cut one of 'em up real bad and wasted another one, and then they threw a couple of them dopeheads off the goddamn roof. Just airmailed 'em into the blue.

"The Skulls had the bodega owners around Southern Boulevard in the palms of their hands. Those dudes had to sign contracts, man, saying they agreed to be protected for fifty a week or something. Those bodega owners *knew*. They paid up or the bodega got torched. And most of 'em never said a goddamn word and there was nothin' the Man could do about it.

"Another time, these two girls, two sisters on the way to the doctor or the dentist or something, was taken by some of the girl Skulls over to the clubhouse, you know? The girls chopped off the sisters' hair and knocked 'em around and then the guys ran a train on 'em—got it on with 'em. That time, the Man pulled five or six of 'em in for kidnapping, I think, for kidnapping and rape, and they did a little time upstate.

"Then there was this dude in the Spanish Mafia. Don't know what he did exactly, chopped down one of the Skulls or something, for no reason. So the Skulls tied the mothafucka up in an empty basement on Longwood and put a starved German shepherd in the room. That dog had worked up an appetite, you know. Another time, they mugged this old lady. She'd been gettin' on their case, I guess, talkin' to the Man, so they mugged her, took her to her apartment, beat her, and poured rubbing alcohol in her wounds. Locked her up in the closet, but her neighbors must've heard her, 'cause they got her out before she died. Those Skulls were something, man. *Mean*."

Snoopy took no particular pleasure in reciting the horror tales. They were a part of his past, just stories, commonplace. Besides, he was sick and tired of the gangs, of running and hiding and telling the cops he was a real good guy. "They're a real low-class gang," he said. "Them Skulls are crazy and I ain't takin' the count for no man." Just after his sixteenth birthday, Snoopy decided to start his own gang. He had not settled on a name, but one thing was sure: his gang was getting into motorbikes. Big ones, big black

"Fort Apache is the underside of the Bronx, a benighted precinct that only becomes visible, the cops like to say, when someone kicks over the stone."

Harley-Davidsons. It was going to be a stand-up gang, with heart and with what Snoopy imagined to be style.

In the meantime, Snoopy just hung out. He worked part time, hit the pinball in the candy store, watched the trick box now and then, shot a little stick in the poolroom, got it on with his girlfriend, avoided the cops, got high, and slept a lot. There was nothing else to do in the ghetto.

*****

I spent some five weeks in the South Bronx, much of it in the company of three plainclothes cops. They were an amiable trio, embittered by their lot but more or less immune to it, and they had the tough, indifferent air of cops who have spent their careers in the ghetto.

The Forty-First Precinct is known as Fort Apache because of an attack on the station house by a band of bellicose residents. Fort Apache is the underside of the Bronx, a benighted precinct that only becomes visible, the cops like to say, when someone kicks over the stone. It has one of the highest crime rates in the world. On Fox Street, the odds of living to old age are said to be nine-to-one against. One of the cops read that figure somewhere and had been surprised the odds were so favorable.

The three cops worked out of Fort Apache's Anti-Crime Unit, patrolling the precinct's sixty miles of streets. Artie Murray, a short, balding man of thirty-nine, had been with the Anti-Crime Unit since its inception in 1972, but he had been in Fort Apache since 1968. His partners were Jack Marchesi, who was thirty, and Billy Coyle, who was twenty-nine. Coyle thought himself particularly ill-favored; he had been dispatched to Fort Apache right out of the Police Academy, the only member of his class to be rewarded in that way.

The three men were concerned with street crime, anything to do with the street, within the precinct's two and a half square miles. They locked up about 150 people a year, but they could be involved with as many as five hundred crimes a year, or about two a day. In 1975 the team was rated one of the best

HOFF
BEVERA
GESTAPO
NEW YORK

anti-crime units in the city and was commended by the police department. “We got an ‘attaboys,’” said Billy Coyle. “In other words, we were told to keep up the good work.”

Fort Apache’s station house is one of only three buildings in that particular block of Simpson Street that are still intact. Of all the precincts in the city, Fort Apache has been the most violent. But because of the widespread burning and the rapid exodus of the neighborhood’s population, the level of crime has fallen in the last two years. Fox Street, once thought to be the street with the densest population in the country, is burned out and practically deserted now; 95 percent of its population is gone. The Forty-First Precinct still has a population of some 170,000, predominantly Puerto Rican and black; 40,000 are on welfare.

Murray, Marchesi, and Coyle normally patrol the ghetto’s streets in an unmarked GM van. For emergencies, there is a red flashing light on the floor and the police radio crackles continually. From the street, the vehicle looks like just another private van. The three men split the driving. During the last two years, their job has become somewhat monotonous. “We used to get fifty, sixty jobs a tour,” said Billy Coyle. “Now, it’s a lot closer to twenty. The population isn’t here anymore. The activity has almost disappeared.”

Even so, two precinct cops have been killed in that time and many others wounded. Last year, less than fifty yards from the station house, Billy Coyle was mugged by a man with a knife. Both Coyle and Murray have been shot at, occasionally by snipers, but have not been hit. It is still a dangerous area, and the plainclothes cops are armed, often with two guns. Artie Murray wears the usual .38 Police Special on his hip and a .38 five-shot Smith & Wesson Chief strapped just above his right ankle. The gun, one is told, will stop a buffalo at thirty paces.

Except for a quick lunch and a coffee break at Moshman’s Bakery, the three men spend their eight-hour tour of duty taking calls on the radio and talking among themselves as they cruise the derelict streets. Having a writer in the van was an unexpected and passable diversion and they made the most of it.

Particularly Billy Coyle. Coyle has a wry, dispassionate sense of humor. The dingy world of Fort Apache does not really interest him anymore; it contains no real surprises; it is merely grotesque and sad and funny. Coyle's laughter is his first line of defense and it always sounded like a necessary precaution.

On our first day together, Coyle turned around in the van and said, "You know, the last writer came up here—wasn't it a year or so ago, Artie?—we took him out and introduced him to the neighborhood and to a few of the Savage Skulls. I remember all those cameras and notebooks he had. Well, one afternoon, we left him with the Skulls—he wanted to go and live with them for a couple of days—and that was the last we ever saw of him. No writer, no article. That was about a year ago." The cops laughed. Billy Coyle lighted a Marlboro. "You think I'm kidding, don't you?" he said.

In spite of the dozens of days I was to spend in Fort Apache, I can still recall that first day with an odd and startling clarity. We drove through the streets: nearly every block contained an empty lot or two; the buildings had been burned and razed and the vacant lots were filled with mounds of rubble, garbage, bricks, and broken glass. On the main streets, between the few occupied buildings, there were gutted bodegas, shops, and grocery stores, their scorched and twisted signs still intact. In block after block, the burned-out buildings leaned like empty coffins against the more substantial sky. The cratered streets were filled with crippled mongrel dogs, limping down the gutters or rooting in the vacant lots. In the middle of Kelly Street, a black beggar pushed a grocery cart piled high with wood and copper piping. Dirty children crawled through abandoned cars, stripping them of seats and steering wheels. On a bridge above the railway tracks, a long, narrow sign requested: HELP KEEP HUNTS POINT CLEAN. Someone had added: AND SAFE, but most of the message had been obscured by coarse graffiti.

When Artie Murray had come to Fort Apache nine years ago, an empty lot was a rarity. There were twenty-six synagogues in the precinct then; now there are two. Billy Coyle points out that in the areas around Fox Street the rats are as big as tomcats. It has been a terrible winter, and the ice, aided by gushing fire hydrants, has piled high in the gutters. Here and there, on street corners and in empty doorways, fires flare up from garbage cans. A heavy haze hangs in the air. It is an evil place, dead but unburied. It is less than a hundred blocks north of Tiffany's.

Driving down Longwood Avenue, Billy Coyle suddenly pulled the van to the curb. "There's Ali," he said, "there, going into the candy store." Ali was not unmemorable. He wore a dirty yellow Arab headdress that flowed around his black leather jacket. One of the older Savage Skulls, Ali was half demented from sniffing glue. "Most of his brain is gone," said Coyle. "He's in there reading a paper, see?"

"He reads?" said Artie Murray.

A few doors down the street is the Bella Capri Pizzeria and Donut Shop. Two years ago, after the Skulls had ransacked the shop, its owner threatened to testify against them in court. The next day, Ali walked into the pizzeria, picked up the owner's cat by the tail, and gutted it with his knife. "This is what will happen to you if you testify," said Ali. Dropping the dead cat to the floor, Ali stuffed some doughnuts in his pockets and walked out the door. The owner did not testify.

"That's what you're up against here," said Coyle. "That Ali, he's a snake, a syphilitic snake. He's got open sores all over his body. He's the only Savage Skull who doesn't get laid in the gang bangs."

"You won't see too much action up here this time of the year," said Marchesi. "It's pretty quiet now because it's winter. Those kids hate the cold. They hibernate. You should be here in the summer when they hit the streets in force."

"The greatest prevention of crime is mother nature," said Murray. "Storms, the snow, the cold. Result? No crime."

Driving through the intersection of Fox, Simpson, and Barretto Streets, Coyle stopped the van. "This location is called the drugstore," he said. "There isn't a drug in the world you can't get right here." At night, the dealers light fires in garbage cans, and after midnight the cars with New York, New Jersey, and Connecticut license plates pull up and negotiate. At dusk, the dealers can be seen in the doorways of the abandoned buildings, smoking and awaiting the first arrivals. Because of citywide cutbacks, the police don't have the manpower to deal with the problem, and, besides, the official policy currently is to concentrate on the big busts and leave the street dealers alone.

Going down Intervale, the van slowed. The street, rutted with deep holes and pools of melted ice, was almost impassable. The burned-out buildings stretched as far as the eye could see and there was no sign of habitation anywhere. "Do you know where I'd like to go?" said Coyle, looking around the deserted city. "I'd like to go to Jackson Hole, Wyoming."

He grinned. Murray and Marchesi laughed.

"I've never been there," he said, "but I've seen photographs. I've got them in my locker at the station house. I like the sound of Jackson Hole. Trouble is I don't think there's much call for three anti-crime cops in Jackson Hole, Wyoming."

The van passed beneath Bruckner Boulevard and out into the comparatively peaceful Hunts Point market area. Coyle calls Bruckner Boulevard the DMZ. Standing like hitchhikers along the market's main thoroughfare are groups of gaudy prostitutes. Most of the girls are run by Heavy, the most successful pimp in the South Bronx. Heavy, an amiable black man with a weakness for diamonds and long, low limousines, is usually to be found across the road in his station wagon; he is always accompanied by two bodyguards, Pitman and Stan. Heavy has controlled this corner since 1969. This winter, he is running thirteen girls—seven in Hunts Point, three in Manhattan, one who is on pregnancy leave, and two others who do a little babysitting and light housework at his home in Mount Vernon. Heavy, in fact, owns two homes in what he likes to call "beautiful, congenial Westchester."

Some 150 to 200 tractor-trailer trucks drive into the market every day, and Heavy's more seductive girls, such as Brandy, can earn $300 a day. Baby, his star white girl, can earn as much as $500 a day on a slightly longer shift. Heavy pays the girls' medical expenses and all their fines. When the girls are picked up by the "pussy squad," as they frequently are, they are usually fined between $50 and $200. "I run a class operation," said Heavy. "None of my girls get *cheap* fines."

The girls live in Heavy's eleven-bedroom Mount Vernon home and he gives them "twenty-four-hour supervision around the clock. All my girls own their own cars," said Heavy. "They don't use drugs and none of them have done time. I stay on top because of my father image. I don't know whether my girls are men, women, chicken, or child, but I assume they're girls and I'm their daddy. I treat 'em sweet and good. I'll tell you, if I ever get to the promised land, it'll be because of what I do for my girls."

"What percentage do you take?" I asked.

"Percentage?" Heavy grinned and slapped Stan, the stickup man, on the knee. Stan smiled uncomfortably. "What do you mean, percentage? I take 100 percent, man. I take it *all*. There's an old saying in this business: Never leave a girl a dime; she might take it and call Mamma." Heavy sighed. He liked to imply that it wasn't easy for a young man to make his way in the world. "You see, there's so much crime up here, the dealers, the muggers, those goddamn gangs, but this is a victimless crime. *Victimless*. No victim. The johns are looking for love and I give 'em gratification. It's like you and me shaking hands, flesh touching flesh, no emotion, no more than that. You dig? It's what they call free enterprise."

A few years ago, Heavy drove a big white Cadillac. It had a television and a telephone. But he gave it up because "in a place like this, I didn't want to corrupt the morals of the young." But he changed his mind, and recently he purchased an $18,000 gold Lincoln Continental with a sliding-glass roof. "They expect it from me, you know," he said. "It goes with the territory."

Heavy works the girls in shifts around the clock. At dusk, the girls gather wood and stack it in high piles along the thoroughfare. Around midnight, the piles are set afire to keep the girls warm and so the johns can see the girls more easily.

Two blocks away, another group of girls stands along the road. They are not as well dressed as

Heavy's girls and not as many tractor-trailers pass that way. Billy Coyle waved as we drove by and the girls, almost in unison, waved and tittered among themselves. "See them girls?" said Coyle. "Last year, we picked up twenty-one of them one night and eighteen of them were guys."

*****

Fat Louis Soto is probably the most notorious figure in Fort Apache. He is the Supreme President of the Dirty Dozen, one of the biggest gangs of the early '70s; but due to police raids and intergang wars, the Dirty Dozen had been cut to fewer than ten members. Fat Louis was now twenty-eight and devoted most of his time to stealing cars. It is said that, excepting one police expert, Fat Louis knew more about doctoring stolen cars than anyone else in the city. Fat Louis claimed he did not have a gang and he called his clique the Dirty Dozen Racing Team. I had heard a lot about Fat Louis, most of it bad, and I wanted to meet him. Artie Murray and Billy Coyle agreed to introduce us.

"Take what he says with a grain of salt," said Artie Murray as we drove away from the station house. "He'll tell you he's not a bad guy, it's the rest of them that are bad guys, that he's into stealing cars and not much of that either, that he runs a garage and behaves himself. But he's done his share of raping and killing. You'd better believe it."

Fat Louis lived with his wife and child above his garage on the corner of Fox and Leggett. His arrest sheet showed more than thirty arrests for stealing cars. "The last time Fat Louis was in jail," said Billy Coyle, "they fixed his teeth and put him on a diet. Three weeks after he gets out, all his teeth are gone again and he's pushing three hundred pounds. And wait'll you see his wife." He and Artie Murray laughed. "She's a dead ringer for Fat Louis."

We pulled up to Fat Louis's apartment building. Taking out their guns, Murray and Coyle moved into the darkened hallway. Assuring themselves that it was clear, they motioned for me to follow. Louis's flat was on the first floor, and rather tentatively, I knocked. After almost two minutes, a chubby woman with no teeth opened the door. Behind her, the floor of the apartment was strewn with bits of newspaper and cardboard. At her feet, two mongrel dogs copulated jerkily. Fat Louis was summoned and soon appeared, a large, unsmiling man with no teeth. He had the cool and crafty look of a successful opportunist. He wore a butterscotch-colored leather coat. We went down to the waiting van.

Coyle explained who I was and what I was doing in Fort Apache. Fat Louis looked out the window. He appeared to be bored. Now and then he would smile, almost painfully. "Now, Louis," Murray explained, "he's a nice guy, you understand? We want you to handle him real well."

"Sure, man," said Fat Louis. "How do you want me to handle him?"

"We want him back," said Coyle.

Fat Louis and the two cops laughed. It was all very funny. Fat Louis shrugged and said I could come and see him in the morning. "But not before eleven, man. I work nights."

"You got yourself a job?" said Murray.

"Yeah, a *steady* job. With lots of opportunity."

"He's ambitious, Billy," said Murray. "I think he'll go far."

"As far as Rikers Island," said Coyle.

Fat Louis was not at home the next morning and no one, neither his wife nor his gang, knew where he was. Two days later, his wife admitted he had gone into Prospect Hospital. Fat Louis, it seemed, suffered from bleeding ulcers. "Makes sense," said Billy Coyle. "He's had a lot to worry about."

But there was no Louis Soto registered at Prospect Hospital. Only later did I discover that he had registered under a pseudonym.

I found Fat Louis, who had registered as Luiz Sanchez, in his bed on a third-floor ward. There were six other patients in the room. "When you check into the hospital," he explained, "it pays to come in on an alias. You gotta take precautions."

Murray and Coyle had explained that Fat Louis was not a well-loved man in the neighborhood.

The cops had often warned me that the real danger of consorting with Fat Louis was not Fat Louis himself but his enemies, who might take potshots at him at any time. On more than one occasion, gang members had strolled into hospital wards and blown away the opposition. Fat Louis had not lived to twenty-eight without taking extravagant precautions.

But he did not seem especially concerned. "R.C. won't fuck with me," he said, shifting his bulk in the bed. "I can handle myself and the dude knows it. What's he gonna do? Send that punk gestapo around?" He laughed. "Besides, the Dirty Dozen ain't dead yet. We can still take good care a things if we have to."

As we talked, other members of his gang came in and out of the ward. Fat Louis showed me the ugly scar from his ulcer operation and the scar from an old bullet wound in his leg. Fat Louis would not discuss his future plans. The future meant very little to him. Only tomorrow counted. "Got to get outta here first," he said, "then we got to get a lot together. The neighborhood's on the slide, the Skulls are getting outta hand. I ain't getting any younger and we got to get a *grip* on things." Fat Louis laughed. He told me to stop by the house when he got out and his old lady would cook me a real cool meal.

Murray and Coyle were waiting outside in the van. As I got in, Tiger and Slick, the two top honchos in Fat Louis's gang, walked into the hospital. They wore denim jackets and jeans and white tennis shoes. "A lot of the gang kids wear sneakers," said Coyle. "When they're fleeing, they're *flying*. We call them felony shoes."

Driving back on Bruckner Boulevard to the station house, Billy Coyle spotted a large camper some fifty yards down the road. "I'll lay you odds the man driving that camper's got a big smile on his face," he said.

Artie Murray asked him how he knew.

"Because he's heading west, Artie, on his vacation."

"To Jackson Hole?"

"Yeah," said Coyle, "to one or another of them goddamn towns."

This article inspired filmmaker Gary Weiss, then making short films for Saturday Night Live, *to make a documentary for NBC News about the Savage Skulls and Bronx street gangs. Although it was too raw for broadcast,* 80 Blocks from Tiffany's *(1979) developed a cult following and was eventually released on DVD in 2010. It is worth tracking down.*

The Death of a Reporter Who Knew Too Much

New York, September 6, 1976

"It's hard enough coping with the fact that your husband was murdered without thinking it was all in vain."

Don Bolles wanted to be the best reporter in Arizona. That was all he wanted. It had always been enough for him. By all accounts he was an old-fashioned man, steeped in such Calvinist beliefs as industry, thrift, and piety. He would not have had much in common with what are known in Arizona as "eastern slickers." Above all, Bolles was a shrewd reporter, a writer of cautionary tales—tales to which few of his readers paid much attention. Alive, he was engaging, but taciturn, difficult to know. Dead, he is the sort of man of whom others now say, "Oh, he wasn't like that at all, you know." Suffice it to say that Don Bolles lived for little more than his work and his family. He did not die satisfactorily.

Bolles had been an investigative reporter for fourteen years and the term always amused him, particularly after it had come into fashion, since it seemed to him redundant. He prided himself on his accuracy. It was a quality on which he placed the highest value. Since going to work for the *Arizona Republic* in 1962, Bolles had rapidly become the state's leading journalist.

The *Arizona Republic* is published by Nina Pulliam, the widow of Eugene C. Pulliam, who purchased the paper in 1946. It has a daily circulation of 235,000. A conservative paper, the *Republic* has many of the hallmarks of provincial journalism. Its front page carries "Today's Chuckle" and "Today's Prayer." In the lobby of the *Republic-Gazette* building in downtown Phoenix, there is a bronze plaque that quotes Eugene Pulliam. It says IF YOU FORGET EVERYTHING

ELSE I'VE SAID, REMEMBER THIS—AMERICA IS GREAT ONLY BECAUSE AMERICA IS FREE. Arizona is a state in which such words are still capable of stirring occasional passions.

Over the years, Don Bolles wrote hundreds of stories attacking the erosion of those freedoms in the "Valley of the Sun." In 1965 he was nominated for the Pulitzer Prize for his investigations of bribery and other irregularities in the state tax and corporation commissions. In 1967 a Bolles series was the *Republic*'s first major effort to expose land fraud in Arizona. During the late '60s and early '70s he wrote extensive pieces on Emprise Corporation, the Buffalo-based firm that, along with the Funk family of Arizona, controlled the state's dog tracks. In 1974 Bolles received the Arizona Press Club award for a series exposing a conflict-of-interest scandal in the Arizona Legislature. He was perhaps best known for revealing the infiltration of Mafia figures into Arizona in a series entitled "The Menace Within."

Don Bolles had always wanted to be a newspaperman. The son of an Associated Press reporter, he was born in Milwaukee in 1928. He attended high school in New Jersey and graduated from Beloit College in Wisconsin in 1950. Following a stint with the army in Korea, he worked for nine years as a sports editor and rewrite man for the Associated Press. At the *Republic*, rarely a week went by when Bolles and such colleagues as Al Sitter, Bernie Wynn, and Paul Dean did not attack the spreading network of crime and corruption that had mushroomed in Arizona since the war. But toward the end of 1975, Bolles began to lose his taste for battle. Because of his articles, his life had been threatened many times. In fact, the lives of all the *Republic*'s leading reporters were threatened repeatedly. Paul Dean once received a piece of chemically impregnated paper that said, "Put this under water and see what will happen to you." When Dean put it under a faucet, the paper burst into flame. Bolles's wife, Rosalie, often pleaded with him to take their name from the Phoenix telephone directory and Bolles had always said, "No, people have to be able to get hold of me." Only late last year did Bolles finally accede to her request.

In the months before he died, Bolles had taken to referring to a policy of "official gutlessness in town." He told his colleague Bernie Wynn that "no one out there cares." He had grown tired of threats. He had grown tired of public apathy and official incompetence. He had grown tired. Late last year, he asked Bernie Wynn if he could rejoin Wynn's capitol bureau and report on the legislature. And when asked if he intended to continue his investigative reporting at some future date, Bolles replied, "No, no more of that. Nothing ever happens."

Bob Early, the *Republic*'s city editor, is very proud of his paper's investigative work, particularly in the areas of consumer fraud and governmental corruption. A tough editor, he has been known to tell young reporters, "Kid, I want you to go out and talk to that guy and come back with an objective story that'll hang the son of a bitch."

Early sympathized with Bolles's frustrations. "I've seen the same thing happen to many reporters in many places. After about ten years of investigative work it gets to you and you need a break. Don worked *all* the time, including weekends. Investigative reporting has been glamorized recently. There's nothing glamorous about it. It's little more than patient drudgery. You get untold harassment from lawyers, a lot of nasty rumors spring up around you, and you get enormous pressure from your family. Add to that the frustration of nothing ever happening and all of a sudden you want to lead a normal life."

Thus, when the Arizona State Senate reconvened last January, Don Bolles occupied himself with reporting on the capitol and democratic politics. Beyond his journalism, he devoted himself to church work, to occasional tennis and daily jogging, and to his family. Bolles and his wife had seven children—four from his previous marriage, two from hers, and a six-year-old daughter, Diane, who had been born deaf. At the age of forty-seven, Bolles had wearied of kicking against the pricks, of battling an intractable system, but in the back of his mind he thought he would write a book about Arizona one day—a state, in his view, which promised everything and, for the most part, failed to deliver.

"Bolles got into his car. Reversing a few yards, he cocked the front wheels slightly to the right in order to leave the parking lot. It was then that the explosion occurred."

* * * * *

On Thursday morning, May 27, Don Bolles received a telephone call from a man who claimed to have information concerning a land-fraud deal involving Senator Barry Goldwater, Congressman Sam Steiger, and former GOP state chairman Harry Rosenzweig. Bolles was suspicious but agreed to meet the man. He returned to the senate press room later in the day and told Bernie Wynn that he had met "a sleazy bastard . . . from San Diego" who had had nothing concrete, but who had promised information and documentation at a subsequent meeting.

"That didn't mean that Don had changed his mind about investigative reporting," said Wynn. "He had no intention of doing the story himself. He was going to pass it on to the city desk."

Over the Memorial Day weekend, Bolles spent his time with his family. They remained for the most part at home, though on Monday they visited the Pulliam-owned Lazy R & G Ranch, where they swam and had lunch.

On Tuesday morning, June 1, the informant phoned again and Bolles arranged to meet him the next day. The following morning Bolles left the house around nine o'clock, as he usually did. He was wearing a new blue leisure suit and his favorite white shoes. June 2 was his eighth wedding anniversary, and before he left the house Rosalie had given him a new billfold. They planned to go out for dinner that evening and afterward to a showing of *All the President's Men*. Bolles did not mention his meeting to Rosalie, saying only that he was going to a lunch at Sigma Delta Chi, and, because it was the babysitter's day off, he would pick up their daughter from school that afternoon.

Getting into the white four-door 1976 Datsun he had bought less than a month before, Bolles drove to the state capitol to attend a meeting of the senate. The meeting broke up just before eleven. Bolles went down to the press room, made a few calls, and just after eleven he departed, leaving a note in Bernie Wynn's typewriter which said, "I've gone to meet that guy with the information on Steiger at the Clarendon House. Then to Sigma Delta Chi.

Back about 1:30 P.M. Bolles." He then drove to the Clarendon House Hotel in downtown Phoenix. When obtaining tips of this kind, Bolles always chose public places—hotels or restaurants. He was not a man to take unnecessary chances and had at one time taped the hood of his car with Scotch tape so that he could tell if it had been tampered with.

The Clarendon House on West Clarendon is a smallish, modern hotel that manages to give an air of age and dilapidation. Bolles parked his car in the parking lot to the rear of the hotel. His appointment was for 11:15, and the tall, bespectacled reporter, his fair hair pushed back into a loose pompadour, walked into the hotel punctually. He looked round the tiny lobby and out through the glass doors to the pool beyond, but there was no one there. Judy Holliday, the front-desk clerk, asked if she could help and Bolles said he was looking for someone and would wait on the sofa. Some five minutes later the telephone rang. Miss Holliday answered it, frowned, then, looking at the seated journalist, asked if he was Mr. Bolles. Bolles nodded and the girl switched the call to the house phone. Later, Judy Holliday remembered only snatches of the conversation. She remembered Bolles said something about the capitol, that he had told the male caller to go to the senate office building, or something like that, that Bolles had talked for about two minutes before hanging up. Bolles thanked the girl and left. The appointment, presumably, had been postponed.

Squeezing between his Datsun and a battered purple Volkswagen, Bolles got into his car. Reversing a few yards, he cocked the front wheels slightly to the right in order to leave the parking lot. It was then that the explosion occurred. The blast ripped the car's four hubcaps off, blew out the windshield, and cut a two-foot hole in the floor beneath the driver's seat. Windows in nearby cars were blown out, and a huge cloud of white smoke billowed up from the shattered Datsun. The explosion blew open the door on the driver's side and Don Bolles flopped out onto the pavement.

The first person to arrive on the scene was Lonnie Reed, a young refrigeration technician who had been installing an air conditioner nearby. Lying facedown on the parking lot, Bolles looked up and said, "Help me, help me." Reed took the belt from his Levi's and, using it as a tourniquet, tied it around Bolles's right thigh. Two minutes after the blast, Fire Captain John Albright arrived. A small crowd had already gathered, some of whom had attempted to alleviate Bolles's pain by putting loose dressings on his wounds and tying a belt around his other thigh. He was semiconscious. "His legs were all shattered," said Albright. "The right leg, the kneecap, had been blown off, and part of the calf, and the same on the left. He was . . . trying to get up." But Bolles could not move. Lifting up his head, his glasses gone, his face blackened from the blast, Bolles asked that his wife be telephoned and said that he was a reporter. He then muttered, "They finally got me—the Mafia, Emprise. Find John Adamson." Those were the last words he said.

The news of the explosion was relayed via police radio to the city desk of the *Arizona Republic*. The report said that an unnamed reporter had been driving a cream-colored foreign car. Reporters began gathering round the city desk. At first, city editor Early thought the reporter was Al Sitter. Over the years, Sitter had written several stories a week attacking fraudulent land deals and the men behind them. Sitter had been threatened countless times and he drove a cream-colored foreign car.

A few minutes later, Sitter walked into the newsroom. "When I arrived," he said, "everyone was gathered around the city desk and Early looked up at me and said, 'You're not dead?' I was astonished. I used to drive a white Toyota, but my wife drives it now." The reporters were relieved, but a few minutes later the telephone rang. Early answered it, listened for a moment, then put his hand over his face. "Jesus Christ," he said, "Jesus Christ." Then he told the reporters that the victim was Bolles. The stunned reporters stood round the city desk in silence. "What the hell was he working on?" shouted Early. None of the reporters knew.

Don Bolles was removed from the hotel parking lot to nearby St. Joseph's Hospital, where, in five hours of surgery, the doctors amputated his

It's hard enough coping with the fact that your husband was murdered without thinking it was all in vain.

Rosalie Bolles

right leg above the knee. Following the operation, Bolles remained conscious though in critical condition. Later that afternoon, when Bernie Wynn began to sift through the papers on Don Bolles's desk, he found a note. It said: "John Adamson. Lobby at 11:15. Clarendon House. 4th and Clarendon." He gave it to the police.

The following morning the *Arizona Republic* and the *Phoenix Gazette* offered a reward of $25,000 for information leading to a solution to the bombing. At the hospital, Bolles was conscious though unable to speak. Two police officers showed him a photograph of John Adamson, and by nodding his head Bolles confirmed that he was the "sleazy bastard from San Diego." Again, by nodding, Bolles confirmed that it was Adamson who had made the call to the Clarendon. The thirty-two-year-old Adamson was arrested the next day on an old charge of defrauding an innkeeper. He arrived at police headquarters with his lawyer. A squat and brutish man, he wore dark prescription glasses, a white suit, and white shoes. He looked like the bouncer in a second-rate bar. He listed his profession as self-employed greyhound owner. He was photographed, was fingerprinted, said nothing, and was released on $100 bail.

Oddly, the police did not have him tailed, an opportunity Bob Early did not overlook. As Adamson strolled from the county jail, nearly ten reporters and photographers lay in wait for him. They made little attempt at surreptitious shadowing. Rather, using three cars, they followed him openly. Adamson soon wearied of their pursuit. Careening through light traffic and parking lots, he attempted to elude them. After a thirty-minute chase, two of the reporters' cars nearly collided, and Adamson disappeared. But he was soon tracked down to his favorite haunt, the Ivanhoe Cocktail Lounge. He spent the rest of the afternoon and early evening there, making and receiving telephone calls and sending his shoes out to be shined. He left only once—to have a manicure next door.

John Harvey Adamson is a minor figure in the Phoenix underworld. He had been a model student at Phoenix's North High School, the president of the school's Latin club, and a mainstay of the school band, in which he played trombone. His subsequent career had been obscure. In 1973 he owned a tow-truck operation. The business entailed chaining cars to cement slabs in assorted Phoenix restaurant parking lots and extracting sizable sums to have the chains removed. He was also wanted on at least two charges of defrauding innkeepers, but little more was known of him.

On the afternoon of June 4, Don Bolles received thirty-two pints of blood. Four days later, in order to obviate the risk of further infection, doctors amputated his right arm between the elbow and the shoulder. Bolles had lapsed into unconsciousness and his condition was now described as very grave.

Later in the day Neal Roberts, a Phoenix attorney, told the police that Adamson had been with him fifteen minutes before the explosion and could not possibly have had anything to do with it. Neal Roberts was to become a central figure in the case. Six feet five inches tall and graying, the forty-five-year-old Roberts is not merely suave; he seems almost afflicted with a slick western panache. He claimed to have met Adamson some two years before in the Ivanhoe Cocktail Lounge in that part of downtown Phoenix known as the central corridor. "John raises greyhounds," said Roberts. "I raise springer spaniels, so we started spending some time together." Roberts has a reputation of being one of the best civil attorneys in Phoenix, though how he acquired the reputation is obscure since he is rarely seen in the local courts. An expert cardplayer, he is often to be found in the prestigious Arizona Club playing gin and pitch.

Neal Roberts told the police that Adamson had been in his offices, a five-minute drive from the Clarendon House Hotel, with another man, a certain Henry Landry, who turned out to be a one-legged convict and professional gambler. Roberts remembered the occasion well because his secretary's watch had stopped and she had telephoned the operator for the time. It had been 11:18. He and Landry, Roberts explained, had driven to the airport in order to send a greyhound to a distant track. Adamson had gone his own way and had seemed in no particular hurry. Police later learned that the airport receipt had logged the dog in at 11:10, which meant that Roberts would have had to have left for the airport at about 10:45. Roberts insisted there had been a clerical error. Roberts described Adamson as "a Damon Runyon character," though when questioned by police he called him "the friendly neighborhood assassin." Despite Roberts's alibi, Adamson was arrested again, this time for not paying a bill of $136 at the Clarendon House Hotel in 1975. Again, he said nothing and was released on bail.

On June 5, the police searched Adamson's apartment and discovered magnets, firecrackers, electrical wire, tape, and a booklet entitled *The Anarchist's Cookbook* published by a radical group. The booklet gave detailed instructions on how to manufacture bombs. On the afternoon of June 10, doctors at St. Joseph's Hospital amputated Don Bolles's left leg. Bolles had now developed pneumonia and his temperature had risen to 104 degrees.

Sunday morning, June 13, he finally died. Two hours later, John Harvey Adamson was arrested in the Ivanhoe Cocktail Lounge and charged with murder. Three days later the lead editorial in the *Arizona Republic* proclaimed, "With the assassination of Don Bolles, the City of Phoenix realizes it has come of age. The slimy hand of the gangster and the pitiless atrocities of the terrorist are part of the current Phoenix scene."

Days later, after the funeral, after the tributes had poured in from across the nation, days later, after the initial shock, for most, had passed, Rosalie Bolles, the reporter's widow, sat quietly in the living room of her Phoenix home. In the next room three plainclothes detectives watched television. Diane, the Bolleses' pretty six-year-old daughter, skipped into the room, speaking in a high incomprehensible stutter—a stutter her mother seemed to understand perfectly. "She was . . . Don's favorite," said Mrs. Bolles. She started to say something else, then stopped and turned away.

"Don always said the Mafia had too much money to think of killing," she said. "They had their lawyers and the courts. They didn't have to resort to gangland tactics in Arizona. I don't know. Even Don's . . . uh . . . adversaries respected him," she said in a low voice.

Again, she looked away. "I don't know what will come of all this," she said. There was no bitterness in her voice, only regret and resignation. "I'm afraid Don made me something of a cynic too. I would hate to think that nothing good will come of his death. It's hard enough coping with the fact that your husband was murdered without thinking it was all in vain."

Two of the three men involved in Bolles's death—John Harvey Adamson and Max Dunlap—served time for their part in the murder (James Robison was acquitted but later pleaded guilty to soliciting a charge of violence against Adamson). Dunlap died in prison in 2009; Adamson, out of prison and in the witness protection program, died in 2002. Bolles is remembered as a hero.

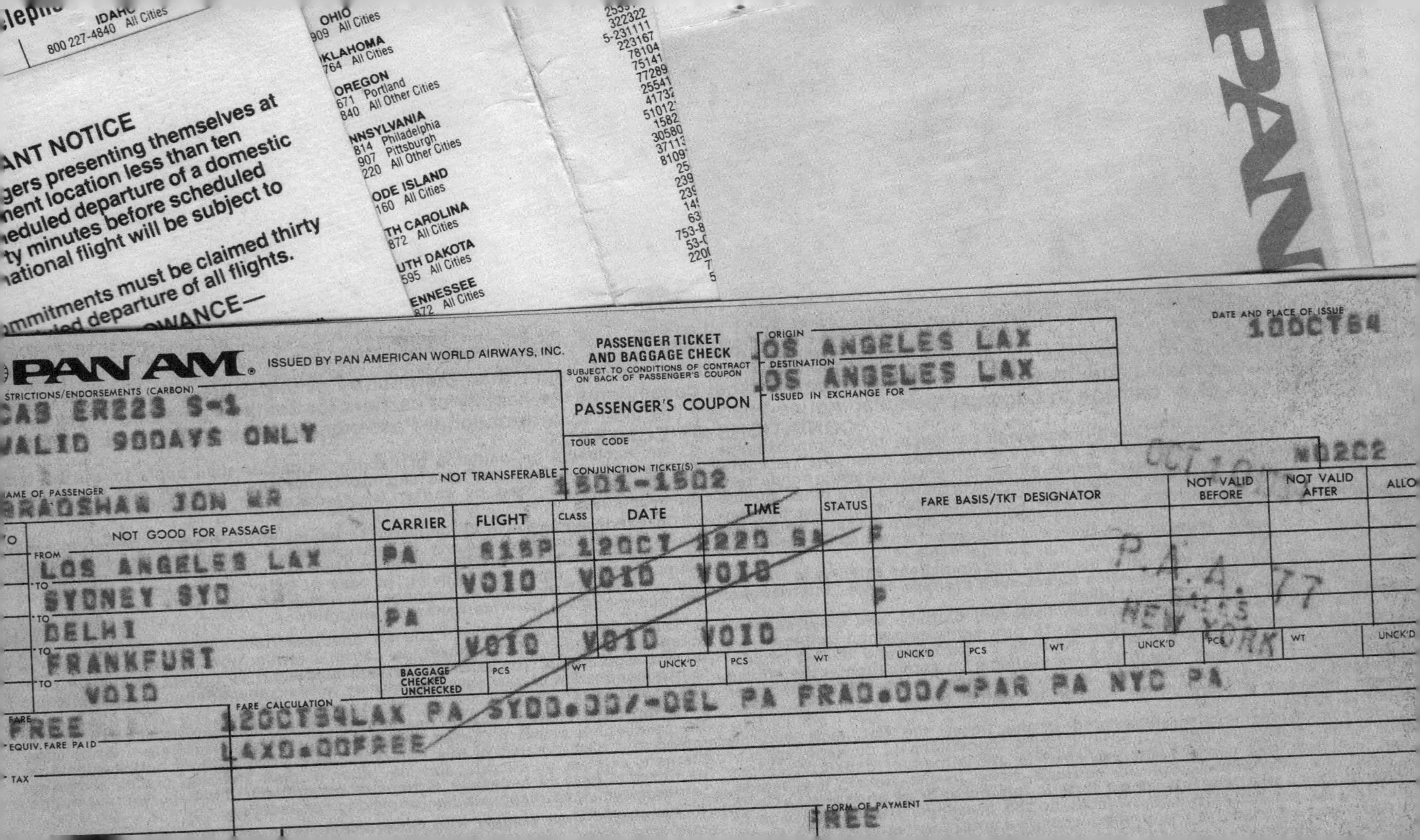
PAN AM
ISSUED BY PAN AMERICAN WORLD AIRWAYS, INC.
PASSENGER TICKET AND BAGGAGE CHECK
SUBJECT TO CONDITIONS OF CONTRACT ON BACK OF PASSENGER'S COUPON
PASSENGER'S COUPON
ORIGIN
LOS ANGELES LAX
DESTINATION
LOS ANGELES LAX
ISSUED IN EXCHANGE FOR
DATE AND PLACE OF ISSUE
10OCT64
TOUR CODE
NOT TRANSFERABLE
CONJUNCTION TICKET(S)
1501-1502
CAB ER223 S-1
VALID 90DAYS ONLY
NOT GOOD FOR PASSAGE
CARRIER
FLIGHT
CLASS
DATE
TIME
STATUS
FARE BASIS/TKT DESIGNATOR
NOT VALID BEFORE
NOT VALID AFTER
FROM
LOS ANGELES LAX
PA
12OCT
VOID
SYDNEY SYD
DELHI
FRANKFURT
BAGGAGE CHECKED UNCHECKED
PCS
WT
UNCK'D
P.A.A.
NEW YORK
FARE
FREE
FARE CALCULATION
LAX PA SYD0.00/-DEL PA FRA0.00/-PAR PA NYC PA
LAX0.00FREE
EQUIV. FARE PAID
TAX
FORM OF PAYMENT
FREE

The Bandit Queen

Esquire, October 1985

"Be wary of her," the policeman whispered, "she's as cold-blooded as they come, but she'll charm the pants off you if she can."

I.

My quest for Phoolan Devi had possessed me long enough. Seduced by tales of her derring-do, I desperately wanted to meet the bandit queen who had been described to me as an avenging angel, more famous in fact than Robin Hood in legend, a beautiful femme fatale who had butchered twice as many men as she had bedded; and, by all accounts, she had been a wanton woman.

I had traveled halfway across the world to find her. Sitting now in the office of the superintendent of prisons in the ancient city of Gwalior, some three hundred kilometers south of New Delhi, I waited impatiently for Phoolan to appear. Only moments before, the superintendent had confided that although it was early afternoon, she had decided to bathe and change her clothes. Phoolan had never met an American journalist before, he said with a thin official smile, and she wished to make a favorable impression.

A wooden fan spun uneasily overhead, and thick curtains hung from the windows and doors to repel the harsh light and the dust that swirled through the air like volcanic ash. During Phoolan's eighteen months in prison she had received a continual flow of visitors—movie producers, policemen and politicians, friends and relatives. Almost daily, loud gibbering crowds of the idle and the curious gathered

Opposite:
Pan Am ticket
for India

beyond the jail's high walls, hoping to catch a glimpse of her as she strolled through the open prison yard with the indifferent aplomb of a potentate. Laughing, the policeman who had arranged our interview referred to Phoolan as Gwalior's most important tourist attraction.

Moments later the door to the interior jail was opened, and, preceded by a burly, mustachioed sergeant of the guard, Phoolan Devi entered the room. "Be wary of her," the policeman whispered, "she's as cold-blooded as they come, but she'll charm the pants off you if she can."

II.

I had first heard of Phoolan Devi some time ago in Australia. Having recently completed a lengthy book and in search of respite and recreation, I had flown to the Land of Oz to visit my friend Richard Neville. Neville, his wife, and child lived high in the Blue Mountains, seventy miles west of Sydney, on a seventy-five-acre estate called Happy Daze, a name that betrayed his partiality for cute and convoluted clichés. We had met many years before through a Bolivian adventuress with whom, unknowingly, we were both having an affair. The dusky trollop introduced us and then disappeared, in search, perhaps, of more pleasurable encounters. Neville and I remained friends.

The forty-year-old Australian was what he liked to call a knockabout nomad, a man who, because he had once been prosecuted unjustly (during an infamous trial in London's Old Bailey), tended to sympathize with those outside the law. Following his departure from England, Neville had wandered across Europe, through Afghanistan, and into India. In India he caroused with cops and investigated criminals, the most notorious of whom was Charles Sobhraj, the French Vietnamese mass murderer. It was in Delhi that Neville had first heard of Phoolan Devi, and now, some years later, he referred to her as "a bloody hellion, mate, a combination of Angela Davis and Jesse James." For the moment, Neville was overly occupied with Happy Daze, "but you," he said grudgingly, "you're free. You ought to track her down."

Astonished that I had never heard of her, Neville sighed, somewhat complacently, and said, "Cobber, next to Indira Gandhi, Phoolan Devi is the most famous woman in India." Then, reaching into a bookshelf, he pulled out a thick scrapbook bursting with newspaper clippings and photographs pertaining to a variety of exotic people and places that appealed to him. He extracted an untidy file entitled "Phoolan Devi, Bandit Queen."

The clippings came from as far afield as *India Today*, the *London Observer*, the *Los Angeles Times*, and the *Bangkok World*. The *Times* piece caught my eye immediately. Neville refilled my glass with cognac, and I began to read.

BHIND, India—In any history of the world's notorious outlaws, Phoolan Devi would need a chapter all her own.

In four years of murder, kidnapping and looting, the diminutive 26-year-old Indian gang leader has fostered a legend as sordid, compelling and romantic as that of the infamous Bonnie Parker, who teamed with Clyde Barrow to terrorize the American Midwest in the 1930s.

Devi is wanted for more than 70 major crimes, including the cold-blooded murder of 20 men she and her gang lined up and gunned down in a 1981 version of the St. Valentine's Day Massacre. . . .

Devi's exploits and her success at eluding a widespread hunt have generated unprecedented publicity in India. . . .

She acquired the nickname "Dasya Sundara" (Bandit Beauty), and Bombay's enterprising film industry decided to make a movie of her life, hiring a raven-haired actress to play the lead.

The other clippings referred to Phoolan's beauty, her cruelty, her nymphomania, her ultimate surrender. The *Bangkok World* reported the fact that as a girl Phoolan had been raped repeatedly by a group of Indian policemen. Newspaper headlines heralded her as LADY KILLER, as MISTRESS OF MURDER, and an Australian tabloid proclaimed, GOOD LOOKS BLAMED FOR NOTORIOUS LIFE OF CRIME.

"But the tale to which I tips my lid," said Neville, "is the one that describes how Phoolan and her ten-man gang drove into Delhi one afternoon to rob a major bank. While her men looted the bank Phoolan climbed up to the roof of the building and sang arias from popular Indian films to the crowds who had assembled in the streets below to hear her sing." He grinned. "I'm told even the cops were mesmerized."

"How often do planes leave for Delhi?" I asked. "I've got to meet her."

Neville laughed. "You will," he said. "You son of a bitch."

It was nearly dawn. As the thick morning mists scuttled down from the peaks of the Blue Mountains, we finished the cognac and Neville said he would ring an acquaintance of his in Delhi, a journalist named Kalyan Mukherjee, who would probably be able to answer my questions. Kalyan had spent considerable time in the Chambal Valley, the bleak area in which Phoolan had committed most of her crimes.

Neville drove me to Sydney Airport the following day. I shook his hand and said goodbye. Neville, adopting one of his favorite poses, that of the world-weary boulevardier, replied, "Don't say that, mate. It's inappropriate. And besides, nomads never say goodbye."

* * * * *

The signs were not auspicious. I arrived in Delhi's Palam Airport at 2:00 A.M., only sixteen hours after Indira Gandhi had been assassinated by two of her Sikh bodyguards. Delhi's avenging Hindu populace had already exacted monstrous reprisals on the capital's Sikh residents, the army had been called out, and a strict curfew had been put into effect, which meant, I was told, languishing in this scruffy airport till dawn.

Palam was glutted with passengers, beggars, huge red-turbaned porters, and scrofulous layabouts, and with British and Australian journalists, most of whom had elected to endure curfew huddled together on wooden benches or slouching against the drab airport walls. I pushed through the crowd and out to the parking lot, where a long line of empty taxis awaited. The Hindu drivers squatted like shadows in the darkness, mute and unresponsive. No one wanted to drive to Delhi till dawn. It was too far, too dangerous.

Stubbornly, I insisted, plying wily blandishments on what appeared to be one of the more impressionable drivers, who finally relented for the not inconsiderable baksheesh of three hundred rupees. "Sahib," he said, "for three hundred rupees, I drive you to paradise." Accompanied by a friend of his, a Hindu youth who got into the passenger seat, we drove away, skirting an unmanned army barricade and turning onto the main Delhi road.

I could not have been asleep for more than ten minutes when I suddenly awakened. The driver and his companion were jabbering between themselves in Hindi, the driver looking nervously to his left and then to his right before swiveling round to peer through the filthy windscreen. The dark boulevards were empty but for the occasional cow munching grass at the edge of the road, and I realized that I had no idea where I was or, indeed, where I was being taken. The driver asked me if I had come to India because of Mrs. Gandhi, and when I explained that I had come to see Phoolan Devi, he beamed and said, "Sure, sahib, she big-time dacoit. I see her in the movies plenty, plenty times. Very powerful, very . . . sexy." And he laughed as if the word itself were titillating. "*Hah*," he added, "I am wishing Phoolan Devi ride with us now."

We had just reached the intersection of Akbar and Nehru Roads when the driver gasped and slowed down. Standing in the darkness some twenty yards ahead was a group of tall, bearded Indians clenching bamboo *lathis* (poles) in their hands. It was

not until the driver shouted, "Sikhs!" that I realized who they were. The driver cursed, attempting to shift the taxi into reverse, but as it coughed noisily, shuddered, and stalled, the Sikhs, some ten or twelve of them, surrounded the car. The youth in the passenger seat yelled and locked his door. The driver furiously twisted the key in the ignition and the engine whirred and whined but refused to turn over. One of the Sikhs swung his *lathi*, smashing the front side window, and, reaching in, opened the door. I leaned forward but was knocked back, and the youth in the passenger seat, screaming horribly, was dragged from the car. Suddenly, the engine started up, and jamming the gear shift into first, the driver accelerated. Just then, the rear window crashed in, showering glass everywhere, and the driver, cursing loudly in Hindi, veered to the left, striking one of the Sikhs, who fell from view as we sped away. Looking back through the shattered window, I could see the Hindu youth lying on his side, his knees drawn up, his hands clasped around his head. In the darkness it was just possible to see the blurred rise and fall of the *lathis* as they beat him.
He had stopped screaming.

The driver dropped me off on Janpath Road, and I walked the few hundred yards to the Sikh-owned Imperial Hotel. Skirting an overturned taxi that was still in flames, I hurried through the archway and into the hotel, where I registered and retired to my room. But I couldn't sleep. The night was punctuated by the defiant cries of a multitude of Sikhs who had gathered below. Leaning out the window, I could see them as they rushed, swords drawn, in pursuit of real or imagined enemies from the parking lot to the swimming pool and back again. Occasionally, the sounds of gunfire could be heard, distant explosions, the urgent screech of steel against stone. I double-locked my door. As I fell asleep the alarm clock rang.

* * * * *

Kalyan Mukherjee arrived in the bar at noon. A slim, bearded youth from West Bengal, he spoke the gruff, rough-and-tumble English of a man who had spent his childhood in sleazy cinemas watching

Gwalior – Bhind

Morning at the hotel —

The Gwalior Jail – First sight of Phoolan Devi.

Drive to Bhind – sixty miles away in the Chambal Valley – By police jeep with Kalyan

The afternoon in the ravines —

Night at the Bhind Circuit House – Kalyan –

spaghetti westerns. He insisted on taking me to lunch at the Moti Mahal, a rowdy restaurant near the thieves' market in Old Delhi. We took a taxi, and as we chugged through the still and ominous city streets Kalyan explained that he had little time, that he had a train to catch that afternoon, but he had dispatched a telegram to a deputy superintendent of police in Gwalior announcing my arrival.

Like the rest of Delhi, the Moti Mahal was nearly empty. We sent out for beer and ordered tandoori chicken, raita, sabzi, and rice. Employing his right hand like a miniature shovel, Kalyan scooped up his sabzi with chunky pieces of naan. I told him that Neville had shown me a number of clippings about Phoolan from Delhi newspapers. "I hope you don't believe our city-slicker press," he rasped between mouthfuls of food. "Those guys hate Phoolan Devi. Truly. They created her myth, and now they're furious because they can't blow it away. Listen," he said, pointing a drumstick at me like a dagger, "the main thing to understand about Phoolan Devi is that her story is a classic Indian myth, an Eastern western, a fabulous yarn of love, betrayal, and revenge. Peasants in the countryside think of her as a Robin Hood, stealing from the rich to give to the poor. Truly. Now, don't take me wrong, mister. I don't necessarily believe the myth, but I'm hog-tied by it. And late at night with a couple of shots in my belt, I sometimes think it's true. Sometimes belief is better than investigation."

Kalyan grinned. "But you want the facts, I suppose? 'Just give me the facts, ma'am.' Isn't that how it goes? Well, I'll tell you what I know." And reaching across the table, he plundered the last drumstick from the plate. "*Mmmmm! Mmmmmm!*" he said. "This grub is good.

"Phoolan Devi comes from a small village in the state of Uttar Pradesh. Her name means 'goddess of the flowers.' She grew up speaking Bundelkhandi, a low dialect of Hindi. Her father, a poor man, a Sudra of the Mallah—the ferryman and fisherman subcaste—worked as a farmer on a small plot—not much more than two acres of land. She never learned to read or write and spent her childhood at home, fetching water from the village well, gathering firewood. You know. The usual household chores.

"The Hindu Marriage Act states that girls cannot be married before they're fifteen, but such laws matter little in rural India. When Phoolan was eleven, her father made arrangements for her to marry a guy called Puttilal, a widower, a Mallah from a nearby village. Phoolan told me that Puttilal was twenty-eight, 'an old man, and I was just a kid in knickers.' But she went along with her parents' wishes anyway.

"After the marriage ceremony Phoolan stayed in her own village, because it's only when a girl reaches puberty that she actually goes to live with her husband. But a few weeks later Puttilal insisted she come immediately. Despite Phoolan's father's reluctance, an arrangement was made—Puttilal returned a portion of Phoolan's dowry—and she was carted off to her husband's village lock, stock, and barrel. She was frightened, but her mother explained that she had raised her daughter like a little bird and that one day she would fly away. And, mister, that day had come.

"'About a week later,' as Phoolan put it when I met her, 'Puttilal behaved improperly to me in the night,' which meant of course that he'd raped her, and when she screamed, he beat the sacred shit out of her. Phoolan's mother criticized him publicly, and the village council told Phoolan's parents to retrieve the dowry. But Puttilal refused to return it. He claimed he'd been humiliated. A few months later the bastard married again, this time to his niece, who was already pregnant with his child. When Phoolan grew up, she swore she'd kill them both. Hang 'em high. But first she was going to cut off Puttilal's balls, she told me, and chop off his new wife's nose. And she would've," Kalyan said. "Sure as grits is groceries.

"For the next seven years Phoolan lived at home with her family, but the news that she'd been deflowered had reached the ears of village gossips long before. They ridiculed the poor girl unmercifully. One of them, Suresh, the headman's son—I guess he thought she was an easy mark—whispered about her to his friends, and now and then he tried to embrace her and touch her tits. Phoolan always slapped him and pushed him away, and the cocky bastard swore revenge. 'Unmarried at sixteen, I was fair game,' Phoolan told me. And I'll never forget what she said to me then. 'It was a difficult time, but the difficult is to be endured.'

"A few weeks later Phoolan went to a nearby village to visit her younger sister Ramkali. In Phoolan's absence, a robbery was committed in her village, and Suresh put the blame on Phoolan. Because Suresh was the headman's son, the cops believed him. He must have imagined that Phoolan would go to jail, that she'd be beaten, that she'd become less headstrong, more amenable to his advances.

"When Phoolan returned to her village, she was arrested, thrown into jail, and the cops kissed her, fondled her breasts, and beat her. Now, Phoolan wasn't the first girl to have been sexually abused by the police. In the Chambal Valley and in the Bundelkhand, villagers fear them even more than they do dacoits."

"Dacoits?"

"Yeah. Outlaws. Bandits. Anyway, Phoolan was eventually released, and in I think it was July of 1979, there was a full moon, a dacoit called Vikram Mallah and his gang crept into Phoolan's village disguised as policemen. Phoolan was sleeping when they burst into her house. Vikram woke her and dragged her from her bed. 'So you were insolent enough to slap the headman's son,' he shouted while slapping her. 'I've been told you keep yourself away from men. I will teach you what a man is. I am Vikram. I am your master.' And then they took her away."

"What happened then?"

Kalyan grinned. "Slow down. I'm full. It's hot. And I have to catch a train to Jaisalmer. Near there, in the northern deserts of Rajasthan, there is said to be a roving band of houris, beautiful gazelle-eyed women, who prey on all male wanderers and slowly, exquisitely, over a period of time, screw them to death. Like the myth of Phoolan, is it true or false?" Kalyan laughed. "It *must* be true. I can hardly wait. In the meantime, you need to go to Gwalior. You'll find what you're looking for there."

"The main thing to understand about Phoolan Devi is that her story is a classic Indian myth, an Eastern western, a fabulous yarn of love, betrayal, and revenge."

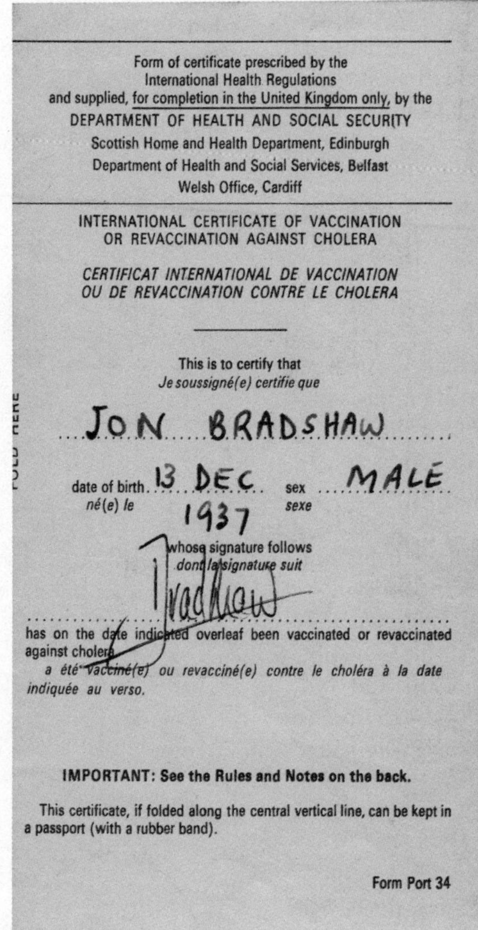

Form of certificate prescribed by the
International Health Regulations
and supplied, for completion in the United Kingdom only, by the
DEPARTMENT OF HEALTH AND SOCIAL SECURITY
Scottish Home and Health Department, Edinburgh
Department of Health and Social Services, Belfast
Welsh Office, Cardiff

INTERNATIONAL CERTIFICATE OF VACCINATION
OR REVACCINATION AGAINST CHOLERA

*CERTIFICAT INTERNATIONAL DE VACCINATION
OU DE REVACCINATION CONTRE LE CHOLERA*

This is to certify that
Je soussigné(e) certifie que

JON BRADSHAW

date of birth 13 DEC 1937 sex MALE
né(e) le *sexe*

whose signature follows
dont la signature suit

J Bradshaw

has on the date indicated overleaf been vaccinated or revaccinated against cholera
a été vacciné(e) ou revacciné(e) contre le choléra à la date indiquée au verso.

IMPORTANT: See the Rules and Notes on the back.

This certificate, if folded along the central vertical line, can be kept in a passport (with a rubber band).

Form Port 34

Bradshaw's cholera vaccination papers

We left the restaurant and found a taxi. Turning onto Lai Bazar, the driver attempted to avoid the shards of broken glass that blanketed the road, accelerating between the fire-blackened frames of taxicabs and three-wheeled scooter rickshaws. A green-clad army column in full battle gear trooped wearily in single file down the side of the road, their recoilless rifles slung carelessly over their shoulders. In the distance, huge clouds of gray smoke curled over the eastern and southern suburbs of the city.

Approaching a roadblock, we were ordered to turn back by the armed guard. To circle through side streets to New Delhi involved a detour of nearly a mile, so, brandishing my press card, I demanded to be let through. The soldier hesitated, then shrugged, waving us on. Kalyan whooped with laughter. He seemed genuinely and inexplicably pleased. "Pardner, you have already learned a very valuable lesson," he said. "In India, one either gives orders or takes them." He laughed again. "There's nothing in between."

* * * * *

New Delhi Station looked like a refugee camp, the crowds spilling in and out of its broad portals with little sense of urgency or direction. Boarding the *Punjab Mail*, I entered a second-class compartment and, using my leather case as a pillow, stretched out on the hard wooden bench. On the bench opposite, a Hindu civil servant in a frayed blue suit sat cross-legged and barefooted, his shoes having been placed neatly below on the floor. He was reading the *Times of India*, the banner headline of which proclaimed: ORGY OF VIOLENCE AND LOOTING CONTINUES. As the train pulled out of the station we began to speak of what the civil servant, who had inherited not only the accent but many of the clichés of the British upper middle classes, called the current unpleasantness in Delhi.

Sighing and smiling sadly, as though he were talking to a backward child, he explained that the Hindus were not a violent people. Nonviolence, after all, was *the* Gandhian ideal. "We are not *Muslims*," he said bitterly, as though he'd been gulled into uttering a profanity. "It's just that these outbursts have to happen from time to time. It's a matter of cleansing, of purification," and he seemed to imply that they had been necessary, inevitable. On the contrary, I argued, the Hindus were a vehement people, their religion rampant with vengeful gods and barbarous goddesses, their mythology replete with monstrous multiheaded and many-armed beasts. To claim the Hindus were nonviolent seemed to me naive. "Ah, you Westerners," he said, smiling sadly again, "you will never understand." And then, quoting Emerson, as Gandhi himself had liked to do, he added, "Consistency is the hobgoblin of little minds."

When the civil servant discovered I was traveling to the Chambal Valley to see Phoolan Devi, he suddenly became meek and withdrawn. "I wouldn't," he said, almost inaudibly. "It's not advisable. Even with a single arm—you know she only has one arm—she's savage, a river in flood. To grapple with her is to drown." Rising from the wooden bench, he put on his shoes and, without a goodbye, hastily left the compartment. Only later, on meeting him again, did I learn that his nephew had been one of Phoolan's victims.

* * * * *

As the train pulled into South Delhi's Nizamuddin Station, I took out my notebook and prepared to write a letter to Richard Neville in Australia. Not only had I promised to send him up-to-date reports of my journey, but it would help me to sort out the details of Phoolan's life while they were still fresh in my mind.

The Punjab Mail
Saturday—

My dear Neville,

In my note of yesterday, I think I brought you up to the point at which Phoolan was kidnapped by the dacoit Vikram Mallah. There's a Chambal Valley saying I've heard continually that goes: If there are three brothers in a family, one will till the land, another will join the army, and the third will take up arms and become a dacoit. By 1979 Vikram was the leader of the most troublesome gang in the trans-Yamuna tract of Jalaun. He was young, only twenty-six, and a bounty of ten thousand rupees had been placed on his head. Vikram was clever and was supported by his fellow caste men, the Mallahs, who possessed a hawk's eye for faces and a bat's ear for accents. The Mallahs shielded Vikram from the police.

For the first months of captivity, Phoolan longed to escape, but the gang watched her carefully and did not permit her to carry a weapon. Only once did she leave the ravines. Six months after she'd been kidnapped, she began to suffer from a chronic pain in her side, a benign tumor as it turned out, and Vikram took her by bus and bullock cart to the hospital in Gwalior, admitting her under the pseudonym of Guddi (doll). Phoolan told the doctor she'd been kidnapped by dacoits but he didn't believe her, and it was only later Phoolan discovered that Vikram had paid him five hundred rupees to keep him quiet. She continued to dislike Vikram, although she hadn't been treated harshly by him, and would've been happier if he'd been captured or killed in Gwalior. She told our friend Kalyan she'd have killed him herself if she'd had the chance. "And she would've," Kalyan told me. "She'd have skinned him alive."

There is an Indian adage that makes an outrageous claim: Love always leads to ruin. And yet that is the fate suffered by Phoolan Devi from the moment she found herself warming to Vikram. Explaining her change of heart to Kalyan, she said, "Vikram was very kind to me, and slowly, I fell in love with him. He was seductive and his love began to overcome my fear of men. After that, I accepted Vikram as my husband."

What happened afterward now seems to have been inevitable. Vikram taught Phoolan how to shoot a gun, a twelve-bore, single-barreled shotgun, at which she soon became expert. During the next few months, the gang committed only robberies, but often two or three a night, walking fifteen to twenty kilometers through the dark ravines, looting gold and silver and money. And Phoolan was permitted to accompany them.

In December of 1979, the gang raided the village of Gufiakhar in Etawah. They had been in the village for only twenty minutes when a police patrol of some dozen men turned up unexpectedly. A gunfight ensued in which three constables lost their lives. As the dacoits retreated, Vikram suddenly leaped up on the village well and, as a kind of salute to Phoolan, he shouted through his megaphone: "This is the gang of Phoolan Devi." The next day a warrant was issued for Phoolan's arrest and a bounty of two thousand rupees was placed on her head. Back in the safety of their camp, the dacoits shouted: "Long live Putli Bai. Long live Phoolan Devi"—Putli Bai being a reference to the famous bandit queen of the '50s. The gang, at last, had accepted her, and Phoolan was thrilled. . . .

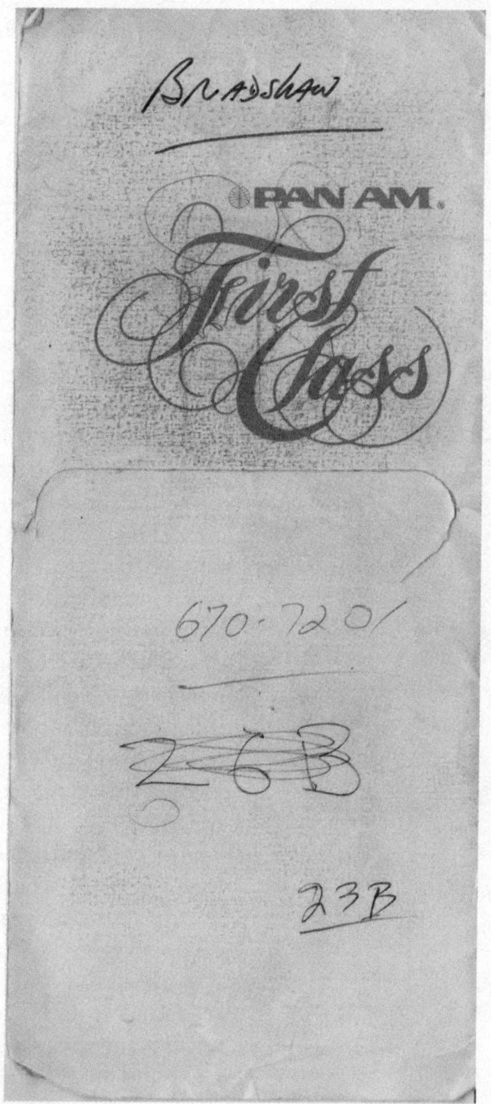

Pan Am ticket for India

. . . It was here, my friend, in the arid ravines that Phoolan's fortunes, if one can call them that, began to sour. Some weeks after the raid at Gufiakhar, a new recruit joined Vikram's gang—a young girl named Kusma Nain. A Sudra of the lowly barber subcaste, Kusma soon became romantically involved with a gang member who was of the noble warrior caste—a Thakur—named Sriram Singh. Phoolan, who had been friendly with Kusma, now began to avoid her. Like everyone else in the gang, she disapproved of liaisons between members of different castes.

Vikram opposed the liaison too. Shortly after it began he beat Kusma in front of everyone and told her she would have to end the affair or leave the gang. Two nights later, near the small village of Baijamau, Phoolan and Vikram ate their evening meal, and afterward Phoolan walked out beyond the camp to relieve herself. She had not gone far when she heard shots. Rushing back to the camp, she was told by Sriram that they were being attacked by a

I became distracted by a small commotion in the next compartment. The skirmish ended quickly, but looking out the window, I could see that we had entered the Chambal Valley, and because I had decided to leave the train at the small market town of Morena, I hastened to finish my letter.

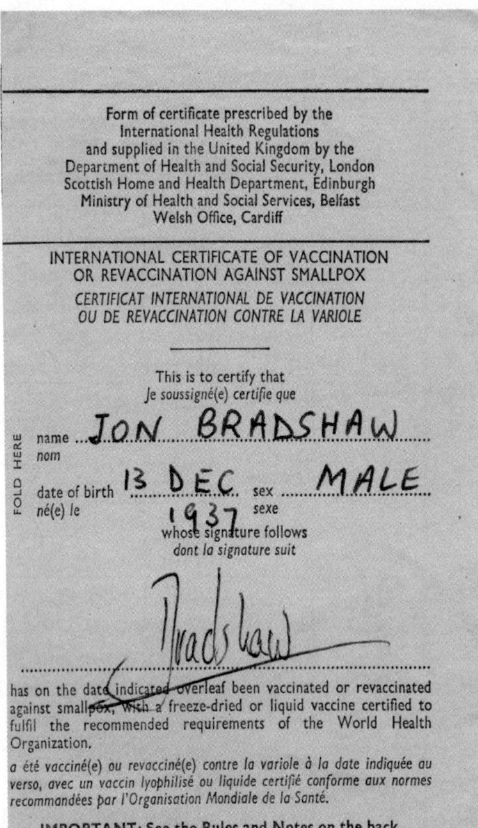

Form of certificate prescribed by the
International Health Regulations
and supplied in the United Kingdom by the
Department of Health and Social Security, London
Scottish Home and Health Department, Edinburgh
Ministry of Health and Social Services, Belfast
Welsh Office, Cardiff

INTERNATIONAL CERTIFICATE OF VACCINATION
OR REVACCINATION AGAINST SMALLPOX

CERTIFICAT INTERNATIONAL DE VACCINATION
OU DE REVACCINATION CONTRE LA VARIOLE

This is to certify that
Je soussigné(e) certifie que

FOLD HERE

name / *nom* ... JON BRADSHAW

date of birth / *né(e) le* ... 13 DEC 1937   sex / *sexe* ... MALE

whose signature follows
dont la signature suit

Bradshaw

has on the date indicated overleaf been vaccinated or revaccinated against smallpox, with a freeze-dried or liquid vaccine certified to fulfil the recommended requirements of the World Health Organization.

a été vacciné(e) ou revacciné(e) contre la variole à la date indiquée au verso, avec un vaccin lyophilisé ou liquide certifié conforme aux normes recommandées par l'Organisation Mondiale de la Santé.

IMPORTANT: See the Rules and Notes on the back.

This certificate, if folded along the central vertical line, can be kept in a passport (with a rubber band).

983845 Dd 233338 5,000M 11/73 StS

Bradshaw's smallpox vaccination papers

police patrol. The gang raced down to the Yamuna River where their boats were moored, and it was only when sitting in one of them that Phoolan realized Vikram was missing. She tried to return to shore, but Sriram clubbed her with an oar, declaring that he had killed Vikram, that he was sick of taking orders from scum, from a fisherman. "You have been spared because my brother Lalaram wants you for himself," he shouted.

They sailed down the dark river for several miles, stopping finally at a Thakur village called Behmai, where Phoolan was held captive. She was locked inside a filthy hut. That first night she cowered on the floor, crying out for Vikram. Shortly after midnight the door opened and a man whom she could not see came in. He beat her first and then, as she lay on the floor, ripped off her clothes. Phoolan screamed, striking out at him, but he was too strong. Holding her down, the stranger raped her. They came in one by one after that—tall, silent Thakur men—and raped her until at last Phoolan lost consciousness.

For the next three weeks, Phoolan was raped several times a night, and she submitted silently, turning her face to the wall. Some time later—she had lost all sense of time—the door opened and bright sunlight poured in. Blinded, she put her arm across her face, and a loud voice summoned her outside. Sriram and Lalaram Singh and a group of Thakurs, some of whom she felt she recognized, stood round the village well. There were no women anywhere. Sriram ordered Phoolan to fetch water for him from the well, and when she refused, he ripped off her clothes and kicked her savagely. At last she limped to the well while her tormentors laughed and spat at her. The naked girl was then dragged back to the hut and raped again.

That night, the twenty-third of her captivity, Phoolan heard a knock at the door and Santosh Pandit, a priest from the nearby village of Simra, crept in. The priest and Phoolan were old friends. Putting his arm around her, he said, "I know what they have done to you. Everyone in the village knows. But there was nothing I could do till now. The Singh brothers finally left Behmai this morning and the villagers are all asleep. Come, let me get you out of here." Phoolan began to cry hysterically. The priest carried her outside—"She was as light as a sack of feathers and bone," he recalled—and took the girl by bullock cart to Pandri, one of Phoolan's contact villages, where, he knew, she would be nursed and safely concealed.

Well, Neville, that's as much as I know of the elusive Phoolan at the moment. But I'm beginning to think she's a figment of all our imaginations. I'm meeting a man in Morena (an unsavory gunrunner, I'm told) who has agreed, for a price, to tell me more.

One last aside: for the next month Phoolan recuperated. She mourned for Vikram, her slain lover, and plotted her revenge. You can imagine how she must have felt, but could you have guessed what form her vendetta would take? As I may have said before, love and revenge are the dual themes of Chambal Valley. There is a local adage I'm fond of that goes: One who has enemies will not be able to sleep in peace; disgrace is the reward for those who forget them. Phoolan had numerous enemies now, and to paraphrase yet another Chambal axiom, a cobra would give birth to kittens before she'd forget them. . . .

"Famed for her beauty and reknowned for her lust, Phoolan Devi captivated an entire nation with her bloody vendetta of honor."

I spotted Shiva Muhti immediately—the seediest character in the bedraggled, flyblown crowd of waiting passengers at Morena Station. A knave if ever I saw one. A Delhi lawyer had put me onto him, and how he—a genteel Brahmin with easy, elegant manners—could ever have crossed paths with Shiva Muhti was a mystery, except, as he had pointed out, that Muhti, when he was not running guns, masqueraded as a country lawyer. Perhaps jurisprudence had brought them together. A tall, thin, angular Sikh with a face like a rusty ax, Muhti took my luggage. "It is you?" he said. "I thought so. Come, we must hurry. They burned seven Sikhs to death on this platform two days ago. It is best to keep out of the public eye. The public eye is bloodshot but watchful."

I had hired Muhti to drive me to Behmai, which was the site of Phoolan's degradation and the place of her ultimate revenge. "As a Sikh, I am taking plenty of risks with my paltry life," he said in his eerie snake's rattle of a voice. He explained that should any Hindu constables discover that he was unarmed in broad daylight on open ground, "*Well* . . ." and he drew his finger across his throat.

Muhti claimed to have sold guns to Phoolan's gang—shotguns, revolvers, and Browning automatics—and that they had become, if not friends, then casual acquaintances. "I have obtained much useful—and expensive—information. But let us stop quibbling," he said before I had said a word. "I can see that you are a man of honor and means. Let us agree on a price of a thousand rupees." When I refused, Muhti smiled, his snaggled, betel nut–stained upper teeth protruding over his lower lip. "Good," he said. "Then it's settled."

As we left Morena, rattling through the hilly wastes of the Chambal Valley, Muhti described the swift and violent course Phoolan's vendetta had taken.

Having recovered from her ordeal, Phoolan trekked deep into the ravines to Gulaoli, the village of a famous dacoit named Baba Mustaqim. She offered to join him, but Mustaqim, a Sunni Muslim, did not approve of unattached women in his gang. "I will accept you only if one of my men wishes to harbor you," he said. Phoolan looked around the campfire at the more than twenty bandits sitting there, but there was only silence. Finally one of them rose, a tall, dark man with flowing locks and a well-groomed mustache and beard. "I will harbor Phoolan Devi," he said, and he held out his hand in a gesture of allegiance.

His name was Man Singh Yadav. A Sudra of the milkman subcaste, the twenty-seven-year-old dacoit was born in the Jhansi district of Uttar Pradesh. Phoolan liked him immediately but pointed out there could be no question of any sexual or emotional involvement between them; she required his strength, his expertise with firearms, and his loyalty in helping her to exact revenge on the Thakur village of Behmai. Less than a week later, following an altercation with Mustaqim, Phoolan and Man Singh decamped and, with a large group of their own caste men, formed a new gang.

During the next few months Phoolan and Man Singh terrorized the ravines, perpetrating dozens of robberies and kidnappings. Her defilement at Behmai had turned Phoolan into a merciless woman. "She was cruel," said Muhti. "She was passionate. She was filled with a terrible rage, like a deep thirst that cannot be slaked. I remember going to her camp on the other side of the Chambal River to sell her guns and ammunition. She wasn't there. She was out on a robbery. I had never seen her before, and when she returned my heart went to my head. I was dizzy with desire. She was nearly six feet tall, believe me, at least, and her hair was the color of dried blood. I swear to you, on the head of my son, a night with that woman would be like drinking the most delectable and deadly poison." At this, Muhti hungrily smacked his lips.

In early February 1981, four of the most powerful Chambal gangs, some eighty dacoits in all, gathered on the east bank of the Yamuna River to discuss the appropriate punishment to be meted out to the Singh brothers for the murder of Vikram Mallah. It was decided that these Thakur dogs, as they were called, had acted dishonorably, and they were sentenced to death. Summoning their informers from all the nearby villages, the gangs were told that Sriram and Lalaram Singh would be in Behmai in five days' time. And so it was agreed that a Sudra gang led by Phoolan Devi would strike the village of Behmai on February 14, a date that would become—Neville's clipping had been correct—India's version of the St. Valentine's Day Massacre.

* * * * *

The monsoons had ended, and the short winter afternoons were parched with heat and dust—weather, in Muhti's view, fit only for the dead or the dying. As we entered Behmai—indistinguishable from the dozens of other dilapidated hamlets scattered like scarecrows along the banks of the Yamuna River—Muhti clutched a filthy handkerchief to his face. It was on an afternoon like this and along this same dusty road that Phoolan, Man Singh, and thirty other dacoits climbed out of the ravines and, trooping across the open fields of wheat and yellow mustard flowers, entered Behmai at noon.

At first, Behmai villagers mistook them for just another platoon of the anti-dacoit police force that patrolled the area, since all but one of them were dressed in police uniforms. That afternoon Phoolan wore her favorite disguise—a peaked cap and cartridge belt, North Star tennis shoes, and a khaki uniform with the Ashoka emblem on the shoulders, two gold stars on the epaulettes, and a small plastic badge on the left breast with her name inscribed in Hindi. It was the uniform of a senior superintendent of police.

Phoolan leaped up onto the village well, the same well from which she had been ordered to fetch water by Sriram Singh, and, brandishing her .315 Mauser rifle, shouted through her megaphone: "Round up all the men in the village. I want every one of them." The gang split into three groups, the first standing guard over the twenty-six Thakur men who had been herded into the village square, the second patrolling the main northern road, while the third group drifted through the mud-and-brick huts looting valuables and cooking utensils and searching for any additional male Thakurs who had concealed themselves. As the villagers pleaded for their lives, Phoolan screamed, "If anybody

> "Peering closely at him, Phoolan thought she recognized him as one of her rapists; he had certainly tormented her as she had been paraded naked through the square. Without hesitating, Phoolan shot him through the leg."

interferes or resists, he will be shot down like a dog." And Man shouted, "Today is the day we take our revenge!"

When all the male villagers had been assembled before her, Phoolan looked carefully at each of them. "Where arc Sriram and Lalaram Singh?" she shouted. "Where have you hidden the bastards?" Suddenly, there was the sound of shots. One of the Thakurs, armed with a rifle, had climbed into a nearby tamarind tree and had begun to fire on the dacoits. Dropping the megaphone, Phoolan aimed her rifle at the tree and shot the Thakur in the leg. He fell to the ground, then rose on one knee and begged Phoolan for mercy. Peering closely at him, Phoolan thought she recognized him as one of her rapists; he had certainly tormented her as she had been paraded naked through the square. Without hesitating, Phoolan shot him through the other leg.

As he toppled to the ground Phoolan smiled and began to taunt him—singing the lyrics of a song from a famous Hindi film called *Mera Gaon, Mera Desh* (My Village, My Country): "*Maar diya jaiye. Ya chor diyajaiya*," she sang ("Should I kill you or should I set you free?"). Looking up at her, the Thakur cringed, and Phoolan shot him in the face. He flopped back on the dusty ground.

The twenty-six villagers were then driven toward the river, where they were ordered to kneel in a row with their hands raised. The dacoits lifted their rifles, then hesitated, and Phoolan shouted, "Kill them. They're nothing but Thakurs." The kneeling villagers began to moan. And then the firing started.

One of the survivors was to claim the shooting had lasted for twenty minutes, another said thirty, but that was almost certainly an exaggeration. When the cordite fumes had cleared, however, twenty of the Thakur villagers lay dead, their bodies sprawling in and out of the bloody river. Huddled in their huts, the Thakur wives sobbed and beat their breasts, and Phoolan shouted, "This is only the beginning. I'm coming back for Sriram and Lalaram." And then, waving to her men, Phoolan led them from the village.

*****

In Behmai, sitting on the raised stone-columned well from which Phoolan had begun her rampage, Shiva Muhti and I could see the hut in which she had been violated; the mud-brick hovels in which the Behmai survivors, who had subsequently shaved their heads in mourning, lived; and, beyond, the murky Yamuna River where their Thakur relatives had been slain. Even now, and well after the event, Behmai seemed a forlorn and haunted place.

It had been the worst dacoit killing in modern Indian history. Never before had so many high-caste Hindus died at the unclean hands of their inferiors. Phoolan Devi was the first dacoit and certainly the first woman to puncture the invincibility of the Thakurs, and by killing them she had violated all ancient caste laws.

Sitting now at the Behmai village well, Shiva Muhti said, "In India, almost nothing has changed for centuries. And it never will. Caste is thicker than cow shit, thicker than blood." And then, turning toward me, his moist brown eyes rolling somewhere in the distance above my head, he asked for his fee.

"Muhti," I said, "in cases of this kind, I have a standard policy. One thousand rupees for the truth, two hundred rupees for lies, and five hundred for exaggerations."

I gave him the money and Muhti smiled. "Thank you, sahib," he said. "The five hundred rupees will help to put my mythical son through school."

* * * * *

Youth is considered a drawback in India and is not taken seriously except by the young. The first appearance of gray in an Indian's hair is real cause for celebration, a promising portent of substance, wisdom, and solemnity. As if to imply he was no longer some artless tenderfoot, A. N. Pathak stroked his graying temples and feigned a convincing air of gravity. But nothing could conceal the gentleman's youthful charm.

The forty-five-year-old Pathak was the most decorated police officer in India. He had been involved in police encounters in which more than a hundred dacoits were killed; he had shot twenty-four of them himself. And for the past three years Pathak had been the town's deputy inspector of police.

The morning after I arrived in Gwalior, Pathak and I drove by Jeep to the Chambal Valley—"Phoolan's lair," Pathak called it. The Chambal Valley, covering an area of eight thousand square miles, lies in the extreme northwestern portion of Madhya Pradesh, forming a boundary with the adjacent states of Uttar Pradesh and Rajasthan; it is India's last remaining bandit country. There is a belief that the Chambal River, which loops down through Madhya Pradesh like a hangman's noose, bestows on those who live on its banks a natural streak of rebellion. It is called the River of Revenge.

We parked at the edge of the ravines and stumbled down the steep bank, pocked with acacia shrubs, the thorny karil, and the thin, shapeless pipal trees, to the crocodile-infested Chambal River. "There are even more crocodiles in the ravines than there are in the river," Pathak observed, alluding to the dacoits.

The Chambal Valley is reminiscent of the Dakota badlands—a harsh and desolate land, scarred by the sun, the deep-set, ribbed ravines falling away from the river like brittle earthen skeletons. "'Where the sun beats,'" said Pathak, "'and the dead tree gives no shelter, the cricket no relief, and the dry stone no sound of water.'" I peered at Pathak quizzically. I had heard that line before but could not place it. Wiping the sweat from his brow, Pathak laughed. "'The Waste Land,'" he said. "T. S. Eliot." He paused. "And you thought I was just another policeman."

The jagged ravines stretched out before us as far as the eye could see, and it seemed to me that one might easily conceal a whole army there. "Is that how Phoolan managed to elude the police for so long?" I said.

"Oh, Phoolan was a wily one," said Pathak, almost admiringly, and there was a trace of regret in his voice that he had not been her adversary. He implied that they would have been worthy foes.

"In the weeks following Behmai," he said, "Phoolan split up her gang. They traveled through the ravines in twos and threes to escape detection. They

Previous: Bradshaw and Tasneem Zakaria Mehta at Indira Gandhi's funeral

made forced marches of up to twenty kilometers a day, making their presence known in one village, then moving rapidly cross-country to confuse the police. Classic guerrilla tactics. Once or twice a week, the gang reconvened, slipping through the night to plunder landowners and rich shopkeepers, to kidnap wealthy farmers—and killing any policemen who got in their way. By the end of 1981, Phoolan was wanted for nearly seventy associated crimes involving robbery, kidnapping, assault, and murder, and a bounty of twenty-five thousand rupees was placed on her head. On two occasions she was nearly caught, but Phoolan led a cat's life and she always escaped."

During this period police officials did not even know what she looked like. Ultimately they released a photograph of Phoolan to the Indian newspapers, which the Associated Press transmitted to the rest of the world. It was subsequently discovered that the photograph was a composite of pictures of a well-known Indian actress and Phoolan's younger sister Ramkali.

Following Behmai, Phoolan became a famous woman. The Indian press mythologized her; ballads were composed, the lyrics of which usually asserted that Phoolan had sacrificed everything for love. Clay statues of her were hawked in Chambal towns and villages for ten or twelve rupees apiece and, according to the *Times of India*, sold "like hotcakes."

Three weeks after Behmai, police were alerted that Phoolan had slipped into the city of Lucknow to see a popular dacoit film. The theater was sealed off and the audience was screened one by one. That night, a rumor that Phoolan had been captured alive spread through town. But much to police embarrassment, it was discovered they had arrested a local eunuch dressed up in drag to resemble the bandit queen.

In urban India, Phoolan suddenly became a symbol of the new woman, depicted as a brash Amazon who had risen above her caste and the traditionally subservient position of the Indian female. In Delhi and Bombay, Phoolan appeared to represent the ideas expressed by such feminists as Kate Millett,

Betty Friedan, and Germaine Greer—writers who have become popular in India only in the last six or seven years.

In addition, the Bombay film industry deified Phoolan. There had been films about dacoits before, notably *Chambal Ki Kasam* (I Swear by the Chambal), *Putli Bai*, and the extremely popular *Sholay* (Flames), but never before had there been two films about a single dacoit—*Outlaw*, *Phoolan Devi* and *The One with Courage*, both of them nationwide hits. "There is an amusing story," said Pathak, "that a third film was to appear. It was produced by a well-known Bombay mogul who hired a voluptuous beauty to

play Phoolan. All but the final sequences were shot, when the mogul received a note from Phoolan saying if she didn't like the film she would come to Bombay and cut off his nose. The mogul, I am told, decided not to release the film."

Hidden deep in the Chambal ravines, Phoolan was happily unaware of her fame. Nor did she know that the Uttar Pradesh state home minister had threatened his senior police officers with dire punishments if Phoolan and her gang were not captured within fifteen days. But the fifteen days passed, and Phoolan remained at liberty. She would be a fugitive for the next two years, and despite numerous official "sightings," Phoolan seemed to have disappeared.

"During that period," said Pathak, "a superintendent of police for the Bhind district in Madhya Pradesh called Rajendra Chaturvedi was making every effort to contact Phoolan in the ravines. He believed that giving dacoits an attractive alternative to certain death (in this case surrender) was a more effective means of clearing up the dacoit problem than spending vast sums of state funds to hunt them down. And I agreed."

"But why would Phoolan have surrendered?" I asked. "Surely, by then, she must have believed she would elude the police forever. If you'll forgive a vulgar Western expression," I said with a smile, "she'd made monkeys of all of you."

Pathak grinned. "Truly vulgar," he said. "But I accept your criticism. 'Each captain, petty officer, and man is only at his post when under fire.'"

"*The Dynasts*," I said. "Thomas Hardy."

Pathak beamed. "You know Hardy? Good. *Very* good." He paused. "But you miss the point. Surrender was the *only* solution. And Phoolan knew it. Life in the ravines is grueling. Few dacoits live to see thirty. Hungry. Huddling in caves during the long monsoons. Furtive. Pressed and pursued." He shook his head. "A rat's life is preferable."

Through Chambal informants Superintendent Rajendra Chaturvedi arranged a clandestine meeting with Phoolan. Traveling all night by foot and motorcycle, he was led to her camp deep in the ravines. Phoolan awaited him and listened quietly to his proposal. When he had finished, she exploded: "You ass-licker. Do you really think you can just come and ask me to surrender? I am Phoolan Devi. I could kill you now."

But Chaturvedi was a patient man. The superintendent arranged a second meeting for the following month, and in the intervening weeks Phoolan almost lost her life in two separate police encounters. At the second meeting she finally agreed to surrender, provided the Madhya Pradesh police comply with all her written conditions: that she not be hanged; that she be granted the status of a political prisoner and be guaranteed three meals a day in jail; that she not be handcuffed and that her cases pending in Uttar Pradesh—where her safety was not assured—be tried in a special court in Madhya Pradesh; that her family be given new accommodations in Madhya Pradesh; and, finally, that her cow and goats be transferred to Madhya Pradesh as well. "If you keep your vows, I'll keep mine and give myself up with dignity," she said.

And so, on February 12, 1983, Phoolan's nine-man gang formally surrendered at the Special Armed Forces Ground in Bhind, a market town some seventy-five kilometers from Gwalior. A twenty-three-foot-high wooden platform had been erected for the ceremony, and at Phoolan's insistence, framed portraits of Mahatma Gandhi and the awesome, ten-armed goddess Durga had been placed near the microphones. Shortly after 9:00 that morning Phoolan, Man Singh a step behind, mounted the high platform—a red woolen shawl draped over her

"I couldn't believe my eyes. It was almost impossible to imagine that this little girl was the cruel and fearsome Phoolan Devi."

khaki uniform, a red bandanna around her head—and placed her cartridge belt and her .315 Mauser rifle before the garlanded portraits of Gandhi and Durga. Rising, she faced the large crowd that had gathered to see her, placing her hands together and raising them high in salute. The crowd began to clap and cheer, but one of them, a Thakur student, rushed toward the platform shouting, "This is not the surrender of the dacoits, but that of the state minister." The police dragged him away.

Moments later Phoolan, Man Singh, and the rest of the gang were escorted to a waiting bus. As the bus pulled away, lurching south under armed escort to the Gwalior Central Jail, Phoolan Devi, a faint smile on her face, waved shyly to the adoring crowd.

III.

Pathak had made arrangements for me to meet Phoolan that afternoon, and we returned by Jeep to Gwalior. As we entered the superintendent's office in Gwalior Central Jail, I asked him about Phoolan's alleged nymphomania, producing the tabloid clipping that stated, "For every man this girl has killed, she's slept with two of them." Pathak laughed. "You'll see," he said. "Phoolan's moody and difficult, but verbally she's quick, spontaneous, a typical jungle girl. There's a lot of violence and sudden sex in her. It floods from her like a river—*whoosh*—but between you and me"—and he smiled and winked—"I think it's mostly show."

As we waited for Phoolan, Pathak explained that she had been tried in Madhya Pradesh for possession of unlicensed firearms for unlawful purposes and had been sentenced to seven years. Although many people believed she would then be freed, Pathak claimed that she would ultimately be tried for all her crimes.

It was rumored that Indira Gandhi had saved Phoolan's life. Following the dacoit's surrender, the state minister for Madhya Pradesh had been in close consultation with Mrs. Gandhi, who said that Phoolan Devi was a wayward village girl and urged that she be treated leniently. Pathak had arranged for

Phoolan and Man Singh to live in an open jail and, fulfilling a promise he had made to Rajendra Chaturvedi, looked after her needs as best he could. Phoolan was indebted to Pathak, and it was because of him that she had agreed to see me.

Phoolan was certainly taking her time. More than forty minutes had passed since we had entered the jail, and there was still no sign of her. I had waited too long and come too far to see Phoolan Devi, and I began to fear that now, at the eleventh hour, she had changed her mind.

Moments later the door to the interior jail was opened, and, preceded by a burly, mustachioed sergeant of the guard, Phoolan entered the room. We were introduced, and clasping her hands together in the traditional Hindu gesture of respect and allegiance, Phoolan bowed and sat down, rearranging her sari over her bare brown legs.

I couldn't believe my eyes. It was almost impossible to imagine that this little girl was the cruel and fearsome Phoolan Devi. Concerning her beauty, her size, and her bloodred hair, the newspaper accounts had been exaggerated. Kalyan had transformed her into Calamity Jane; the perfidious Muhti had blatantly lied; and finally, my own imaginings had deceived me most of all. In the flesh Phoolan was about five feet tall and looked to be no more than seventeen. With her short black hair, high cheekbones, and broad, snubbed nose, she might have been a Nepali girl from the frontier. Most alarmingly, perhaps, she possessed not one arm, but two. Legend, it appeared, had confused her with Putli Bai, the famous one-armed dacoit of the '50s.

Stunned, I turned to look at Pathak, and my astonishment must have loomed from my face like a flare. "Illusions must not be destroyed too quickly," he said with a smile, "but they must be destroyed."

Dressed in a stained and tattered lavender sari, Phoolan wore plastic bangles on her arms, hooped earrings, and silver anklets. She had the sly face of a wild leprechaun and she spoke in a high, stuttering singsong voice, speaking in what Pathak called her "*pourbi* lingo"—a low dialect of Hindi.

She began to talk, but, she said, she wanted one thing understood. She would have preferred that none of this had happened, "but it was not my lot, it was not my destiny. What happened to me was meant to be."

Phoolan believed herself to be the equal of any male, if not his better. Even so, I asked her if she had not found it difficult being the leader of an all-male gang. "Certainly not," she retorted angrily. "Doesn't a woman lead India?" And then, remembering that Mrs. Gandhi was dead, she lowered her eyes and her voice trailed off.

"In the ravines," she began again, "gang leaders pissed in their pants when they heard my name, and they shit when they encountered me in battle. I was never afraid. Why should I have been? Bullets came out of their guns just as they did out of mine, but mine were more accurate. As for the peasants, I don't know whether they feared or respected me, but when I walked into their villages the headman would come to me with garlands and touch my feet."

The tale of Neville's that had first seduced me—of how Phoolan's gang had looted a bank in Delhi while she sang arias from the rooftops to her fans below—turned out, like so much else, to be apocryphal. But it amused her, and drawing her sari across her face, Phoolan giggled, her dark eyes darting mischievously between myself and Pathak. "I have never been to Delhi," she said, "and I am not the singing kind. The only time I sang was at Behmai, and even then it was more of a shout than a song."

Concerning her sins, as she called them, she said, "I am a sinful woman, but I have done nothing but take revenge. My crimes were crimes of the heart. What else? I only regret that I did not have the chance to kill Sriram and Lalaram Singh. I would have nailed them to a burning cross. And if I had tracked down that bastard Puttilal, my husband, I would have killed him too. I went to his village once, but he had disappeared, so I burned down his house. Now I will try and take him to court and get my dowry back."

Since I was catching the late train to Delhi to attend Indira Gandhi's funeral, I rose to leave. Phoolan asked me to place a flower on Mrs. Gandhi's bier, and then, in order to prove to me that she had learned to write in prison, she signed her name in Hindi on a hundred-rupee note. It was *nazrana*, she said with a smile—an Urdu word meaning "gift" and signifying respect.

I in turn thanked her. Phoolan was not what I had expected. But I was not disappointed. I did not agree with Kalyan's premise that belief was better than investigation. For me, knowing is always better than believing.

As I turned to leave, Phoolan Devi bowed; then, looking up, she said, "One thing more. I learned all this cruelty after I joined the gang. I was not like that before. I don't know what the world thinks of me. Left to myself, I'm an ordinary Indian village girl." She paused. "But I think I'm capable of anything."

Phoolan Devi was released from prison in 1994, and two years later she served as a member of the Indian Parliament. She was assassinated by three masked gunmen in July 2001. She was thirty-seven years old.

Closing Time in the Garden of Eden
Esquire, October 1977

"One wants something unusual, I suppose, and the privacy to enjoy it. That's what drove me out of America. It was the bloody sameness of it all."

Monday: I am sitting high in the hills on the island of Mahé and looking out at what the local brochures call the turquoise-and-sapphire sea. I have come a long way and the view is obscured by clouds. It is difficult to say why I have come so far for so short a time. I have no plans. I have no expectations. Suffice it to say that I am on the largest of the Seychelles islands, in the middle of the Indian Ocean, some one thousand miles east of Mombasa, some two thousand miles southwest of Bombay.

Until the late '50s, only one ship a month called at this remote island. Before the airport opened in 1971, one came by ship from Mombasa or Bombay. I arrived from New York late yesterday on the Air France inaugural flight via Paris, Marseilles, and Djibouti. I might just as well have come by ship. It was a thirty-nine-hour journey from New York.

When the airport opened, James Mancham, who was then president, claimed that his young republic was no longer a thousand miles from nowhere, but halfway to everywhere. Even so, one has an acute sense of isolation here. The next Air France flight does not leave for another seven days. I am, temporarily at least, marooned. Look upon this as the note in the bottle.

It has rained gently but ceaselessly all day. Given the rain and the long trip, I have spent the day drinking rum and bitters on the veranda of Timbertin Lodge. Secluded in the hills above the town, the lodge has three bedrooms and fewer guests. Everything

"It takes a lot of experience to learn to do nothing well. I'm rather good at it."

pleases. Timbertin. I even like the fine French roll of its name. Or I did this morning. This afternoon, Madame Cormier, the lodge's fierce proprietress, explained she had called it Timbertin because it was built of timber and tin. She felt my naïveté deserved a drink and called for another noggin.

Madame Sylvia Cormier is an Englishwoman in her early fifties, and she built and operates the lodge with Abel Morel, her twenty-four-year-old friend and confidant. Abel is a white Seychellois, what is known in the islands as a *grand blanc*. He is descended from one of the island's older French families. His slight but muscular stature and wispy beard give him more than a passing resemblance to Pan. Madame Cormier and Abel live at Timbertin with a couple of cats, the chickens in the yard, the goats, three kids, and two mongrel dogs called Eight and Nine. The hilltop is heavily forested, but the bush has been cleared from the yard below, and through the palms, the vanilla and cinnamon trees, and the bougainvillea, one can see, if one could see, the sea. It is a good place in which to disappear.

The Seychellois call Sylvia Cormier "Madame Bourgeois." It is the Creole name for "boss." Although English is the official language, the locals speak a guttural and incomprehensible patois. Madame Cormier first came to Seychelles in 1967. She bought some land, left, and then came back in 1970 to stay. "There were only about a hundred cars when I first came, and no buses," she says. "I took the boat from Bombay, and when I first saw this island, I really thought I would never leave."

A large woman, Madame Cormier always wears worry beads round her neck and shoes only when absolutely necessary. Despite the worry beads, she believes that everything that happens to her is for the best. She is resigned to a kind of fitful optimism.

"This used to be a quiet place," she says. "But the airport has changed everything. Seychelles is the new mecca of the package tour. Bloody tourists. Bloody hell." She looks out toward the sea. "Wait till the rain stops and I'll show you round what's left of it."

Wednesday: To spend time at Timbertin Lodge is like spending a weekend at the country

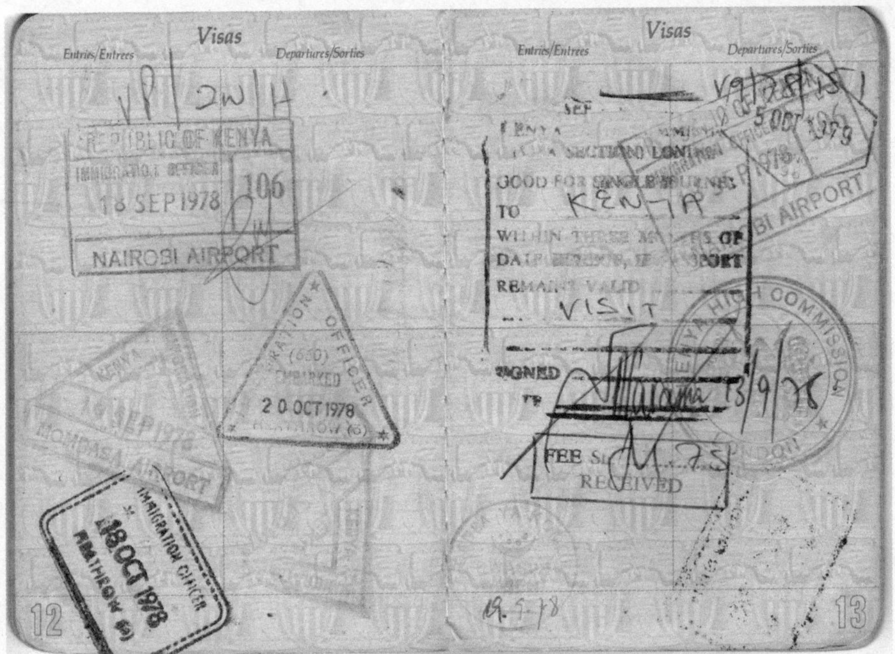

Bradshaw's visa to Kenya

home of a bizarre but rather amiable maiden aunt. It is comfortable without being fussy, charming without being cute, all the drinks are doubles, and most eccentricities are, if not encouraged, condoned. Over breakfast, Madame Cormier delicately explains that to find the real beauty of Seychelles, I should drive as far from Victoria as possible. "The island itself is beautiful," she says. "The rest is gormless." (Gormless: pathetic, not up to par, lacking gorm.) And that is that.

There is one road that nearly encircles the island before petering out in the bush. Three other roads twist and turn across the mountains from sea to sea. Most of the larger hotels are clustered together on the eastern side of the island. There are only five or six of these, but they obtrude from the landscape like exclamation points. In 1971 there were just four small hotels in Mahé. Tourism, of course, is now the island's main source of revenue and caters primarily to package tours from England and the Continent. But already Mahé seems overrun with Europeans. It is an all too familiar story.

The Seychellois are unaccustomed to these invasions. When the five-story Mahé Beach Hotel opened last year, its elevator proved to be the main attraction. Most Seychellois had never seen one before. Today, there is a guard posted in the hotel lobby to stop them from taking free rides.

Madame Cormier likes to tell of the time she took her friend Abel to New York. "He had never been off the island before," she says. "We checked into one of the larger New York hotels. When we arrived, there was a crowd round the registration desk. One of the men had a casket with him, beautifully carved, with silver handles. He said the man in the coffin had a reservation. But the hotel refused to honor it. 'We don't take dead people, sir,' the desk clerk said. 'It's all right,' said the man with the casket. 'He's a vampire. He'll be up tonight.' Abel couldn't believe it. He wanted to come back to Mahé right away."

At the southern end of Mahé, all intrusions are left behind. Here the island is as it must always have been. The huge palms and forest ferns loom up from the volcanic rock, concealing empty white beaches and tiny, almost inaccessible coves. No people, no noise. On a little beach between Police Point and Anse Intendance, a narrow stream bisects the beach. And beyond, as far as one can see, is the limitless ocean. Again, one senses just how isolated one is here and remembers this has always been a place for exiles and deportees. Over the years, the British exiled to Seychelles such dissidents as the Sultan of Perak, King Prempeh of the Ashantis, the Kabaka of Buganda, and Archbishop Makarios, who spent a year in exile here in 1956 and 1957. It is still a beautiful, untrammeled place.

Friday: In Victoria, the fashionable hostelry for lunch is Frankie's Place. Here the island's British expatriates gather almost daily for Frankie's fifteen-rupee lunch. Before the airport opened, few tourists came, but the hills around Victoria were dotted with the villas of wealthy Englishmen and the homes of ex-colonials out of Uganda, Kenya, and Tanzania. The days of the empire may be gone, but one still finds hearty English ex-colonials drinking pink gin and beer in country clubs from Port of Spain to Singapore.

I think he really did like the living aspect more than making a living. Making a living really didn't mean much to him, because he was so clever, he could always make a living. That was never even an issue.

A. Scott Berg

In Seychelles, the expatriates are presided over by Frankie Chaston, a beautiful thirty-year-old Englishwoman who came here on her honeymoon in 1970, stayed, divorced, and stayed on. Madame Cormier comes two or three times a week to Frankie's Place for the fifteen-rupee lunch. Sitting with her is Honest Jack Causton, the local realtor. "He's a brilliant drinker," says Madame Cormier. In his early fifties, Honest Jack sits with his young Seychellois wife. Formerly a sergeant major in the British army and attached to the Uganda Rifles, Honest Jack taught Big Daddy Amin to box in the late 1950s. He is also a self-professed psychic who has helped Scotland Yard track down missing bodies and stolen goods in his time.

At another table is Miss Grace McClean. At seventy-two, she teaches in a private nursery school, drinks beer for breakfast, and employs a maid called Jungle Bunny. For thirty years, she was a children's nanny aboard the *Kampala*, a cruise ship of the British Indian Line. A tall, striking spinster, she sits erect in Frankie's Place, and when she requires another drink, she taps her empty glass on top of her head.

Other regulars include Roy Marsh, a pilot who flies for the brother of the Shah of Iran. It was Marsh who piloted Hemingway in Kenya in the early '50s when the plane crashed and the world believed the writer dead for several days. In another part of the room is Eddie Condon, an American with artificial legs who runs the nearby Moses' Bar. Condon tells complicated tales of his long friendship with Howard Hughes.

These expatriates have been in Seychelles for years, and when they first arrived from Mombasa or Bombay, they claimed the islands would be their final stopover. But with the coming of the airport and the tourist boom, the conversations at Frankie's Place are filled more and more with moody talk of moving on. Talk of other islands, unsullied, unrecognized, beyond the reach of the multitude. There are numerous references to the Maldives and the New Hebrides at Frankie's Place this day.

Saturday: Madame Cormier and I are sitting in the Rendezvous, a particularly ugly bar in downtown Victoria. It is drinks time, but there is no one in the bar except for a Chinese man snoring in a chair by the door. A fan whirs overhead and the young Seychellois barmaid has played Rosemary Clooney's "How Much Is That Doggie in the Window?" on the ancient jukebox. It's that sort of bar.

I don't really wish to leave Seychelles despite the fact that I feel I've been here for several years. A real torpor has set in. The plane leaves in twenty minutes and we are at least that far from the airport. "Have another toddy," says Madame Cormier. "The planes rarely leave on time."

As a kind of beau geste, I have taken to drinking the local grog. The toddy is made from the sap of the coconut palm. It is wonderfully intoxicating and should be drunk immediately after bottling, although it is better used as paint remover. I have had five or six this afternoon. As I get up to order another, I can hear them slopping back and forth in my head. It is a hideous sound. "It's time to go," I say to no one in particular.

"I am always going," says Madame Cormier. "Moving on. One wants something unusual, I suppose, and the privacy to enjoy it. That's what drove me out of America. It was the bloody sameness of it all. The madras trousers three inches above the ankle, all those alligator shirts, and, worst, the millions of lawnmowers starting up on Sunday mornings. You have no idea. They tried to turn me into a real American mother, the bitchiest bitch that ever bitched, but one morning I suddenly came to my senses, got on a plane, and left.

"And I'm leaving again, this time for Praslin. Praslin is still one of the most beautiful islands in the world, you know. And it's protected—there's nothing to do. Tourists don't like that, they don't like it at all. It takes a lot of experience to learn to do nothing well. I'm rather good at it."

We go outside to the Mini Moke. The plane was scheduled to leave some fifteen minutes ago. I'm becoming petulant. "Look on the bright side," says Madame Cormier. "There's another plane leaving in seven days."

Jonathan Routh's painting of Knutsford Great House—the Bradshaw home in St. Ann, Jamaica

"Bradshaw loved islands," says Carolyn Pfeiffer. "In those days you had to get visas to travel to many foreign places. He had those accordion passports where they added pages to include all the visas. His ambition was to visit every major island in the world."

EDITOR'S NOTE

Magazine stories are fallible records at best. What makes a story impactful in its moment is often irrelevant to succeeding generations. Bradshaw wrote when magazines put the "long" in "longform" and readers had an entire month to consume an issue of *Esquire* with fewer distractions than we have today. So, for the sake of offering the widest variety possible, only these pieces have escaped abridgment: "Holding to a Schedule with W. H. Auden," "Tom Stoppard, Nonstop," "Hunter Thompson, on a Bat," "A Bold Gossip," "You Used to Be Very Big," "Haiti's Gingerbread Palace," and "The Bandit Queen."

04–05
The final photograph of Bradshaw with his daughter Shannon
Image © Carolyn Pfeiffer

21
Libby Holman Book Cover
Image © Jonathan Cape UK, Photographer Mary Lou Saxon

26
Young Bradshaw
Image © Estate of Gene Moore

36
W.H. Auden letter agreeing to an interview
Image © Estate of W.H. Auden

50
Bradshaw's journal 1977
Image © Estate of Jon Bradshaw

62
Bradshaw playing softball with expats in London
Photographer unknown

72
Bradshaw's journal 1977
Image © Estate of Jon Bradshaw

76
Richard Goodwin inscription
Image © Estate of Richard Goodwin

97
Articles Bradshaw sold in 1965 / 1966
Image © Estate of Jon Bradshaw

100
Nigel Dempster By David Levine
Image © Matthew and Eve Levine

108
Bradshaw. Photograph by Patrick Lichfield
Image @ Estate of Patrick Lichfield

113
Bradshaw and Carolyn's wedding
Image © Nathalie Delon

120
Bradshaw with A. Scott Berg at Bradshaw's annual birthday dinner
Image © Martha Luttrell

137–138
Letter from Gore Vidal
Courtesy the President and Fellows of Harvard College

143
Bradshaw on the cover of New York Magazine
Image © The Estate of James Moore
Courtesy *New York Magazine*

148–149
Hugh Hefner letters regarding Bradshaw's gambling debt
Images © Estate of Hugh Hefner

153
Bradshaw's journal 1975
Image © Estate of Jon Bradshaw

157
British first edition of Fast Company
Image ©Harper UK, Illustration Willie Feilding

168
Bradshaw's journal, 1977
Image © Estate of Jon Bradshaw

173
Bradshaw's travel bag
Image © Mary Lou Saxon

202–203
On the road
Photographer unknown

204
Contact sheet
Image © Estate of Gene Moore

209
Assorted envelopes from Paul Bowles
Image © Estate of Jon Bradshaw

222–223
Bradshaw, Chris Blackwell and Nathalie Delon celebrating at Blackwell's home in Nassau
Image © Lynn Goldsmith

235
The Man Who Would Be King
Images © Estate of Julian Allen

237
Bradshaw's Visa to the Comoro Islands
Image © Estate of Jon Bradshaw

Bradshaw's writing chair

ACKNOWLEDGMENTS

My first debt of gratitude goes to publisher Michael Zilkha, who suggested this anthology in the first place, and without whose unflagging support and steady guidance this book would not exist.

I'm hugely grateful to Carolyn Pfeiffer for her trust, partnership, and myriad contributions. Carolyn makes things happen and her enthusiasm is infectious. She facilitated all sorts of connections and was ever attentive, cheerful, and galvanizing. She is a force of nature and a pleasure to work with—the consummate professional. The kind of person who makes you better by being in her company.

Carolyn and Michael rallied Bradshaw's friends and colleagues, who were all generous with their time and recollections. We'd like to thank: Olinda Adeane, Martin Amis, Ken Auletta, Chris Blackwell, James Bradshaw, Joan Juliet Buck, John Byrne, Dick Clement, Nik Cohn, Nathalie Delon, Rob Fleder, Anne Taylor Fleming, Rick Guest, Anthony Haden-Guest, Sally Henzell, Marilyn Johnson, Ian La Frenais, Lewis Lapham, Barbara Leary, Fiona Lewis, Martha Luttrell, Terry McDonell, Jim McMullan, Lindon "Ian" Mills, Lady Fiona Montagu, Thom Mount, Dan Okrent, Alan Rudolph, Fred Schruers, Emma Soames, Winston Stona, Amanda Urban, Teresa Vargas, Gary Weiss, and Anna Wintour.

Special thanks to A. Scott Berg, who went above and beyond in sharing his memories and impressions of Bradshaw and making sure our portrait was on the mark.

I'd also like to thank Lucas Wittman and Sarah Bumstead at Ze Books, With Projects Inc., as well as Chris Heiser and Olivia Taylor Smith at Unnamed Press. A nod of gratitude and appreciation goes to Victoria Allen, Lili Anolik, Don Belth, Matt Blankman, Jeremy Collins, Jim Fissel, Mike Fox, Kelsey Hurwitz, Malcolm Jones, John Kenney, Brad Lappin, Mary Lou Ledden, Matthew and Eve Levine, Mike Sager, Mary Lou Saxon, John Schulian, Deanna Shapiro, Glenn Stout, Alex Wolff, and Hilma Wolitzer. Finally, huge thanks to my wife Emily Shapiro for her love, encouragement, warmth, and inspiration.

—Alex Belth

Next:
Bradshaw and Carolyn on the beach at Shelter Island

ACKNOWLEDGMENTS